Violence and Defense in the Jewish Experience

*Papers prepared for a seminar on violence and defense
in Jewish history and contemporary life
Tel Aviv University, August 18–September 4, 1974*

CONTRIBUTORS *Yohanan Aharoni
Salo W. Baron
Graenum Berger
Haim Cohn
Michael Confino
Ben Halpern
Joel L. Kraemer
Yuval Ne'eman
Harry M. Orlinsky
Emanuel Rackman
David Schers
Shimon Shamir
Shlomo Simonsohn
Uriel Tal
Ephraim Urbach*

THE JEWISH PUBLICATION SOCIETY OF AMERICA

PHILADELPHIA 5737/1977

SALO W. BARON
GEORGE S. WISE
Editors

LENN E. GOODMAN
Associate Editor

Violence and Defense in the Jewish Experience

Copyright 1977
by The Jewish Publication Society of America
First edition   All rights reserved
ISBN 0–8276–0092–5
Library of Congress catalog card no. 76–52664
Manufactured in the United States

Designed by Adrianne Onderdonk Dudden

CONTENTS

Foreword

GEORGE S. WISE

The Yom Kippur War of October 1973; the rapid changes in the fortunes of that war; the treacherous attack of the Arab countries; the heroic defense by the Israeli army; the repulsing of the enemy and the successful counterattack, which not only threw the enemy back in Syria but also led to the entrapment of a whole Egyptian army corps on the eastern banks of the Suez; the foreign pressures which compelled Israel to give up a victory gained by the spirit, determination, and blood of her best sons—these somber events, and the equally somber reflections they evoked, prompted the idea of a symposium on violence and defense in the Jewish experience.

Violence has always existed, and the Jews have been its victims for thousands of years in all parts of the world and in all periods of history. The destructive wars against Israel in the ancient period, the bloody centuries of Christian Europe, the Inquisition, the massacres in Western and Central Europe, the barbarous era of the pogroms in the Ukraine, Russia, and Poland in the so-called modern period, and the Holocaust under Hitler—these were all stages in the martyrdom of the Jewish people.

What has been the Jewish response to violence? We recall with pride and sorrow the deeds of the Maccabees, the sacrifice at

Masada, the endurance of the Marranos, the tragic uprising in the Warsaw Ghetto. We are also justifiably proud of Israel's victories in the wars of 1948, 1956, 1967, and 1973. But two questions still remain unanswered: what has been the traditional Jewish attitude toward violence and defense, and why must Jews defend their right to defend themselves? May not the Jews, like the other nations of the world, be allowed to enjoy the fruits of their well-earned victories when they successfully fight off premeditated, brutal attacks by enemies sworn to their destruction, as in the present case of Israel?

Such questions, it was apparent, had come to preoccupy Jews throughout the world. I therefore decided to assemble the basic data on the Jewish millennial tradition concerning violence and defense. To my surprise, I found that the existing literature on the subject was wholly inadequate. In order to fill this lacuna, it appeared imperative to invite leading scholars in various fields of Jewish studies to gather for a colloquium in Israel to discuss the three-thousand-year record of Jewish thought and action on the subject. It seemed to me that the experience of the Jewish people, who through the ages have suffered much more from violence than any other people, might provide a lesson as to how mankind might possibly avoid the damaging impact of the spreading violence and, when unable to stop it, how best to survive.

I turned to Salo W. Baron, a distinguished friend and one of the great Jewish historians of all times, to chair the colloquium. I take this opportunity to express to him my appreciation for his advice and guidance, which has assured the success of the project. I would also like to thank all the scholars in Israel and in the United States who joined Professor Baron in this effort. Some of them have been friends for many years and some have also been my colleagues at Tel Aviv University. The fruits of their deliberations are presented in this volume.

Opening Remarks

YUVAL NE'EMAN

This seminar on the subject of violence and defense in Jewish history and contemporary life has been initiated by George S. Wise, the lifetime chancellor of Tel Aviv University, to mark the inauguration of the university's Chaim Rosenberg School of Jewish Studies. We meet in Tel Aviv, the city which—with all due respect to the capital, Jerusalem—can be regarded as the center of the modern Jewish national rebirth. Indeed, the city of Tel Aviv, the seat of our university, is today the hub of all Israeli life and activity. It is also the center, as it always was, of the country's defense system. We need only recount that in prestate days Tel Aviv was the headquarters of the various defense organizations; and it is in keeping with the city's tradition that when a university was established here among the first departments to be created was a department of military history. There are altogether about fifteen such academic departments throughout the world, and the only one in Israel is to be found at our university.

It is out of his profound historical sense that George Wise has called this conference into being. He has grasped the need for some kind of recapitulation of Jewish attitudes toward the issues of violence and defense, particularly in the wake of the Yom Kippur

War. The Yom Kippur War marked the first time since antiquity that an enemy attacked a Jewish state on a day that is holy to Jews. We have to go back to the history books to find another such occasion, to the Maccabean period when the Syrian Greeks launched armed attacks on the Sabbath. Thus past and present are joined.

Self-defense has been the distinguishing feature of Jewish life not only in Israel—a fact that is well known—but in the Diaspora as well. There is the heroic, heartrending example of the Warsaw Ghetto uprising and of the other ghettos that took up arms against the Nazi murderers. Earlier in Jewish history we recall the revolt of Mar Zutra in Babylonia, in 513 C.E., who succeeded in holding the province of Mahoza for seven years against the Persian oppressors. There was also the Jewish revolt in 115–117 C.E. in Cyrenaica, which spread to Egypt, Cyprus, and other parts of the Roman Empire. All these examples bear out the theorem which states that force is proportional to some power of an exerted oppression.

Finally, I take this opportunity to welcome to our midst Professor Salo W. Baron, a dear friend of Tel Aviv University, and to extend greetings to all the participants in the seminar.

Violence and Defense in the Jewish Experience

SALO W. BARON

Introduction

With respect to the subject matter of our forthcoming discussion, I regret to say that we have not agreed upon any definition of either violence or defense. However, as in other matters of wide concern, artificial attempts at definition are likely to obfuscate rather than enlighten the significance of terms that everybody seems to understand.

There is an ever-accumulating literature on violence. Unfortunately, violence has been with man since his very beginnings. After all, the Bible itself quite early relates the story of Cain and Abel. According to the biblical narrative, the very first generation of man witnessed the slaying of a younger brother by an older brother. Since at that time the victim was supposed to have constituted one-fourth of the world's population, Abel's destruction might be regarded as a sort of genocide committed on 25 percent of the human race then in existence. Not surprisingly, that slaying had serious repercussions for generations thereafter, as I shall have occasion to explain in some detail.

Violence and defense can be approached from various perspectives. Psychologists have studied it from their point of view. I need but mention Erich Fromm's recent book, which analyzes the various forms of destructiveness in both individual and group life.[1] Hannah Arendt has dealt with the subject from the political perspective. Richard Hofstadter, together with Michael Wallace, has edited a large volume on violence in the United States.[2] His documentation, I am sorry to say, is very substantial.

Surprisingly, however, although most of us have been convinced that the United States, with its deep-rooted tradition of violence, is one of the most violent countries in the world, a 1969 presidential commission examining worldwide violence found that, at least with respect to the assassination of leaders, the United States was only thirteenth in the list of eighty-three nations under review. Even so, there has been a great deal of violence of every kind in America.[3]

Coming from America, as do most of the participants in this seminar, we are regrettably attuned to thinking of various kinds of violence. So greatly have we been concerned with the civil and human rights of every race and minority that we have sometimes neglected the protection of the natural rights of man. It would seem, for example, that the laws of nature would ensure anyone the right to walk freely through the streets and parks of a city at any time of day or night. But I do not dare to do it. Nor, I am certain, do my colleagues here venture to rely on that natural right. The situation has become so tragic that this effective denial of a basic natural right has become a phenomenon of daily life which is simply taken for granted.

Thus, without trying to start from any arbitrary definition of the scope of violence and defense, we shall try to analyze some factual developments, as well as the attitudes of Judaism and the Jewish people relating to human violence and the rights and forms of defense against it.

Violence has reigned supreme during the twentieth century, probably the bloodiest century in all the history of man; there have been wars almost constantly. True, in the seventeenth century there were only some twenty-odd years during which there was no major international conflagration, and the late Middle Ages saw the Hundred Years' War. But, compared with the twentieth century, there have never been such widespread and sanguinary conflicts between vast coalitions of states at the same time—conflicts, moreover, which directly affected the civilian populations as much as the armed forces. Admittedly, during the Middle Ages spring was known as the season when kings go to war. Today, however, wars may break out on any date—October 6, for instance. There have been wars almost continuously from the beginning of this century: the Boer War (1899–1902), the Russo-Japanese War (1904–1905), the Italo-Turkish War (1911), the Balkan War (1912–1913), World War I (1914–1918), which in geographic extension and battlefield casualties (eight million dead) overshadowed all previous armed conflicts, and, finally, World War II, which surpassed its predecessor, as it directly affected almost all of Europe, the United States, Brazil, the British Empire countries, China, and Japan—indeed, the overwhelming majority of mankind. Never in the past had so many nations participated in such bloodshed, and the number of civilian dead far exceeded that of the military.

The postwar world, too, has been filled with violent encounters. It suffices to glance at the publications of the Institut Français de Polémologie to realize how extensive and constant the disruptions in the peaceful coexistence of peoples have been in our time.[4] That Jews have participated in many of these clashes as both combatants and victims goes without saying. We rejoice that the Jews of most countries have been emancipated during recent generations, but the price paid for such equality was a high one. For instance, German Jewry, which numbered some 525,000 persons in 1910 (having diminished by more than 40,000 during the preceding three years), lost about 12,000 Jewish combatants in World War I. This despite the fact that anti-Semites were shouting from the housetops that Jews were shirkers and had for the most part successfully evaded military service. In fact, after that war the German Jewish war veterans were able to publish a list of 10,623 names of Jews who had sacrificed their lives for the German "fatherland" in the battles of 1914–1918. There must have been at least 1,000 more such victims whose Jewishness could not be ascertained because their names did not sound Jewish and because of the other recognized difficulties in making positive Jewish identifications. In addition, there was an even larger number of wounded personnel, many of them crippled for life, while more than 30,000 Jewish men won decoration for valor in combat.[5] I can personally testify to the difficulties of identifying Jews because I served during World War II on the National Bureau of War Records, which tried to assemble the data pertaining to all Jewish participants in the American armed forces during the war. With the help of local leaders familiar with the residents of their areas, we found that a great many Sullivans, Farrells, Donovans, Johnsons, and Talmadges were Jews, whereas quite a few Cohens, Cowans, and the like were not.[6]

Emancipation, with all its undeniable benefits, was not obtained without a price in other countries as well as Germany. The hundreds of thousands of young Jews who lost their lives on behalf of Russia, the United States, and other countries of Jewish settlement, especially during the two world wars, together with the millions of other war fatalities, have already stamped the twentieth century as perhaps the bloodiest in history. And a quarter of this century is still ahead of us, with all its horrible potentialities for destruction. In fact, all prospects for the future are overshadowed by the ever-present menace of atomic warfare. The very proliferation of atomic power plants among more and more nations—now made doubly necessary by the energy crisis, though at this time still employed for peaceful purposes—greatly magnifies the perils of an atomic holocaust before this century draws to a close.

Under these circumstances the widely quoted saying of Karl von Clausewitz, that war is essentially but a continuation of diplomacy through other means, may no longer be true. It applied in most earlier wars, which ended more or less as they had begun while the underlying civilization continued intact. This fact had become so obvious that in the 1930s there was a general tendency to minimize wars and to say that "they settled nothing" because life thereafter as a rule continued along accustomed lines. Now, however, there is a real danger that the next world war, if it comes, would no longer be a prolongation of diplomacy but would spell the end of all existing diplomatic relations, indeed of our civilization as a whole. Albert Einstein's reply to a pertinent inquiry on this subject has often been quoted. When asked with what weapons men would fight their third world war, Einstein supposedly answered that he could not foretell that, but that he was sure their fourth would be fought with ordinary clubs. He thus intimated that after a third world war society would again become so primitive that all the more advanced methods of warfare would disappear.

Remarkably, despite the great importance, even urgency, of understanding the varying attitudes to war, those of the Jewish people, in both theory and practice, have never been satisfactorily examined. There is no significant literature on the basic Jewish ideology as it was formulated over the ages by the Bible and Talmud, by medieval rabbis and modern thinkers, as well as by the actual historical experience of Jewish participation in wars, both passively and actively. From time to time telling quotations from various classical Jewish sources have been cited, and preachers have delivered sermons on war and peace, especially during one or another raging conflict. But these statements are so sporadic and unsystematic that they may not be considered historical or philosophical research.[7] I hope, therefore, that this volume may give rise to some serious investigations of Jewish attitudes toward war.

At the same time, we should also consider other forms of group violence, particularly revolutions, of which the twentieth century has had an abundance. This century has witnessed the great Russian Revolution, which rivals, perhaps even exceeds, in importance the English, American, and French Revolutions because, positively or negatively, it has influenced the whole thinking of mankind, with far-reaching repercussions in all corners of the globe. Moreover, "revolution" has become so popular a word that even conservatives now employ it, not as a term of opprobrium but, rather, in claiming to have started some sort of a revolution of their own.

Revolutions, too, have often caused much bloodshed. To be sure, there have been numerous assertions to the contrary, and Karl Marx himself often made a special point of denying that violence was an integral part of the coming socialist revolution. Rather, it was pre-Marxian utopian socialism which had emphasized violence, just as Lenin, Trotsky, and the New Left today have glorified it and preached that violence should be utilized to the full as a means of social action.

In the United States we recently have had such domestic upheavals as the burning of urban areas in an unprecedented fashion. Some of us like to think that economic prosperity generates peace. Yet the 1960s, the most prosperous period in the history of the United States, perhaps also in the history of the world, witnessed for the first time the tragic spectacle of mobs burning their own cities, as happened in Los Angeles, Detroit, and Newark. Curiously, tempers calmed down with the onset of an economic recession.

Another revolutionary upheaval took the form of the much heralded student uprising of the late 1960s. In its international scope this movement was also in many ways unprecedented. I still vividly remember the session of a committee of the overseers of Harvard University, which happened to take place on the day when President Nathan Pusey announced that he would close the university. At the reception following the meeting I was asked by some concerned graduate students whether, as an historian, I had noticed any serious differences between the student revolt then raging and those which had occurred in earlier periods of history.

Although I had not given any real thought to the comparison, I replied that offhand I saw two noteworthy differences between the involvement of students in "revolutionary" movements today and in the past. First, in the past students used universities as a base for operations, since these were the only places where they could debate their problems and plan activities in comparative freedom. Even in absolutist countries, universities usually enjoyed a measure of autonomy, which included provisions against the police entering their premises without authorization by the university authorities.

At one such meeting in the hall of the University of Vienna in 1918, for example, a great many students assembled to discuss revolutionary action, while outside the university a score or more of policemen marched up and down the Ringstrasse but did not enter the hall. In youthful exuberance, one of my colleagues, standing on the third step above street level, shouted to the policemen: "Long live the world revolution!" One police officer, thus provoked, could only reply, "You come down the steps and I shall take care of you." But he did not dare to extend his arm, drag the boy down the steps, and arrest him.

In short, the university was a good place from which to start a revolution; yet no one thought of destroying the universities themselves, which was a very easy thing to do, particularly in the United States with the relatively few guards and helpless administrations, often divided against themselves. But all the organs of government —the President, the Congress, the courts, the army, the police, as well as the media of mass communication—were still intact and could effectively resist any revolutionary change. One could foresee that such student upheavals might bring about reforms in curricula and administrative methods on the university level (some legitimate student grievances, indeed, required remedial action), but they would have had little bearing on the general revolutionary goals of the student radicals.

Secondly, I saw a serious weakness in the American student uprising of the 1960s inasmuch as it often started with the idea of amnesty. Students in revolt were supposed to be free to do whatever they pleased, but when the uprising was over they were to be granted full amnesty. In my opinion, no revolution could prove successful if its protagonists were not prepared to pay the price for failure. As a result, indeed, even some perfectly legitimate grievances of the students produced only minor remedies. On the whole, except for greatly damaging many universities to the disadvantage of the students themselves, this movement ended in utter futility. There were some Jewish aspects to that movement, insofar as Jewish student leaders played a disproportionately large role in the

United States, France, and other countries; but they left few marks on the Jewish community as such.

Another element to be considered is the violence employed by the state against its own citizens. This is a sort of revolution from above. Any state is of necessity an organ of enforcement—Georg Jellinek called it a *Zwangsordnung*—and all, except the anarchists, have agreed that without a state there would be a *bellum omnium contra omnes*. In order to keep peace and order among the various groups of the population, the state is needed to enforce the law. Hence Leon Trotsky was not quite wrong when he bluntly declared that all states are based upon violence. He made that assertion at a time when the Soviets had to submit to German power in the peace treaty of Brest-Litovsk. But he did not foresee that his own country, the Soviet Union, would become before long the worst sinner in using violence against its citizens and suppressing opposing points of view, in defiance of its own constitution.

As a matter of fact, the Soviet Union has clearly in many ways become (or reverted to being) a continuation of the czarist empire, for it bears many of the unmistakable earmarks of czarist authoritarianism. Suffice it to cite the famous definition of Count Sergei Uvarov, Minister of Public Enlightenment to Nicholas I in the 1850s, concerning the basic principles of Russian policy in order to see their fundamental similarity to those of the new Soviet regime, particularly in the early 1950s. A century ago Uvarov declared that orthodoxy, autocracy, and nationality were the three pillars on which the czarist empire rested. "Orthodoxy" referred, of course, to the Russian Church, to which all other faiths were to be subordinated; "autocracy" indicated the unlimited power of the czar, while "nationality" meant that the Russian nationality was to prevail over all the other ethnic groups. Soviet policy, especially under Joseph Stalin, has basically been the same. Soviet autocracy is, in fact, much more powerful than czarist despotism because it extends over all the domains of life and, through the nationalization of the means of production, in effect controls the entire economy. Orthodoxy in the traditional religious sense is rejected, along with all other faiths, as an "opiate" of the people. But there is a new orthodoxy: you have to be a believer in Communism or else you are not tolerated at all. While the czarist empire accepted the presence of millions of Catholics, Protestants, Jews, and Muslims, the Communist regime does not tolerate any deviation from the Communist line. With respect to nationality, it appeared for a while that the Soviet Union would radically depart from the staunch Russian nationalism of the czarist period and grant full self-determination to the national minorities. This was, indeed, one of the first laws enacted by Lenin after he came to power. Yet, in the course of the last decades the great latitude given to the minority cultures has been whittled down continually. It has become increasingly clear that the immense power of government, especially in the large Russian republic, was used to promote russification as in the days of the czars.[8]

We have here an example of the power of the state used against the people. In such cases there usually is much miscarriage of justice in the courts and misinterpretation, or even outright violation, of the existing laws.

Frequent failures to enforce the law, on the other hand, due to negligence, overwork, excessive clemency, or outside influence, may be equally damaging to the reign of law. There are statistics indicating that only 57 percent of reported crimes in the United States lead to any investigation, and of these only 20 percent actually result in arrests. Moreover, only 75 percent of those arrested are brought to trial, and only 60 percent of such defendants are actually sentenced. Prison sentences, too, are often greatly reduced by lenient parole boards. In short, a criminal act is more than likely not to be punished at all. Conditions are quite similar in Italy, where 41 percent of those arrested are ultimately sentenced, and in France, where 57 percent are condemned.[9]

In contrast, in the Soviet Union, someone who is arrested (not merely temporarily detained for questioning) is almost certain to be sentenced. Sometimes even someone who has committed no crime is also sentenced.

The power of the state to use violence against purported criminals, including various forms of police brutality, is part of the perennial story of violence and defense. Some Jews, too, have been involved both as victims and as perpetrators. In its early years the Soviet secret service, known as the Cheka, included a very large number of Jewish agents, although this aspect has never been investigated in detail.

In addition to these forms of violence occurring in relations among states and between states and their citizens, there also have been violent outbreaks between groups of citizens, even if they did not assume the dimensions of regular civil wars. Throughout history such sanguinary conflicts were fought between classes and ethnic groups. But some of the most extreme forms of extermination were inspired by religious fanaticism. Jews were, of course, the most frequent and long-enduring victims of pogroms, which, even if in part motivated by secular socioeconomic antagonisms, became utterly virulent when they were disguised as attempts to eliminate contagious religious infidelity.[10]

These and many related problems will be explored by the papers in this volume.

NOTES

1. Erich Fromm, *The Anatomy of Human Destructiveness* (New York, 1973).

2. Hannah Arendt, *On Violence* (New York, 1970); Richard Hofstadter and Michael Wallace, eds., *American Violence: A Documentary History* (New York, 1970).

3. Staff Report of the National Commission on the Causes and Prevention of Violence (Washington, D.C., 1969), p. 119; Monica D. Blumenthal et al., *Justifying Violence: Attitudes of American Men* (Ann Arbor, Mich., 1972), pp. 2 ff.

4. See in particular its *Etudes Polémologiques,* which include regular reviews of the "Chronique de la violence mondiale." For instance, a recent issue of April 1974 covers the period from November 1973 through January 1974 (II, pp. 114–24). See also "Une bibliographie sélective chronologique sur la guerre et la paix," ibid., pp. 108–12.

5. See the brief summary of "Die Hauptergebnisse der Berufszählung vom 14 June 1907 im deutschen Reich," *Zeitschrift fur Demographie und Statistik der Juden,* VI (1910), 164 ff; *Jüdisches Lexikon,* II (Berlin, 1928), p. 147; *Die jüdischen Gefallenen des deutschen Heeres der deutschen Marine und der deutschen Schutztruppen, 1914–1918, Ein Gedenkbuch,* published by the Reichsbund Jüdischer Frontsaldaten (Berlin, 1932). Of considerable human as well as political interest is the selection of letters published by that organization under the title *Gefallene deutsche Jüden, Frontbriefe, 1914–1918* (Berlin, 1935).

6. National Bureau of War Records of the National Jewish Welfare Board, *American Jews in World War II: The Story of 550,000 Fighters for Freedom,* compiled by I. Kaufman, I. Dublin, and S. C. Kohs, 2 vols. (New York, 1947).

7. The extent to which Jewish preachers, like their Catholic and Protestant confreres, were swayed by the patriotic fervor of the belligerent countries during World War I was described by me in an address on "The Impact of Wars on Religion," delivered at the American Historical Association's annual meeting in 1950 and published in the *Political Science Quarterly,* LXVII (1952), 534–72. (It is reprinted in my *Steeled by Adversity: Essays and Addresses on American Jewish Life,* ed. by Jeannette Meisel Baron [Philadelphia, 1971], pp. 417–53, esp. pp. 434 ff.) The homilists' attitudes during World War II, and still more during the changing constellations of the protracted Vietnam war, were far more varied.

8. See my "Cultural Reconstruction of Russian Jewry," The Allan Bronfman Lecture, Montreal, 1971, and Westmount, Quebec, 1971; and my *The Russian Jew Under Tsars and Soviets* (New York, 1964), particularly in its greatly revised and updated 1976 edition.

9. See *On Violence,* pp. 98 ff.

10. Outside of Jewish history, the best known example of such bloodthirsty clashes are the European wars of religion in the sixteenth and seventeenth centuries, on which there exists an enormous literature accumulated during recent generations. On one major episode, namely the St. Bartholomew Day Massacre, see Natalie Zeman Davis, "The Rites of Violence: Religious Riot in Sixteenth-Century France," *Past and Present,* no. 59 (1973), 51–91, and the selected literature listed there. The literature of anti-Jewish pogroms is likewise very large. Suffice it to mention here the

excerpts from the earlier records assembled by Simon Bernfeld in his *Sefer ha-Dema'ot* ("Book of Tears"), 3 vols. (Berlin, 1923–1926); and on the Holocaust of the 1940s, Jacob Robinson and Philip Friedman, *Guide to Jewish History Under Nazi Impact* (New York, 1960), with forewords by Benzion Dinur and Salo W. Baron; and other bibliographical compilations of that joint documentary project of the Yad Vashem and the Yivo.

Part One

The Ancient and Medieval Periods

SALO W. BARON

1 The Ancient and Medieval Periods: Review of the History

In considering Jewish attitudes toward violence and defense during the ancient and medieval periods, one must be aware initially that it is difficult to determine exactly when these periods of Jewish history come to a close. While all periodization is arbitrary, that of medieval Jewish history as ending with the French Revolution was quite widely adopted by nineteenth-century Jewish historians, beginning with Leopold Zunz, and this view was by and large followed by their early twentieth-century successors. Among nineteenth-century scholars the struggle for Jewish emancipation loomed very large, and it thus became customary for them to consider the medieval period of Jewish history as continuing up to the French Revolution. More recently, some American scholars have suggested that the American Revolution marked the true beginning of the emancipation era for Jews and therefore the beginning of the modern period of Jewish history. Only Heinrich Graetz, with his deep interest in intellectual history, took Moses Mendelssohn and the Berlin Haskalah as the starting point of modern Jewish life.

For my part, I have always felt that, however significant these major eighteenth-century developments were, even with respect to the Jews, Jewish emancipation itself represented a much slower process extending over many generations before 1789 or 1776. Generally speaking, legal emancipation, like law as a whole, often followed rather than preceded the more basic economic, demographic, and cultural evolution. Of course, once enacted, law itself became a major social force, accelerating as well as modifying the earlier trends. Regrettably, neither social, economic, nor cultural epochs are easily datable. One can arbitrarily select an author or book as representing an important cultural turning point. For a long time, for example, Moses Hayyim Luzzatto's minor dramatic work *Migdal Oz* ("Tower of Strength"), written on the occasion of a friend's wedding in about 1727, was taken as a convenient starting point for modern Hebrew literature. But discoveries of earlier works of this type in both Italy and Holland, belonging essentially to what I call the Italian and Dutch Haskalah, led many recent investigators to give up that artificial beginning date. In the economic sphere it is even more difficult to pinpoint a particular event as setting in motion the new forces shaping the productive processes and the corresponding social responses in a nation or a group of nations.

Ever since the publication of the first edition of *A Social and Religious History of the Jews* in 1937, I have consistently advocated the abandonment of these rigid chronological divisions and proposed that the emancipation era be seen as a gradual unfolding of factors which in the cultural sphere operated from at least the sixteenth century and in the economic area came strongly to the fore by the seventeenth century.[1] This process was not completed until the twentieth century, if then. We must never forget that at the beginning of this century Jews residing in czarist Russia (half of world Jewry) as well as those living in Rumania, the Ottoman Empire, North Africa, and elsewhere, had not yet attained even formal emancipation. Those countries which had emancipated their Jewries, such as the United States, France, and the lands of the British Empire, embraced a multitude, often a majority, of Jews born and bred in countries without emancipation. The outlook on life of most such recent settlers was conditioned by their earlier experiences in the "old countries" much more than by their new environments. It was, therefore, more for the sake of convenience and to allow investigation of a problem of genetic history that in the new edition of *A Social and Religious History of the Jews* I suggested the middle of the seventeenth century as the major dividing line between the emancipation and pre-emancipation eras.

One consideration that I think we should bear in mind throughout our deliberations is the distinction between what German philosophers like to call *Sollen* and *Sein*. Both, to be sure, have a history, and both are of the highest relevance to our inquiry; but the two do not always perfectly correspond, and our sources are very often much more concerned with *Sollen* than with *Sein*. The Bible, Talmud, and other classical sources are filled with discussions about the norms of behavior and with occasional illustrations of events which shed light both on the minutiae of the norms and on their practical application. As is well known, the Bible is supposed to contain 265 positive and 348 negative commandments, or a total of 613, the famous *taryag mitzvot*. There has never been a universally accepted enumeration of these commandments, even in those medieval tracts which bore the title *Sefer Ha-Mitzvot;* yet good halakhists essentially knew what was to be considered proper adherence to such regulations. Historians must always ask what actually happened and how the facts of life corresponded with the postulates, and in this respect our sources are by no means as informative as we might desire.

To cite only one significant example: some of us have long been accustomed to look to the responsa literature of medieval and early modern times as better reflections of historical realities than debates over legal requirements, some of which may not even have been considered applicable to the time and locality in which they were conducted. However, because of their principal concentration on the legal aspects of a case—and this was, after all, the main purpose of the responsa—the authors often neglected the detailed factual aspects as not quite relevant. That is why they sometimes summarized the actual events that had occasioned the inquiry in a few lines, often failing to mention even the names of persons or localities involved and substituting for them such stereotypes as "Reuben did this" and "Simon reacted in such and such a way." In modern times reported inquiries became so relatively brief and factually uninformative that in many cases one is not even sure whether they reflected actual events or merely presented hypothetical cases so as to introduce elaborate replies. In this way authors could speculate about juridical details of some legal postulate as a guide for the future, regardless of whether they were to determine what course of action was to be adopted in a particular case.

Nevertheless, law, even if not immediately reflective of life, has often helped shape living conditions for the future. This is particularly true of religious law, the normative force of which is strengthened by the emotional appeal it has to the hearts of believers. The same holds true of myths. The actual doings attributed by legends to historical figures may not be factually true, yet the very fact that the narratives are widely believed has often made them new vehicles for setting examples of behavior. At times the impact of both law and myths has assumed major historical dimensions.

Suffice it to quote here one example from the biblical story of Cain and Abel. This narrative of the reputed first murder in history immediately conveyed an important lesson to future generations. While Cain's act did not go unpunished, it did not lead to the culprit's execution. According to the biblical record, God told Cain, "You shall become a ceaseless wanderer on earth" (Gen. 4:12).* But he was to be protected against attacks by any third party through the divine threat that "if anyone kills Cain, sevenfold vengeance shall be taken on him" (Gen. 4:15). True, the Bible itself did not adopt this principle as a norm applicable to all subsequent murders. What is in effect capital punishment, *mot yamut*, frequently appears among the penalties for criminals in the pentateu-

---

*Unless otherwise specified, biblical citations throughout refer to the latest translations issued by the Jewish Publication Society of America.—ED.

chal legislation. Nevertheless, the legend of the first slaying in human history, the notion of enormity attached to this crime and God's treatment of the criminal, doubtless contributed to the reluctance of the later talmudic sages to carry out the biblical provisions for capital punishment. They hedged the trial procedure in capital crimes by so many formalities regarding evidence, especially through the so-called *hakirot* and *bedikot,* the very complicated examination of witnesses, that sentencing criminals to death became a rarity. The majority of rabbis followed the view of Rabbi Joshua ben Qarha who, speculating on 2 Samuel 8:15 and Zechariah 8:16, taught that in issuing any judgment one ought to combine justice with charity (*tzedakah* in its new meaning) and truth with peace. By the third century the Palestinian Rabbi Johanan could announce: "Jerusalem was destroyed only because the judges had based their sentences upon the law of the Torah and failed to modify it inside the line of the law [according to the principle of equity]."[2] It was, therefore, not only Roman legislation which removed capital jurisdiction from the Jewish courts of justice (according to the Talmud, this happened forty years before the fall of Jerusalem); but also, in view of its own internal evolution, ancient Judaism gradually abandoned this form of retaliation, a procedure adopted once again by the modern State of Israel.

Equally far-reaching was the homiletical interpretation of the Cain-Abel story by the Christian Church Fathers and their medieval successors. They shared with the Jewish Aggadah the assumption that the Bible was not a mere storybook and that each narrative contained therein was intended to convey an important lesson. Owing to their own belief that the ultimate rise of Christianity was foreordained by God and that it even preceded the creation of the world—as early as the beginning of the second century St. Ignatius of Antioch could paradoxically claim that Christianity did not believe in Judaism but Judaism believed in Christianity—they saw in Cain and Abel prototypes for the subsequent struggle between Judaism and its nascent daughter religion. In this view Cain represented Israel, the older brother whose sacrifice was ultimately repudiated by God in favor of that of the younger brother, that is the Christian faith. Thereupon the older brother, that is the Jewish people, crucified the younger brother, that is Jesus, the founder of the Christian religion. For this crime, allegedly committed by their ancestors, Jews were to suffer a severe and long-enduring penalty. However, according to the biblical injunction, Cain was not to be slain. This meant that the Jewish people was not to be exterminated and that all those demanding "Cain's" death would suffer a seven-fold revenge. The only retribution to be derived from the biblical story was found in *na ve-nad ba-aretz,* the idea that the Jew would be a permanent fugitive and migrant on the earth, not allowed a permanent home anywhere, at least not until the ushering in of the messianic age shortly before or during the second coming of Christ.[3]

This doctrine saved many Jewish lives during the Dark Ages and helped preserve the Jewish people in Christian Europe, despite all the antagonisms and the ensuing massacres of hundreds, or even thousands, of Jewish victims in some localities or regions. So widely accepted was this homily, reinforced by the prophetic predictions of the ultimate restoration of the Jews from all corners of the earth to the Holy Land, that even hostile Church teachers had to find a justification for its disregard. For one example, John Duns Scotus, the famous thirteenth-century scholastic often styled the *doctor subtilis,* was gravely prejudiced against the Jews by his environment in France and England prior to the expulsions of 1290 and 1306, and he had to seek some justification for expelling Jews despite their expected survival to the end of days. In a desperate attempt at harmonizing these conflicting postulates, he suggested in his commentary on Isaiah that one might provide sufficiently for Jewish survival by placing a small group of Jews on a distant island and maintaining them there until the second coming of Christ.[4]

Needless to say, the notion of Israel as Cain did not prevent bloodthirsty individuals from attacking Jews. But this general homiletical view of the Jew's role in history has endured into the modern period and was taken over by the Protestant churches as well. In fact, some Protestant clergy belonged to the most ardent advocates of the restoration of the Jews to Palestine, though under the general assumption that such a restoration (combined with the Jews' conversion to Christianity) was necessary in order to usher in the second coming of Christ.

Legends, and more generally historical illusions, have often exercised a greater power over the minds of men than historical facts as such. The great German poet, Johann Wolfgang von Goethe, witnessed toward the end of his life the first flowering of historical criticism, particularly in the fields of classical and biblical studies. As a poet, he felt that humanity was impoverished by the work of these harping critics who "through some pedantic truth, displace something great which is of superior value to us." Disconcerted by the work of his contemporaries, especially the historian of ancient Rome, Berthold Georg Niebuhr, Goethe objected, for example, to scholarly repudiation of the veracity of narratives concerning Mucius Scaevola and Lucretia. He exclaimed: "If the Romans were great enough to invent such stories, we should at least be sufficiently great to believe them." When a legend appeared under a religious guise, its rejection was often considered by pious Christians as an outright sin. This was also the prevailing attitude of most Jews, including many of their enlightened leaders, against anyone trying to dispute the historicity of an Aggadah. Moreover, legends had the additional virtue of facilitating the harmonization of obvious contradictions in the classical sources which defied purely rational explanations.[5]

Among the reinterpretations by the later biblical writers of the historical events connected with the Israelite conquest of Canaan have been the bloodthirsty descriptions of the total destruction of the native population by the conquerors, reflecting their desire to emphasize the absolute rejection of idolatry under any guise. Not surprisingly, these descriptions have often been used by anti-Jewish historians and theologians to attribute a basic proclivity toward genocide to the Jewish people. Even today, some Jew-baiting Soviet writers, such as Trofim Kichko and Yurii Ivanov, quote not only the numerous pertinent passages in the Book of Joshua but also many prophetic predictions about the future as evidence of the "Zionist" drive toward both world domination and total elimination of opposing faiths. Ivanov, for example, cites the well-known predictions of Deutero-Isaiah: "Aliens shall rebuild your walls, their kings shall wait upon you. . . . For the nation or the kingdom that does not serve you shall perish; such nations shall be destroyed" (Isa. 60:10–12). Quite apart from overlooking that what the prophet had in mind by the term "serve" was primarily the idea of the conversion of the conquered population to the religion of Israel and their worship of the true and only God of the universe, the Soviet critic ignores the fact that what the seer evidently envisaged here was the advent of a messianic age—of eternal peace and harmony among men and, what is more, of peace in nature.[6]

Historians, however, have realized that these later reinterpretations of ancient history, as well as predictions for the future, did not quite reflect historic reality. The Bible itself preserved the historical record that many Canaanite groups had survived the Israelite conquest and were living among the new settlers "unto this day." These passages, particularly in the Book of Judges, undoubtedly stemmed from the period of the Israelitic monarchy when the process of assimilation between the older and the newer inhabitants was far from complete. The rabbinic tradition, too, seems to have preserved a dim memory of what may actually have happened. According to Rabbi Samuel, a rabbinic sage of the amoraic age:

Joshua sent three missives to the Land of Israel before the people entered the country. [He informed the natives] that he who wants to depart may do so, he who wishes to surrender shall secure peace, and he who wants to fight shall be subdued. The tribes of Girgushites departed, believing in the Holy One blessed be He, and settled in Africa. . . . The Gibeonites surrendered and made peace. . . . The thirty-one kings offered armed resistance and were subdued.

Other talmudic texts speak of the native Amorites proceeding to Africa, undoubtedly echoing the historic memory of the Phoenician colonization of North Africa. We know that "Carthage" was none other than *karta hadeta* (the new city), ruled, like the Israelitic tribes, by what the Romans called *sufetes* (the equivalent of the Hebrew *shoftim,* or judges) and generally continuing much of the Semitic tradition brought from their Canaanite homes. In fact, deep into the medieval period some of these North African tribes claimed to have been ousted from their native country by "Joshua the robber" and, at least in theory, demanded the restoration of the country to them. (This parallel to the modern Palestine Liberation Organization is quite noteworthy.[7])

Far more typical of the biblical outlook was the legislation concerning man's responsibility toward his neighbors, even enemies. To be sure, the main objective of the legislator was to regulate the relationships among the Israelites themselves. However, many provisions are also made for the treatment of "strangers" in the Land of Israel and that of neighboring tribes or countries, particularly in war time. Though writing many centuries later and somewhat handicapped by his apologetic attempt to present Judaism to the Greek-speaking world in its most favorable light, the historian Josephus quite accurately summarized the prevailing doctrines of the biblical lawgivers. In his reply to the Egyptian Apion—whose demagogic appeal to mass prejudice earned him the designation of *cymbalum mundi* (the world's cymbal) from Emperor Tiberius—Josephus wrote:

We must furnish fire, water, food to all who ask for them, point out the road, not leave a corpse unburied, show consideration even to declared enemies. He [God] does not allow us to burn up their country, or to cut down their fruit trees, and forbids even the spoiling of fallen combatants; he has taken measures to prevent outrage to prisoners of war, especially women.

The curious emphasis here on pointing out the road to strangers was undoubtedly a reaction to the accusation, widespread in the Roman Empire, that Jews, as sworn enemies of gentile nations, were unwilling to extend even the courtesy of pointing out the road to non-Jewish strangers. More important was the biblical injunction against burning enemy countries or cutting down their fruit trees. Because of the long interval between the planting of trees and the bearing of their fruit, such destruction might cause starvation to an enemy population long after the cessation of hostilities.[8]

In fact, too, the Jewish kings often differed very greatly from their confreres in other lands in their generally merciful attitude, for which they seem to have gained some reputation among their neighbors. The First Book of Kings furnishes us with an interesting illustration in the story of the Aramean king Ben-hadad, who, after his defeat at Aphek, went into hiding. Thereupon his advisors assured him: "[W]e have heard that the kings of the House of Israel are merciful kings" and persuaded him to surrender. In answer to a messenger, King Ahab is supposed to have exclaimed, "Is he [Ben-hadad] yet alive? he is my brother!" (1 Kings 20:31–32). Even in their private lives the kings of Israel seem to have abstained from the sport of hunting animals, a diversion widely indulged in by other Middle Eastern royal families.[9]

Not surprisingly, wars between Israel and Judah were often more violent than those with other neighbors. In many respects these confrontations resembled civil wars rather than wars among strangers. Even after the separation of the two Jewish states upon the death of King Solomon, the unity of the monarchy established by David surpassed the differences created by the division that the biblical narrator attributes to Rehoboam's rashness. During the two centuries of separation, the boundaries between the two countries were so fluid that modern scholars have had difficulty in ascertaining their location. The designation "from Dan to Beersheba" remained the standard description of the extreme points north and south covering the whole area of the two states. As soon as the occasion arose after the fall of Samaria, King Josiah of Judah embarked upon the ambitious enterprise of reconquering the territories which had formerly belonged to Northern Israel. Yet, technically, each country was sovereign. For instance, the prophet Amos, of Tekoa in the south, felt free to preach in Samarian Bethel in the name of the God of both Israel and Judah, but he could readily be expelled by Amaziah, the priest of Bethel, as an undesirable alien (Amos 7:10 ff.). Moreover, in one such fratricidal war, we are told, the Israelite king Pekah, son of Remaliah, slew 120,000 "valiant men" of Judah and carried away 200,000 women, sons, and daughters of Israel's "brethren" captive to Samaria (2 Chron. 28:6–8).

These internecine wars were but episodes in the more difficult defenses set up first by the Northern Kingdom and then by Judah against the inroads of the great neighboring powers of Assyria-Babylonia and Egypt. It was fortunate for the Israelite people, and indirectly for the world at large, that in the struggle of these two "superpowers" of the ancient Middle East there was a long hiatus of some three centuries when, preoccupied with their own internal dissensions and other difficulties, the countries bordering on the Nile or on the Euphrates-Tigris, played a relatively minor role in Middle Eastern affairs. It was during that period that Israel consolidated its hold on the country and laid the foundation for its unique culture with its memorable contribution to world civilization. By the ninth century, however, first Assyria and then Babylonia resumed their expansive march; Egypt, too, however ineffectually, tried to reassert its former lordship over the land of Canaan, then greatly fragmented among mutually hostile smaller kingdoms of Ammonites, Moabites, Edomites, the five Philistine city-states, as well as Northern Israel and Judah.

Jewish participation in belligerent moves did not cease with the fall of Jerusalem. Although the restoration of some exiled Jews to Palestine and the erection of the Second Temple proceeded apace with relatively few armed clashes with the local population and largely followed a nonviolent course, aided and abetted by the central powers of the Achaemenid Empire, some Jews, at least on the periphery, were still engaged in occasional combat. Best known is the case of the Elephantine military colony, where an organized force of Jewish soldiers was established by the Egyptian kings to defend their southern border against attacks from what is now Sudan and Ethiopia. It was in this context that the famous collection of Aramaic papyri, preserved in Egypt's favorable climate, revealed much of the story of the expanding Jewish dispersion which had begun long before the fall of Jerusalem. Later on, too, according to Josephus, detachments of Jewish soldiers were often involved in Egyptian campaigns down to the Ptolemaic age.[10]

Needless to say, Jews also fought in behalf of their own country. The heroism of the Maccabees, of the fighters for independence during the great Roman wars against Nero, Vespasian, Trajan, Hadrian, and, as late as the seventh century, against Heraclius, is fully attested to by the historical records. Suffice it to say that Rome had to marshal a force of four legions, parts of two other legions, twenty cohorts of allied infantry, and eight squadrons of cavalry, together with a strong contingent of Arabs "who hated the Jews with all the hatred that is common among neighbors" (Tacitus), to subdue the Jewish uprising of 66–70 C.E. Large forces under the command of Rome's ablest generals were needed to overcome the resistance of certain Diaspora Jewries in 115–117, and again that of Simeon bar Kokhba and his troops in 132–135. In contrast, only three legions were able, with much less effort and time, to conquer the large kingdom of Armenia. Shortly after the war of 66, which ended in the fall of Jerusalem and Masada, Josephus could boast before the Graeco-Roman public that it had been "the greatest [war] not only of the wars of our own time, but so far as accounts have reached us, "well nigh all that ever broke out between cities or nations." More significantly, in none of these cases did the Jewish people in the land and abroad act in unison in opposition to the overpowering force of Rome.[11]

Such disunity may be explained, in part, by internal ideological differences and, in part, by Roman policies. One of the major reasons for the downfall of Jerusalem was the dichotomy between the Roman treatment of Jews in the vast dispersion and their attitude toward Palestinian Jewry. In Palestine, where the Jews were in the majority, Rome treated them as a subject population with all the harshness of a conqueror and the greed of a colonial exploiter. What was said of Ventidius Cumanus, governor of Syria (of which Palestine was a subdivision)—that he had "entered rich Syria poor, and left poor Syria rich"—also applied to many other Roman officials in Palestine and elsewhere. On the other hand, the Jews of the Roman dispersion were often viewed by the Roman authorities as welcome allies, at least until the days of Trajan. They were numerous enough in many provinces to play a significant role in sociopolitical affairs without being interested in any of the local irredentist movements. On the contrary, in Egypt, Syria, and other important areas the Jews were confronted with considerable hostility by the native majorities and considered Rome as their protector. Rome reciprocated by extending to them a large measure of equality of rights *(isonomia)* combined with considerable autonomy in their cultural and religious affairs. It is noteworthy that even in the midst of the Great War, Vespasian and Titus refused to abrogate these Jewish rights when requested to do so by delegations from Alexandria and Antioch. Thus the Roman policy of "divide and rule" was successful not only in regard to relations between the Jews and their immediate neighbors but also with respect to relations between the dispersed communities and those of the Palestinian homeland.[12] One of the great Jewish tragedies of the period was that the millions of Diaspora Jews, while intimately concerned with what was happening in Palestine, did not act as partners in a joint undertaking, except in emergencies, but allowed Palestine alone to make the final decisions affecting the entire people.

Next to the heroism of the fighters in the defense of their country and religion, was the more passive heroism of the religious martyrs. This type of defense was in some respects even more significant and enduring. It has long been recognized that the very idea of religious martyrdom was born at the time of the Maccabean liberation movement. It is not surprising that the surrounding polytheistic nations, particularly the Romans, had full understanding for sacrificing one's life in behalf of one's country. The Romans actually claimed that *dulce et decorum est pro patria mori*—that dying for one's fatherland is both useful and sweet. But sacrificing one's life in order not to worship one or several more gods made little sense to those who believed in a multiplicity of deities. In fact, many conquered populations were convinced that the very fact of the conquest and their own defeat proved that the conqueror's gods were more powerful and, hence, more right than their own. Only the Jewish people, with their staunch belief in the one and only God, would insist that the slightest deviation through recognition of another deity was a cardinal sin, the avoidance of which, even at the price of one's life, was a commandment instilled into Jews from childhood.

Curiously, in time the very Maccabean "rebels" were overshadowed in the memory of the people by the so-called Maccabean martyrs, as exemplified in the story of Hannah and her seven sons in the Fourth Book of Maccabees. While this tract played a lesser role in the Jewish community than in the nascent Christian church, the idea of suffering for one's religion assumed increasing importance in the turbulent period before and after the fall of Jerusalem. The people soon remembered the great "martyrs" of their own tradition, beginning with Abel; the greatest of them all, Isaac, the intended victim of his own father, was increasingly glorified as the supreme example of obedience to God. Abraham himself became more and more the prototype of an exalted martyr in the Aggadah. For her part, Hannah, in exhorting her seven sons to accept violent death rather than surrender their religion, reminded them of their father's instruction:

He read to us of Abel who was slain by Cain, and of Isaac who was offered as a burnt-offering, and of Joseph in the prison. And he spake to us of Phineas, the zealous priest, and he taught you *the song of* Ananias, Azarias, and Mishael in the fire. And he glorified also Daniel in the den of lions, and blessed him; and called to your minds the saying of Isaiah, "Yea even though thou pass through the fire, the flame shall not hurt thee." He sang to us the words of David the psalmist, "Many are the afflictions of the just." He quoted to us the proverb of Solomon, "He is a tree of life to all them that do his will." He confirmed the words of Ezekiel, "Shall these dry bones live?" For he forgot not the song that Moses taught, which teaches, "I will slay and I will make alive." This is your life and the blessedness of your day. [4 Macc. 18:11–17][13]

Compared with this new emphasis on martyrology, even the heroic deeds of Judas Maccabeus and his brothers receded in the memory of the people. It is truly characteristic that the Talmud has little to say about the Maccabean family, and what it does say is chiefly in Babylonian, rather than Palestinian, sources. Even the festival of Hanukkah is disposed of rather briefly in a few paragraphs, whereas the other Jewish holidays, even Purim, are discussed at considerable length from the point of view of their halakhic implications. The great miracle which led up to the restoration of the Temple and national liberation is reduced in these paragraphs to the miraculous story of a small container of oil, the light from which lasted for fully eight days. Some scholars have indeed been led to assume that the later Pharisees and their disciples, the talmudic sages, had so little use for the last Maccabean rulers that because of their semipolitical and semireligious bias against these "high priests" they held their glorification of the Maccabean uprising as definitely secondary to that of the miraculous divine intervention.[14]

Religious martyrdom indeed remained the keynote for the entire Jewish evolution in the medieval period. Medieval Jewry excelled in glorifying its martyrs by following their example in comparable situations when no alternative to death became morally possible. The story of self-immolation on a mass scale by the victims of the Crusaders has few parallels in the history of man. In theory, too, Judah Halevi rationalized the existing powerlessness of the Jewish people—often regarded by Christian apologists as proof for the rejection of the formerly chosen Jewish people by God after the coming of Christ—by insisting that Christians, too, have glorified their martyrs much above their statesmen and conquerors. For this reason, he taught, Israel's "chosenness" has always been connected with its perennial sufferings. "Israel amidst the nations," he exclaimed, "is like the heart amidst the organs of the body; it is at one and the same time the most sick and the most healthy of them." Halevi thus reacted with redoubled effort to the great conflict raging in his time between Christianity and Islam. It had reached a climax in the period of the Crusades when the Christian world declared a holy war on Islam in reaction to the *jihad* (holy war) proclaimed by the Muslim conquerors of the seventh century and continued with much vigor for several generations thereafter.[15]

In this war between titans the Jewish people suffered severely. But the idea of martyrdom had so deeply permeated the masses of the Jewish population that they saw in the massacres a manifestation of the will of God to which one had to submit. True, some Jews resisted. According to Solomon bar Simson of Mainz, the most informative Hebrew chronicler of the First Crusade of 1096, upon the approach of the Crusaders one community successfully organized its defenses. Supported by the local authorities, the Jews killed two hundred assailants and thus saved the entire community. However, this episode meant so little to the chronicler and to other contemporaries that it was disposed of by a brief mention without any clear identification of the locality where it occurred. (The name Shela, given by the chronicler, and possibly misread by a copyist, has long been inconclusively debated by scholars; it might perhaps refer to Vishegrad in Bohemia.) All chroniclers, on the other hand, engaged in lengthy descriptions of the great acts of self-destruction, through a sort of collective ritual *shehitah,* from the Rhineland to Palestine. (At the same time, it must be remembered, most organs of both state and church tried to save the Jews, but they could not stem the outbreak of mass violence.[16])

This tradition of meek submission to the will of God and the acceptance of suffering, including violent death, at the hands of raging Jew-baiters has so permeated the Jewish psyche that many intellectual leaders of the people have long accepted the assumption that suffering has been the outstanding feature of Jewish life in the dispersion. The *Leidensgeschichte* has thus become a leit-motif of Jewish historical writings to the present day. It also helps explain the Jewish acceptance of persecution and suffering as more or less natural phenomena and even makes more understandable to us some attitudes of both the leaders and the masses during the Nazi Holocaust. However, later essays discuss the fact that the popular notion that Eastern European Jewry allowed itself to be "led like sheep to the slaughter" by Nazi extermination squads has overlooked the numerous acts of heroic resistance by both individuals and groups throughout the great tragedy, acts of resistance by no means unprecedented in prior Jewish history.[17]

Many of these aspects will be more fully clarified in the succeeding chapters.

N O T E S

1. See my *A Social and Religious History of the Jews,* vols. I–III (New York, 1937), II, pp. 164 ff. and the notes thereon, III, pp. 129 ff.; and the preface to the 2nd ed., vols. IX–XVI (New York, 1952–1976), pp. v ff. (henceforth cited as *SRH,* 2nd ed. unless otherwise stated); "Jewish Emancipation," *Encyclopaedia of Social Sciences,* VIII, pp. 394–99; "New Approaches to Jewish Emancipation," *Diogenes,* no. 29 (1960), 56–81 (also in French and Spanish). On the beginnings of modern Hebrew literature see also Eisig Silberschlag, *From Renaissance to Renaissance* (New York, 1974).

2. Tosefta Sanhedrin I, 3, ed. by M.S. Zuckermandel (Pasewalk, 1880–1882), p. 415; Babylonian Talmud, Sanhedrin 6b; Bava Metzia 30b, 88ab; and other sources cited in *SRH,* II, pp. 267 ff.

3. St. Ignatius's Letter to the Magnesians, viii–x, in *Patrologia Graeca,* ed. by J.P. Migne, pp. 669 ff.; Tertullian, *Adversus Judaeos,* ii; "Apologeticus adversus Gentes," xxi, in *Migne's Patrologia Latina,* I, p. 451; II, p. 637.

4. John Duns Scotus, *Sententiae,* IV, dist. 4, qu. 9, in his *Opera omnia* (Paris, 1891–1895), XVI, p. 489: "Unde sufficeret aliquos paucos in aliqua insula sequestratos permitti legem suam servare."

5. Goethe's statement is quoted with much elaboration by Mario Krammer in "Die Legende als Form geschichtlicher Gestaltung," in *Geist und Gesellschaft* (Kurt Breisig Jubilee Volume), III (Breslau, 1928), pp. 22–34. More directly relevant to Jewish problems is Isaiah Wolfsberg's "Aggadah and History" (Hebrew), in *Minhah li-Yehuda* (Judah Leb Zlotnik Jubilee Volume) (Jerusalem, 1950), pp. 31–39. See also my remarks in *SRH,* VI, pp. 232 ff., 440 n. 99.

6. On the use made of such passages by modern Jew-baiters to spread their "anti-Zionist," indeed anti-Semitic, propaganda, see, for example,

Trofim Kichko's notorious *Judaism Without Embellishment* (Kiev, 1968); his *Judaism and Zionism* (Moscow, 1968); and Yurii Ivanov's *Beware: Zionism* (Moscow, 1969), in the well-chosen "Extracts" in English translation, published in the *Bulletin of Soviet and East European Jewish Affairs,* no. 3 (1969), 45 ff., 50 ff.; supplemented by "The Kichko Affair, Additional Notes," *Soviet Jewish Affairs,* no. 1 (1971), 109–13. See also the revised edition of my *The Russian Jew Under Tsars and Soviets* (New York, 1976).

7. Judg. 1–2; Palestinian Talmud, Shevi'it VI, 1, 36c; Babylonian Talmud, Gittin 46a; Wilhelm Bacher, "The Supposed Inscription upon 'Joshua the Robber,' " *JQR,* [o.s.] III (1890–1891), 354–57; Alexandre H. Krappe, "Les Chananéens dans l'ancienne Afrique du Nord et en Espagne," *American Journal of Semitic Languages* LVII (1940), 229–43; and other sources cited in *SRH,* I, pp. 176, 374 n. 13; III, pp. 90 ff., 271 n. 23.

8. Josephus, *Against Apion,* II, 29.211–12, with brief comments thereon by H. St. J. Thackeray, ed., in the Loeb Classical Library Series (London, 1926), I, pp. 378 ff.

9. Immanuel Benzinger, *Hebräische Archäologie,* 3rd ed. (Leipzig, 1927).

10. See the numerous sources discussed by Jean Juster in *Les Juifs dans l'Empire Romain; leur condition juridique, économique et sociale,* 2 vols. (Paris, 1914), esp. II, pp. 265 ff.

11. See Tacitus, *Historiae,* II, 4 and V, i; Josephus, *The Jewish War,* I, 1, 1.1; and other sources cited in *SRH,* II, pp. 90 ff., 368 ff.

12. On the complicated problems of the legal status of the Jews of the Roman Empire before and after Emperor Caracalla's *lex Antoniniana de civitate* of 212 C.E., see J. Juster's comprehensive analyses in *Les Juifs;* and some subsequent debates analyzed in *SRH,* esp. I, pp. 238 ff., 402 ff.; II, pp. 108 ff., 347 ff.

13. The ramified problems of ancient Jewish martyrology have been the subject of a large monographic literature. See my observations on the writing available a quarter century ago in *SRH,* I, pp. 230 ff., 399 ff.

14. See esp. Louis Ginzberg, *Ginze Schechter* (Genizah Studies in Memory of Solomon Schecter), 2 vols. (New York, 1928), I, p. 476; and Victor Aptowitzer, *Die Parteipolitik der Hasmonäerzeit im rabbinischen und pseudoepigraphischen Schrifttum* (Vienna, 1927).

15. See Judah Halevi, *Kitab al-Khazari,* II, 33–36, and numerous other passages analyzed in my octocentennial address, "Yehudah Halevi: An Answer to a Historical Challenge," *Jewish Social Studies,* III (1941), 243–72, reproduced in my *Ancient and Medieval Jewish History: Essays,* ed. by Leon Feldman (New Brunswick, 1972), pp. 128–48, 433–43.

16. "Solomon bar Simson's Chronicle," ed. by Adolph Neubauer and Moritz Stern with a German trans. by Seligman Baer in their *Hebräische Berichte über die Verfolgungen während der Kreuzzüge* (Berlin, 1892), esp. pp. 6, 26 (Hebrew); 95, 137 ff. (German); and in Abraham Meir Haberman's compilation, *Sefer Gezerot Ashkenaz ve-Sarefat* (Records of Anti-Jewish Persecution in Germany and France from the Period of the Crusades) (Jerusalem, 1946), pp. 30, 57. Characteristically the chronicler, referring to a female victim and her children, referred to Hannah and her seven children. See in general the chapter on the "Age of Crusades" in *SRH,* IV, pp. 89–149, 283–311.

17. See the extensive documentation presented by Reuben Ainsztein in his *Jewish Resistance in Nazi-Occupied Eastern Europe with a Historical Survey of the Jew as Fighter and Soldier in the Diaspora* (London, 1974).

HARRY M. ORLINSKY

2   *The Situational Ethics of Violence in the Biblical Period*

To understand the phenomena of violence and defense in ancient Israel—whether the use of these actions or their avoidance, even their interdiction—it is necessary to recognize a basic principle that undergirds the entire Bible. The Bible, from beginning to end, is a "Book of Law." I do not mean a book, or a collection of books, in which laws, legal terms, and settings are to be found sporadically or in batches, although that view is true enough and is well recognized. I mean that the whole basis of the Bible, the raison d'être and main thrust of the Bible, is law—more specifically, a contract between two free parties, God and Israel, entirely enforceable by law. This is a contract—"covenant" is the term generally employed in this context—into which these two sovereign parties entered as equals and of their own free will. This contractual relationship between God and Israel, with no third party involved, is the basic principle of the Bible.

It is simply not possible to understand the events, personalities, and concepts that the Bible presents without comprehending fully and keeping in mind constantly the pertinence of the mutually exclusive contract that bound God and Israel to each other forever. No serious attempt to understand the biblical concept of God, for example, of nationalism-universalism, of worship, or of violence and defense can hope to be successful without understanding and applying the biblical concept of covenant.[1]

A Legal Contract Between God and Israel

In the view of the biblical writers, God and Israel had entered voluntarily into a contract as equal partners to serve and further the interests of one another exclusively. God undertook to prosper and defend Israel alone among all the nations of the world, in every aspect of her life—economic, military, political, and so on. Israel, in turn, was to worship God alone and carry out whatever laws and commandments He imposed upon them. Both parties took an oath to fulfill this contract; thus, the expressions "vow," "swear," "promise on oath"—frequently forms of *nishba*—are used for God no less than for Israel in this connection.

Of course, the biblical concept of God initially was such that it was unthinkable that He could or would break the contract; if God were the kind that broke contracts and disregarded His vows at will, Israel would not have entered into a contract with Him in the first place. One calls to mind in this connection the rhetorical passage in Balaam's speech:

> God is not man to be capricious,
> Or mortal to change His mind.
> Would He speak and not act,
> Promise and not fulfill?
> [Num. 23:19]*

Accordingly, whenever a spokesman of God, a *navi,*[2] opened his mouth to rebuke and warn Israel, he began with an accusation

---

*In this essay biblical citations conform generally to the new JPS editions of the Torah, the Five Megilloth, Psalms, Isaiah, and Jeremiah. However, in the case of citations from the other Prophets and Writings, the author has altered some translations in order to modernize the text.—ED.

involving the breaching of the covenant, the breaking of the contract that had been duly accepted by the two signatories, Israel and God. Thus Amos, using the legal term *pesha* (transgression or violation), after building up his case (Amos 1:3–2:3; see further below), charges his fellow Judeans with having repudiated the teaching (*torah*[3]) of the Lord and His laws:

> Thus said the Lord:
> Because of three transgressions of Judah,
> Because of the four, I will not revoke it
>   [viz., the punishment]—
> Because they repudiated the teaching of the Lord,
> They did not keep His Laws . . .
>
> [Amos 2:4]

And Israel, immediately thereafter, is accused of rejecting these laws:

> Thus said the Lord:
> Because of the three transgressions of Israel,
> Because of the four, I will not revoke it—
> Because they sold the one in the right[4] for silver,
> The one in need in exchange for a pair of sandals.
>
> [Amos 2:6]

Isaiah begins at once with such an accusation:

> Hear, O Heavens and give ear, O earth[5]
> For the Lord has spoken:
> I reared children and brought them up—
> And they have rebelled against Me!
>
> [Isa. 1:2]

Micah, Isaiah's younger contemporary, calls upon the whole world —a favorite hyperbole in the Bible—to be witness to God's legitimate and imminent action against His contractual partner:

> Because of Jacob's transgression . . .
> Because of the House of Israel's sins.
>
> [Micah 1:5]

And finally, to include the last of the four outstanding spokesmen of God in the eighth century, Hosea charges Israel with idolatry —for which he employed adultery (i.e., faithlessness, the breaching of a contract) as a symbol:

The Lord said to Hosea:
Go take a woman of harlotry
And have children of harlotry;
For the land has committed harlotry
By forsaking the Lord.
[Hosea 1:2]

In conclusion, it is the legal bond uniting God and Israel that made it possible for God's prophets to address their fellow Israelites in a manner they could not employ for any other nation in the world.

Yet God did have a legal claim upon all the inhabitants of the world—animal as well as human life, and the natural phenomena too—even though that claim was far more limited in scope than that involving Israel. To the biblical writers, from Genesis to the Second Book of Chronicles, God is not only Israel's God alone— exactly as Israel is God's people alone—but He is at the same time, and naturally so, also the God of the universe, the only God in existence in the whole world, the only God who ever existed or will ever exist. He is the sole Creator of sun, moon, and stars; of rain, drought, thunder, lightening, and earthquakes; or sky, earth, and waters; of all living creatures, human and animal alike. All heavenly bodies, all natural phenomena, all parts of the universe inhabited by living beings, all peoples, nations, and individuals alike— all are subject to His direct supervision and will. He is their Master in the fullest sense of the term.

Thus, the God of Israel is the sole God and Master of the universe, even as He is the God of no other nation but Israel. In other words, the *national* God of biblical Israel is a *universal* God but not an *international* God.[6] God never entered into a legally binding relationship with any people other than Israel. To the biblical writers, God was never the God of Moab, Egypt, Canaan,

Assyria, Aram, Ethiopia, or Philistia; He was the God of Israel alone. Just as Israel was to have no other God, so was God to have no other people. Yet, as the Creator and Master of the universe, God did have a legal obligation to all His creation, embracing not only all the non-Israelite peoples of the world but also all the living creatures of sky, earth, and waters and all the heavenly bodies.

✓   What was God's universal legal obligation? The contract that God had made with the world at large bound Him never again to destroy it, no matter how great the lawlessness might become. Indeed, it was the function of the rainbow to prevent God from bringing another flood upon the world:

> And God said to Noah and to his sons with him, "I now establish My covenant with you and your offspring to come, and with every living thing that is with you—birds, cattle, and every wild beast as well. . . . never again shall all flesh be cut off by the waters of a flood. . . . God further said, "This is the sign that I set for the covenant between Me and you, and every living creature with you, for all ages to come. I have set My bow in the clouds, and it shall serve as a sign of the covenant between Me and the earth. When I bring clouds over the earth, and the bow appears in the clouds, I will remember My covenant between Me and you and every living creature among all flesh, so that the waters shall never again become a flood to destroy all flesh. . . . "That," God said to Noah, "shall be the sign of the covenant that I have established between Me and all flesh that is on earth."[7]
>
> [Gen. 9:8–17]

For it was the lawlessness of the world in the first place that had brought on the flood and the destruction of pre-Noahide life on earth:

> The earth became corrupt before God; the earth was filled with lawlessness.[8] When God saw how corrupt the earth was, for all flesh had corrupted its ways on earth, God said to Noah, "I have decided to put an end to all flesh, for the earth is filled with lawlessness because of them: I am about to destroy them with the earth. Make yourself an ark[9]. . . .
>
> [Gen. 6:11–14]

And chapter 8 concludes with this fiat (v. 22):

> So long as the earth endures,
> Seedtime and harvest,
> Cold and heat,
> Summer and winter,
> Day and night,
> Shall not cease.

But while God promised never again to bring destruction upon life on earth, mankind in turn also bound itself to certain rules. It had to respect all living beings; wanton murder and shedding of blood—be it by man or animal against man or animal—was proscribed:

> God blessed Noah and his sons, and said to them, "Be fertile and increase, and fill the earth. The fear and dread of you shall be upon all the beasts of the earth and upon all the birds of the sky . . . and upon all the fish of the sea. . . . Every creature that lives shall be yours to eat; as with the green grasses, I give you all these. You must not, however, eat flesh with its life-blood in it. But for your own life-blood I will require a reckoning: I will require it of every beast; of man, too, will I require a reckoning for human life, of every man for that of his fellow man!

> Whoever sheds the blood of man,
> By man shall his blood be shed;
> For in His image
> Did God make man.[10]

> [Gen. 9:1–6]

The heavenly bodies, the seasons of the year, the natural phenomena—all these now also had their fixed careers in the universe, and none could go beyond the roles assigned to them. These universal laws came to be called by the rabbis "Noahide laws"; others would subsume them under the term "natural law."[11] As for natural phenomena, the heavenly bodies, and the like, Elihu and God offer vivid descriptions of God's control over them in the famous speeches in the Book of Job (36:27–37: 24, Elihu; 38, God).

Coming back to the non-Israelite peoples of the world, chapters 1 and 2 of the Book of Amos provide excellent examples of the biblical concept of God's contract with the gentile nations and the concrete application of the universal Noahide laws. Even a casual perusal of the crimes with which the six gentile neighbors of Israel were charged and for which God, Israel's own God, would punish them, indicates clearly that it is universal laws that were breached. It is the inhuman treatment that Damascus (Aram) meted out to Gilead—"because they threshed Gilead with threshing sledges of iron"—that will result in the former's punishment (Amos 1:3). Gaza (Philistia) will suffer retribution for "carrying off into exile a whole people" (1:6). God will destroy Tyre (Phoenicia) "because they delivered up a whole people to Edom and were not mindful of the covenant of brotherhood" (1:9) and will devastate Edom "because he pursued his brother with the sword and cast off all pity" (1:11). God will lay Ammon waste and exile her leaders "because they ripped up pregnant women of Gilead" (1:13), and, finally, He will cut off the rulers of Moab and their followers "because they burned to lime the bones of the king of Edom" (2:1).

These crimes, involving mass murder (or genocide, as we would call it today), ruthless exile, excessive and unnatural brutality—in short, man's inhumanity to man—are violations of God's universal (Noahide) laws of nature.[12] According to the writers of the Bible, it is Israel's God who promulgated these laws, and it is her God who will punish the violators.[13]

Violence and God's Punishment

Violence and defense in the biblical period are to be understood—so far as the biblical writers were concerned—in the light of the basic concept of God's national covenant with Israel, on the one hand, and of His universal (not international) covenant with the world at large on the other. Thus, what may have appeared as violence or defense to Israel's gentile neighbors was understood by Israel as legitimate punishment at the hands of God for violations of the contract with Him. In other words, generally speaking, when one person kills another it is murder, it is violence in the extreme, it is an illegal act; but when the killer is tried by a duly authorized judge and/or jury, in whatever form (e.g., by Israel's elders "in the gate"), and is condemned to death, his execution is a legal act. In this light, the killing becomes an act by which society defends itself against anarchy and violence; it is not murder but justice.

When Amos condemned the six gentile nations for having committed certain acts against one another—none, in this case, against Judah-Israel—they had, in Amos' view, committed acts of violence in violation of the universal laws proclaimed by Israel's God; for that God would see to it that the violators would be punished.[14] God is not guilty of any violence against the nations, for they, by their violence, bring on His punishment.

Seen in this light, the biblical explanation of the destruction of Sodom and Gomorrah makes sense: the inhabitants had flouted grossly God's universal (Noahide) laws. Israel's tradition had it that the destruction was indeed awesome: "The Lord rained upon Sodom and Gomorrah sulfurous fire. . . . He annihilated those cities and the entire Plain, and all the inhabitants of the cities and the vegetation of the ground . . . and [Abraham] saw the smoke of the land rising like the smoke of a kiln" (Gen. 19:24–28). Clearly, this judgment could have been the consequence only of gross misconduct (18:20): "The Lord said, 'The outrage [or outcry, *tza'akat*] of Sodom and Gomorrah is so great, and their sin so grave!' " And when not even ten just men could be found in Sodom (18:22–32), the fate of the town was sealed. As for the heinous offense of the Sodomites in their attempted treatment of their three guests— forced unnatural acts of lewdness in place of gracious hospitality (19:1 ff.)—that alone justified the harshest retribution.

The experience of the five "cities of the plain" serves as excellent background for the story of the levite[15] (i.e., the seer-priest) and his Judean concubine (Judg. 19). There are several striking parallels, such as the element of sodomy, the offer of the two daughters so as to avoid sodomy and avert violation of hospitality, and even the use of similar phrases (cf., e.g., Gen. 19:8 and Judg. 19:24). What may be noted here is that Israel—in addition to the laws of its national covenant with God—was subject to all universal laws no less than the non-Israelites.

God as Warrior

An instructive example of the biblical view of violence is the war —"holy war" is the concept to which it gave rise—that the Israelites under Joshua waged against the inhabitants of Canaan, following on the ten plagues, the exodus, and the wandering in the wilderness under Moses. To the Egyptians the actions of God against them and their Pharaoh could hardly have constituted anything but violence in the extreme. To the Israelites, however, this constituted prime evidence that God took His mutually exclusive contract with Israel quite seriously; and if the Egyptians lost their Hebrew slaves and experienced the dreadful plagues and then the debacle at the Sea of Reeds, that was their punishment for not having accepted the reasonable proposal made by God's spokesman Moses.

So far as the inhabitants of Canaan were concerned, the Israelite invasion of the Cisjordan part of their considerable sea and land empire—like the invasion of the Transjordanian part by Israel's closely related peoples, the Moabites, Ammonites, and Edomites —was only another act of violence among other invasions that all countries in the Fertile Crescent experienced during the third and second millennia. For Israel, however, this invasion had been determined by their God in accordance with a longstanding promise to Israel's ancestors; no element of violence would be involved in God's fulfillment of His part of the contract with first the patriarchs and then the people Israel.[16]

In keeping with the geography of the territory on both sides of the Jordan and the political divisions of the peoples that inhabited it, the Israelites, after the initial conquest of some of that territory, were to experience continual wars of defense and offense. On the one hand, the previous inhabitants of the conquered areas fought to regain what had been theirs—acquired in much the same way that the Israelites had dispossessed them —while, on the other hand, the individual Israelite tribes and varying groups of tribes attempted, when the occasion seemed to them favorable, to extend their territorial domain.[17] Since the conquest, settlement, defense, and consolidation of the land of Canaan was essentially a military affair, and since their God and contractual partner was the central force in this great and prolonged event, it was natural for the Israelites during this period to emphasize the aspect of war in God's qualities and actions. The prophets of the eighth and seventh centuries could emphasize such other qualities of God as compassion and justice (reward and punishment for obeying and breaking the laws of the covenant), and always God will be reminded by His Israelite partners of the "natural" aspect of His being (rain in season, fertility in agriculture, flocks and herds, children, and the like). However, during the period of the judges, who were military leaders, it was God's military prowess and leadership that received emphasis. These attributes of God are pointed up time and again in subsequent periods of Israel's history, frequently with reference to God's mighty arm and deeds in connection with the Exodus from Egypt (cf., e.g., Ezek. 20:33 ff.; Isa. 42: 25).[18]

Yet, while God is described as a "warrior" (Ex. 15:3), one who "goes forth like a warrior" (Isa. 42:13), and one who is "mighty in battle" (Ps. 24:8), He is never a "man of violence" and is nowhere associated with violence or with illegal and unjust action. In punishing Israel or a gentile nation, no matter how fierce His anger or how violent His retribution, God was always the God of justice (rewarding and punishing justly), the Judge of all the earth who deals justly (cf. Gen. 18:25), always true to His word (Num. 23:19).

Violence brings to mind murder and war, and one extreme form of violence is civil war, in which the desire or need to maintain power or to wrest it from others turns group against fellow group and brother against brother in uninhibited hostility and savagery. An early instance of this may be found in "The Rebellions during the Reign of David."[19] No holds are barred in the struggle for power, whatever justification for the struggle may be advanced. Thus Mephibosheth (Meribaal), son of Saul, and Shimei, son of Gera and a follower of Saul, though rivals for power, nevertheless joined forces with Prince Absalom in his revolt against his father David, for the king was the common and most serious foe at the time. And while the biblical text justifies David's handing over of seven of Saul's sons to the Gibeonites to be executed (2 Sam. 21:1–14), Shimei was not perverting the truth when he publicly accused the king of criminal acts against the House of Saul (2 Sam. 16:5 ff.).

Bloody as they were, the revolts would have been even bloodier if the leaders of the opposition had not come to realize that "what was, was"; history could not be thwarted. It was impossible for the old, clan-centered, tribe-centered, and largely agricultural social structure to check and control the growth of a more centralized, royal-bureaucratic, urban-commercial-agricultural social order. This was even less possible than the prevention of the monarchy, limited as it was under Saul, only a few decades previously. When Samuel, representing the old order, warns the people of the brutal lawlessness—in a word, violence—inherent in the monarchical system, and rebukes them for rejecting God as their sole king, he bases his declaration on his ability to receive directly God's instructions and transmit them to God's covenanted partner. Yet, when the forces of centralized rule triumphed—as they had to in the face of the centralized Philistine threat—it was God, again, who was cited as favoring the monarchy. Thus, to the victor belong not only the spoils but also the determination and interpretation of God's will.[20]

Civil War, Destruction, and Exile

Several additional events of national significance come to mind in connection with violence, such as the permanent break between the North and South, a break which began during Solomon's reign, and the first revolt under Jeroboam the Ephraimite, in association with Ahijah of Shiloh, representing the Shilonite seer-priesthood (1 Kings 11:26–40). What was legitimate—that is, divinely determined—monarchy and rule in the eyes of the Davidic-Solomonic regime was not so regarded by its opponents; David, in the poem of thanksgiving to God attributed to him (2 Sam. 22; Ps. 18), refers to them as *ish hamas(im)* "lawless men," or traditionally, "men of violence." The latter, on the other hand, accused Solomon of breaking the covenant with God by committing idolatrous acts (e.g., Ahijah to Jeroboam, 1 Kings 11:33). The knowing historian will, of course, see readily behind this religious terminology and recognize the real causes of the revolt: forced labor, high taxes, and political corruption.

In fact, "the rebel leaders of northern Israel did not oppose a monarchy, nor did they care about the kind of worship that went on in the Temple and the shrines. They were willing to support one of their own as king, in the hope and belief that this would lighten the heavy burden of taxation and increase their share in the common wealth. But the lower classes . . . had yet to learn that what Jeroboam and the other northern leaders intended was nothing more than replacing the Judean monarchy of Solomon with another equally harsh monarchy of their own."[21]

The repressive acts of the Solomonic regime—would it be unfair to describe them as acts of violence?—brought on an act of violence that ushered in the Divided Kingdom: when Rehoboam, Solomon's son and successor, sent his tax collector, Adoram, to treat with the Israelites under Jeroboam, he was confronted with open revolt. Adoram was stoned to death, and Rehoboam himself barely escaped with his life (1 Kings 12; 2 Chron. 10).

The destruction of the northern kingdom of Israel in 722–721 B.C.E., grievous as it was to all Israel "from Dan to Beersheba," was not as traumatic as the destruction of the southern kingdom of Judah almost a century and a half later (587–586 B.C.E.). Prior to that event there was sometimes good reason and always some hope that Israel would be restored, perhaps even reunited with Judah under Davidic rule; but once Judah lay crushed and quiet all the swirl and clash of centuries had apparently come to naught. Never before had God's covenanted partner—at least the half that had survived the devastation of Israel and her capital city, Samaria —experienced, or even witnessed, such violence against the people, the land, and the fortified as well as unwalled cities. Even more shattering was the incredible fact that God's own sanctuary, His very own Zion, was taken by Gentiles and lay defiled by them.[22] Only two other events in almost four thousand years of Jewish history can be classed with the destruction of Judah and the First Temple and the imposition of the Babylonian exile: the destruction of the Second Temple and Judean sovereignty in 70 C.E. (both commemorated on the same day of the year, Tishah B'Av), and the Holocaust of the six million Jews in our own century.

The author of the Book of Lamentations does not spare words and imagery in describing the violence inflicted on defenseless Judah and Jerusalem:

> Lonely sits the city
> Once great with people! . . .
> Because the Lord has afflicted her
> For her many transgressions. . . .
> From above He sent a fire
> Down into my bones.
> He spread a net for my feet,
> He hurled me backward. . . .
> [Lam. 1:1–13]

God, of course, was merely carrying out his obligation as a covenanted partner when He punished Israel for breaching the covenant:

The Lord is in the right,
For I have disobeyed Him. . . .
See, O Lord, the distress I am in!
My heart is in anguish,
I know how wrong I was
To disobey. . . .

[Lam. 1:18–20]

As Nebuzaradan, King Nebuchadnezzar's representative, is said to have put it to Jeremiah (Jer. 40:2): ". . . The Lord your God threatened this place with disaster . . . because you sinned against the Lord and did not obey Him. . . . As for Babylonia's King Nebuchadnezzar, whose regime and army wreaked God's violent destruction on Judah, the prophet Jeremiah refers to him as nothing less than God's servant, for he faithfully carried out God's purpose in punishing Israel. Indeed, he is the only non-Israelite in the entire Bible so described, and in rabbinic literature he is referred to as a *tzadik*. [23]

Nevertheless, the realities of life's experiences did not permit Nebuchadnezzar and his people to go unscathed. According to Jeremiah, God had decreed that all nations submit to the rule of Babylonia;[24] but in the end Babylonia also suffered the fate of those she had vanquished:

> . . . those nations shall serve the king of Babylon seventy years. When the seventy years are over, I will punish the king of Babylon and that nation and the land of the Chaldeans for their sins . . . and I will make it a desolation for all time. . . . For they too shall be enslaved by many nations and great kings; and I will requite them according to their acts and according to their conduct.
>
> [Jer. 25:11–14]

During the exile the Second Isaiah not only assured his fellow Judeans in captivity that God would redeem them (Isa. 41:14–16) and restore them to their holy homeland (43:3–6) but also proclaimed dramatically the violence and humiliation that Babylonia would suffer in the process (47:5–11; 49:22–26).[25] As the prophet himself put it:

Fear not, O worm Jacob,
O men of Israel:
I will help you—declares the Lord—
I your Redeemer, the Holy One of Israel.
I will make of you a threshing-board,
Sharp, new, with many spikes.
You shall thresh mountains to dust,
And make hills like chaff.
You shall winnow them
And the wind shall carry them off;
The whirlwind shall scatter them;
But you shall rejoice in the Lord,
And glory in the Holy One of Israel.
      [Isa. 41:14–16]

For I the Lord am your God,
The Holy One of Israel, your Savior. . . .
Because you are precious to Me,
And honored, and I love you,
I will give men in exchange for you,
And peoples in your stead.
Fear not, for I am with you:
I will bring your folk from the East,
Will gather you out of the West;
I will say to the North, "Give back!"
And to the South, "Do not withhold!"
Bring My sons from afar,
And My daughters from the end of the earth.
      [Isa. 43:3–6]

Sit silent; retire into darkness,
O Fair Chaldea;
Nevermore shall they call you
Mistress of Kingdoms.
I was angry at My people,
I defiled My heritage;
I put them into your hands,
But you showed them no mercy.
Even upon the aged you made
Your yoke exceedingly heavy.
You thought, "I shall always be
The mistress still". . . .
"I am, and there is none but me". . . .
Evil is coming upon you . . .
Disaster is falling upon you . . .

Coming upon you suddenly
Is ruin of which you know nothing.
                    [Isa. 47:5–11]

Thus said the Lord God:
I will raise My hand to nations
And lift up My ensign to the peoples;
And they shall bring you sons in their bosoms,
And carry your daughters on their shoulders.
Kings shall tend your children,
Their queens shall serve you as nurses.
They shall bow to you, face to the ground,
And lick the dust of your feet. . . .
I will make your oppressors eat their own flesh,
They shall be drunk with their own blood as with wine.
And all mankind shall know
That I the Lord am your Savior,
The Mighty One or: Champion of Jacob, your Redeemer!
                    [Isa. 49:22–26]

In conclusion, the biblical attitude toward violence, whether in rejection or in justification and support, is determined solely by the specific historical circumstances in which the act of violence is practiced. Accordingly, Persia's destruction of Babylonia—and the restoration of Judah—was justified; but Judah's breaking of the covenant with God justified Babylonia's violence against her in the first place.

Violence and the Prophets

No attempt has been made here to discuss those situations in the Bible where acts of violence involve individuals. I have in mind, for example, the common fate of the prophets. Throughout the Hebrew Bible whenever a prophet came before the people to rebuke them for breaking God's covenant, he automatically suffered violence or the threat of it because of the nature of his mission. No prophet ever appeared in order to praise Israel for her justness and uprightness in the eyes of God. With their uncompromising condemnations, the prophets continually risked, and sometimes suffered, abuse and even death at the hands of those they rebuked. Elijah had to flee for his life because of the vehement denunciation of Ahab and Jezebel. Micah was hit in the jaw and imprisoned, and Amos the Judean risked limb and life. Because he bitterly denounced the domestic and foreign policy of his government, Jeremiah was threatened with death, beaten, put into stocks, and thrown into a dungeon, so that he was constrained to cry out, ". . . I was like a docile lamb led to the slaughter" (Jer. 11:19). Ezekiel was told by God, "And you, son of man, be not afraid of them [the prophet's fellow Judean exiles in Babylonia], neither be afraid of their words, though briers and thorns be with you and you dwell among scorpions" (Ezek. 2:6). The prophet Uriah was killed by King Jehoiakim (Jer. 26:20–23), and Zechariah was stoned to death (2 Chron. 24:20–21). Thus these spokesmen of God suffered violence because of the very nature of their calling.[26]

Yet another type of violence occurs when Nehemiah, in his zeal to enforce the laws he regarded as paramount, resorted to physical violence against the transgressors:

> I saw in Judah men treading wine presses on the sabbath, and bringing in heaps of grain loaded on asses, along with wine, grapes, figs, and all kinds of loads—bringing them to Jerusalem on the sabbath day . . . The Phoenicians [literally Tyrians] who lived there also brought fish and all kinds of goods and sold them on the sabbath. . . . But I warned them and said to them, "If you do this again, I'll lay hands on you." And from then on, they did not come on the sabbath. . . . I also saw in those days the Jews who had married Ashdodite, Ammonite, and Moabite women; half of their children spoke Ashdodite, and could not speak Judean . . . I remonstrated with them and reviled [or cursed] them, and I beat them and tore their hair . . .[27]
>
> [Neh. 13:15 ff.]

A Concluding Note

In this discussion the term "violence" has not been confined to cases of physical abuse, for the biblical Hebrew term *hamas* denotes lawlessness as well as physical violence (see n. 8). Thus the term would include violation of a person's rights or repression in any form. After all, repressive laws that bring on violence surely are to be regarded as no less violent than the reactions they engender; oppressive, undemocratically derived laws, even though technically legal—as so many laws of Hitler's Germany and Stalin's Russia were—are hardly to be considered nonviolent when they call forth violence on the part of the oppressed.

In our world today no continent and no major grouping of nations has escaped outbursts of violence on the part of those who see themselves as oppressed by the old order. Since it is not usual for the establishment to give up power peacefully, those who are bent on seizing power, like those who are determined to retain it, must resort to various kinds of violence. In this unprecedented historical circumstance, unprecedented both in its global scope and in its savagery, the Jewish people has again become a convenient target for blame, calumny, and destruction—"again" because, as George S. Wise puts it in his Foreword to this volume, "Violence has always existed and the Jews have been its victims for thousands of years in all parts of the world and in all periods of history."

NOTES

1. Very much has been published in recent years on the biblical concept of covenant. Most of the discussions have revolved about the extrabiblical

origins (Hittite, Assyrian, Canaanite, etc.,) of the biblical idea of covenant and the influences on it, especially individual words and phrases. Emphasis also has been laid on the vassal-suzerain treaties of the Mesopotamian societies as underlying the God-Israel relationship in their covenant. However, I have little sympathy with many of these studies, and I am not aware of a single study of the concept and institution of the biblical covenant that a historian qua historian could accept methodologically. All kinds of Sumerian, Assyrian, Babylonian, Hittite, and Northwest Semitic texts of all historical climes and periods are cited indiscriminately to prove that Israel and God had agreed to a vassal-type treaty. I am not really being facetious when I wonder out loud where the various historians, prophets, psalmists, and chroniclers—not to mention the glossators and redactors —who composed the Bible found the time to compose what they did when they were so busy reading and keeping up with, and making use of, the suzerian-vassal treaties that the Hittities and Northwest Semites were signing and so often breaking.

In point of fact, I am not sure that any scholar has ever proved—worse, I am not sure that any scholar has recently even thought of trying to prove —that the contractual relationship between Israel and God as presented in the Bible was actually one that involved an inferior and a superior in the manner of a vassal and a suzerain. My own impression is that the biblical concept constituted a relationship into which both parties entered not only freely but as equals and that this relationship derived ultimately —since God by the very concept of Him to begin with is the Lord and Israel the servant—from the lord-servant *(adon-eved)* relationship that characterized Israel's (and much of Western Asia's) economy at the time. As for the increasingly numerous "covenant parallels" being discovered between Israel and her Asiatic neighbors, one is tempted to say, with Gertrude Stein: a parallel is a parallel is a parallel. . . . The pity of it is that in pursuing and collecting parallels, scholars think that they are writing history.

Part of the above will be found in my "Whither Biblical Research?" (Presidential Address for the Society of Biblical Literature), *Journal of Biblical Literature* (hereafter *JBL*), 90 (1971), 1–14; reprinted as chap. 11 in my *Essays in Biblical Culture and Bible Translation* (New York, 1974), pp. 200–217.

2. After M. Jastrow, Jr., wrote (*JBL,* 28[1909], 56) that the prophet's "main purpose is to speak out in the name of a Deity, to speak forth rather than foretell. . . ." and such scholars as R. H. Charles two decades later (*A Critical and Exegetical Commentary on the Book of Daniel* [Oxford, 1929]) described the prophet as a "forthteller" rather than "foreteller," it is sad that scholars continue to refuse to distinguish between the diviner-

seer (foreteller) and the prophet (forthteller), i.e., between the likes of an Eli, Samuel, the unnamed "men of God," Nathan, Ahijah, and Elisha (from the eleventh to the ninth centuries)—all of whom were diviners and attached to shrines or to diviner guilds or orders, and constitute a phenomenon common to the ancient Near East—and those like Hosea, Amos, Isaiah, and Micah, who make their appearance after about 800 B.C.E. and are a uniquely Israelite phenomenon. See my "The Seer-Priest and the Prophet in Ancient Israel," in *Judges,* The World History of the Jewish People, vol. III, ed. by Benjamin Mazar; reprinted as chap. 3 in *Essays in Biblical Culture,* pp. 39–63, and bibliography, pp. 64–65.

3. The Hebrew term *torah* has several meanings and nuances; see the comment in my *Notes on the New Translation of the Torah* (Philadelphia, 1969), index, s.v.

4. The traditional rendering for the Hebrew *tzadik* is "the righteous," but this rendering is incorrect and misleading. It is not a moral-ethical term that is involved here but a legal term: it is "the just, the one in the right, the one who acted within the law and obeyed it," that conveys the intent of the Hebrew. Similarly, the well-known phrase *"tzedek, tzedek tirdof"* (Deut. 16:20) is to be translated "Justice, justice shall you pursue"; the traditional "Righteousness, righteousness . . ." fails to reproduce the legal character of the Hebrew, nor will the term "righteousness" be found in any of the standard dictionaries of legal terms. (Similarly, such terms as *rasha* are to be understood as "to be wrong," "commit wrong," or "be guilty," not simply as "be wicked.") See my *Notes on the New Translation of the Torah,* index, s.v. "legal term," p. 276a, and *"tzadak,"* p. 278b. A fine analysis of the problem as a whole is the unpublished master's-ordination thesis by Lennard Thal (Hebrew Union College-Jewish Institute of Religion, 1973) on "The Legal Terminology and Context of the Book of Job." This study served me well in the preparation of a lecture on "The Septuagint in the Light of the Hebrew Bible as a Legal Document," the last of the three lectures I delivered at Oxford (April-May 1974) as Grinfield Lecturer on the Septuagint. As an example of how to analyze the career of a legal concept, see the monographic study by Jacob J. Finkelstein, "The Goring Ox," in the *Temple Law Review* (1972)—a veritable tour de force in our field of research; Finkelstein's overall view can now be gauged in his discussion of the concepts of "World and Man *(olam ve-Adam)* in the Cosmology of the Ancient Near East and in the Bible" (Hebrew), *Molad,* VI (XXIX), 31, 241 (April-June 1974), 122–23.

5. I had sometimes wondered whether the mention of "heaven" and "earth" (Micah 1:2 will involve "peoples" and "earth") constituted the minimum of two witnesses required for legal action against an accused

(Deut. 19:15 specifies that " . . . a case can be valid only on the testimony of two witnesses or more"). Actually these two words—in accordance with common usage in biblical Hebrew poetry—are used in combination to denote "the whole world," as for example, in, Gen. 1:1: "[When God began to create] heaven and earth," i.e., the world, the universe (see *Notes on the New Translation of the Torah*).

6. On the books of Ruth and Jonah, following on an analysis of such "classical" passages as Mal. 2:10 ("Have we not all one Father? Has not one God created us?"), Lev. 19:18 ("You shall love your fellow as yourself"), and Amos 9:7 (" 'You are to Me the same as the Ethiopians, O Israel,' declares the Lord . . .")—not to mention such other passages as Isa. 2:2–4; Micah 4:1–3 ("In the days to come, the mount of the Lord's House shall be established on the highest mountain . . . and all the nations shall gaze on it . . . and say, 'Come, let us go up to the mount of the Lord . . . that He may instruct us in His ways . . .' For instruction [*torah*] shall come forth from Zion . . ."); Isa. 56:7 (". . . For My House shall be called a house of prayer for all peoples"); Isa. 14:1–2; Zech. 2:14–16; and Mal. 1:11—see Orlinsky, "Nationalism-Universalism and Internationalism in Ancient Israel," *Essays in Biblical Culture,* chap. 5, pp. 78–116; the internationalism of Isa. 19:18–24 is also discussed, pp. 90 ff. Chapter 9 of *Essays* (pp. 166–86), " 'A Covenant (of) People, A Light of Nations'—a Problem in Biblical Theology," deals with Jer. 1:5 ("I appointed you a prophet concerning the nations"), with Isa. 42:6 ("I created you, and appointed you/A covenant-people, a light of nations"), and with Isa. 49:6 ("I will also make you a light of nations"). Chapter 6 (pp. 117–43) discusses in considerable detail "Nationalism-Universalism in the Book of Jeremiah."

7. Another version, Gen. 8:20–22 (designated as "J" by scholars, as against "P" for the "rainbow" version), has it that after Noah and his family and the animals came out of the ark, "Noah built an altar to the Lord and . . . offered burnt offerings on the altar. The Lord smelled the pleasing odor, and the Lord said to Himself; Never again will I doom the world because of man. . . ."

8. The Hebrew word rendered here by "lawlessness" is *hamas;* the traditional translation "violence" unnecessarily and misleadingly connotes a limitation of the term to physical force.

9. The parallel version, Gen. 6:5–8 (designated "J" by scholars, as distinguished from "P" for the *hamas* version), reads: "The Lord saw how great was man's wrongdoing on earth . . . And the Lord regretted that He had made man on earth . . . The Lord said: 'I will blot out from the earth the men whom I created . . .' But Noah found favor with the Lord."

10. It is this kind of universal law that Cain violated when he murdered

his brother Abel: "Then [God] said, 'What have you done? Hark, your brother's blood cries out to Me from the ground'" (Gen. 4:10). The scholarly analysis which views the Cain-Abel event as reflecting an ancient struggle between two socioeconomic forces, those who tilled the soil and those who raised herds and flocks, is here beside the point.

11. I have discussed this in chap. 5 of *Essays in Biblical Culture*, pp. 87 ff.

12. It should be added that, in time, blasphemy too became a Noahide transgression. When Isaiah denounced King Sennacherib of Assyria and assured him that God would bring about his ignominious defeat, it was because of his blasphemous treatment of God (2 Kings 19:22 ff.):

> Whom have you blasphemed and reviled,
> Against whom raised your voice
> And insolently raised your eyes? . . .
> Against the Holy One of Israel!
>
> (28) Because you have raged against Me,
> And your tumult has reached My ears,
> I will put My hook in your nose
> And My bit in your mouth;
> And I will take you back by the road
> By which you came.

On the reasons for God's punishment of His servant, King Nebuchadnezzar of Babylon (*N. melekh-bavel avdi,* "N. . . . My servant" (Jer. 25:9, 27:6, and 43:10)), see n. 25 below.

13. It does not appear to be recognized as widely as it should that the fact that God is the Creator of the world automatically made Him—so far as the Bible is concerned—a just God. This is one of the main points in God's speech out of the whirlwind, where the crescendo of rhetorical questions of chaps. 38–39 builds up to God's question addressed to Job in 40:8: "Would you . . . find Me guilty so that you would be in the right?" See the latter part of the Prolegomenon by James L. Crenshaw in the volume of *Studies in the Wisdom Literature* (New York, 1975) that he has compiled for Ktav's Library of Biblical Studies.

14. Amos 1:2–15 ff.:

> The Lord will roar from Zion,
> From Jerusalem He will raise His voice. . . .
> [T]he people of Aram shall go into exile in Kir. . . .
> [T]he remnant of the Philistines shall perish. . . .
> I will dispatch fire against the wall of Tyre. . . .
> [F]ire shall consume the towers of Bosrah [Edom]. . . .
> (2:3) I will slay all her [Moab's] officials. . . .

15. The spelling "levite" (rather than "Levite") is justified by the fact that the term denoted in this period a diviner-priest rather than a member of a tribe called Levi. According to Judg. 17:7, the levite was "a young man of Bethlehem in Judah, of the family of Judah." These levites traveled up and down the country as sojourning (i.e., itinerant) diviner-priests, and they sometimes acquired a permanent post or shrine. See "The Seer-Priest and the Prophet," *Essays in Biblical Culture,* chap. 3, pp. 46 ff.

16. It may be noted in this connection that when reference is made in the Bible to God carrying out His part of the covenant, the phraseology that will be employed very frequently is "I/He brought you up/out from the land of Egypt," and "I/He led you through the wilderness," and "I/He dispossessed/destroyed the Amorites/Canaanites before you"—with the usual variations (cf., e.g., Josh. 24:5 ff.; Judg. 6:13; 1 Kings 8:51, 53; Jer. 2:4 ff.; Ezek. 20:5 ff.; Amos 2:9–10; 3:1 ff.; Neh. 9:6 ff.). The term *b'rit* is used far less frequently than is generally assumed; thus Amos uses this term only once (1:9), not in connection with God and Israel but regarding Phoenicia (Tyre) and an unnamed non-Israelite people, where Phoenicia is accused of having violated a "covenant of brotherhood" *(b'rit ahim);* cf. pp. 86–87 and n. 8 in *Essays in Biblical Culture.*

17. These groupings of tribes or clans were sporadic and ad hoc creations, the product of localized circumstances. Fewer scholars than ever continue to take seriously the idea of an amphictyonic structure of Israel during this period, and some of those who do have been careful to skirt the problem by avoiding the use of the term "amphictyony" and the designation of the specific location of the shrine around which the alleged amphictyony was structured, substituting instead such vaguer terms as "confederacy," "tribal federation," and "league," and making the mobile and elusive Ark the shrine. Indeed, in desperation they have turned to the elusive Midianites and Kedarites and discovered among them "biblical-style leagues"; such crucial matters as time and place and social structure have no meaning for non-historians. See my study of "The Tribal System of Israel and Related Groups in the Period of the Judges," reprinted as chap. 4 in *Essays in Biblical Culture,* pp. 66–77, with a bibliographical addendum on p. 77; and, most recently, A.D.H. Mayes, *Israel in the Period of the Judges* (London, 1974). See also the published abstract of G. Fohrer's paper presented at the Sixth World Congress of Jewish Studies (Jerusalem, 1974, A–76)—"The pre-monarchic period of Israel must be explored anew, because there [was] no amphictyony of the tribes . . ."); and A. J. Hauser, "The 'Minor Judges'—a Re-evaluation,"*JBL,* 94 (1975), 190–200.

18. The description of Israel's concept of her God as "The Divine Warrior" is misleading, unless equal emphasis is given to such other

descriptive titles as "The God of Peace," "The Divine Judge," "The Angry God," "The Compassionate God," "The Jealous God," "The Nature God," "The Fertility God," and the like. These glib, catch-all phrases—defying the context of time and space—do not help one to comprehend properly biblical Israel's understanding of God, history, nature, and the universe; they obfuscate more than they clarify.

19. This is the title of Martin A. Cohen's study, subtitled "An Inquiry into Social Dynamics in Ancient Israel," which appears in *Studies in Jewish Bibliography, History, and Literature in Honor of I. Edward Kiev,* ed. by C. Berlin (New York, 1971), pp. 91–112. His earlier study should be read in this connection, "The Role of the Shilonite Priesthood in the United Monarchy of Ancient Israel," *Hebrew Union College Annual (HUCA),* 36 (1965), 59–98.

20. I have in mind the "conflicting" statements about the role of Samuel, i.e., the Shilonite seer-priesthood, in the decisions to choose Saul and David as kings; see briefly my *Understanding the Bible through History and Archaeology* (New York, 1972), pp. 103 ff. ("The Philistines" and "King Saul") and p. 116 ff. ("David Acquires the Throne of Saul").

21. Both this quotation and the one following derive from pp. 148–50 of *Understanding the Bible.* On forced labor (*corvée*), see, e.g., pp. 98, 126, 134, 140, 143.

22. See in general my "The Destruction of the First Temple and the Babylonian Exile in the Light of Archaeology," *Essays in Biblical Culture,* chap. 7, pp. 144–60; Selected Bibliography, p. 161.

23. See n. 12 above; and my *The So-Called "Servant of the Lord" and "Suffering Servant" in Second Isaiah,* Supplements to Vetus Testamentum, XIV, 1967, pp. 1–133; chap. 1, "The Biblical Term 'Servant' in Relation to the Lord," pp. 7–8, 11.

24. Cf. Jer. 25:8 ff., 27:2 ff., 43:8–13; and in general my "Nationalism-Universalism in the Book of Jeremiah," *Essays in Biblical Culture,* chap. 6 pp. 117–143, pp. 135 ff.

25. As I have stated elsewhere (*The So-Called "Servant of the Lord,"* p. 35), in chap. 47, for the first and only time in all of Second Isaiah, a reason is given for the downfall of a gentile nation, Babylonia; it is the same as that given in chap. 37 (and in the parallel section in 2 Kings 19) for the downfall of Sennacherib and Assyria, namely, that Babylonia ignored the central role of God in making her merely the rod of His punishment of Israel, and, instead, regarded herself as the all-powerful one. In addition, it is charged that she maltreated Israel ruthlessly, beyond the call of her mission.

26. See the section on "The Fate of the Prophets and their Teachings,"

in *Ancient Israel,* pp. 156–57, or in *Understanding the Bible,* pp. 260–62); see also *The So-Called "Servant of the Lord,"* p. 56.

27. See in general the sections "Ezra and Nehemiah" and "The Jewish Theocratic State" in *Understanding the Bible,* pp. 234–46, or in *Ancient Israel,* pp. 134–41.

SELECTED BIBLIOGRAPHY

Berman, Harold J. *The Interaction of Law and Religion.* Nashville, 1974. Its themes: "The separation of and disillusionment in law and religion viewed as the fundamental problem facing society today."

Cohen, Martin A. "The Role of the Shilonite Priesthood in the United Monarchy of Ancient Israel. *Hebrew Union College Annual* 36 (1965): 59–98.

"An Inquiry into Social Dynamics in Ancient Israel," *Studies in Jewish Bibliography, History, and Literature in Honor of I. Edward Kiev,* edited by C. Berlin, pp. 91–112. New York, 1971.

Orlinsky, Harry M. *Ancient Israel.* Ithaca, 1954; reprinted 1960 (paperback reprinted frequently).

———. *Understanding the Bible through History and Archaeology.* New York, 1972. Like *Ancient Israel,* a compact survey of the history of biblical Israel. Its thesis: the modern historian must seek—behind the religious terminology (of the Bible)—the same kind of documented human story, with an examination of its underlying dynamics, that would be his objective in any other field. Unlike *Ancient Israel, Understanding the Bible* is supplemented by pertinent Hebrew passages from the Bible and their translation into modern English, with aids, recent bibliography, and numerous illustrations, maps, charts, etc.

———. *The So-Called "Servant of the Lord" and "Suffering Servant" in Second Isaiah.* Supplements to Vetus Testamentum XIV (1967): 1–133.

———. *Essays in Biblical (and Jewish) Culture and Bible Translation.* New York, 1974. Note especially the chapters on "The Seer-Priest and the Prophet in Ancient Israel" (3, pp. 39–65), "The Tribal System of Israel and Related Groups in the Period of the Judges" (4, pp. 66–77), "Nationalism-Universalism and Internationalism" (5 and 6, pp. 78–116 and 117–43), "The Destruction of the First Temple and the Babylonian Exile in the Light of Archaeology" (7, pp. 144–61), and "Who is the Ideal Jew: the Biblical View" (10, pp. 187–99).

Zeitlin, Solomon. Prolegomenon (pp. ix–xxxv) to Gerald Friedlander, *The Jewish Sources of the Sermon on the Mount*, Library of Biblical Studies, ed. by H.M. Orlinsky. New York, 1969. Now reprinted in vol. III of S. Zeitlin, *Studies in the Early History of Judaism and Christianity*. New York, 1975, pp. 374–400.

Violence: A Religious Perspective. Dimensions Symposium Reprint XV, Union of American Hebrew Congregations, 1970, 20 pp.

Articles on "Law in the Old Testament," by E.M. Good, pp. 704–6; and "Ideas of War," by L. E. Toombs, pp. 796–801. *Interpreter's Dictionary of the Bible,* 4 vols., ed. by George A. Buttrick. New York, 1962. See also the *Supplementary Volume* (1976), ed. by Keith R. Crim.

YOHANAN AHARONI

3 Violence and Tranquility in Ancient Israel: An Archaeological View

Israel's history, according to biblical tradition, begins with the conquest. The next stage, the period of the judges, is viewed as a rhythm of violence and defense, explained in a theological-historical framework. Is this the correct concept of Israel's first step as a nation in its own land? Was the period of conquest and settlement filled by a continuous series of aggressive and defensive actions?

Archaeology draws a very different picture. Tel Aviv University's Institute of Archaeology has carried out excavations at various sites in the eastern Negev, as a result of which the history of the whole region has been revealed. The emerging picture sheds light not only on the history of the Negev but also on that of the whole country. As a border region on the fringe of the desert, the Negev is more exposed to changes and developments than other more protected regions. It appears as a kind of political seismograph, which reveals in the rather brief history of its settlement the main trends of the country's history.

The Bible recalls two pre-Israelite settlements in the eastern Negev, Arad and Hormah. "[T]he Canaanite, king of Arad, who dwelt in the Negev" resisted the children of Israel in the days of Moses, and the battle with him was fought in the neighboring city

Hormah (Num. 21:1–3). Both cities appear in the list of Canaanite cities defeated by Joshua (12:14). No pre-Israelite city is mentioned at Beersheba, the capital of Simeon, the main tribe which occupied the Negev, although the site appears as a center of worship already in the patriarchal traditions.

Unwalled settlements of the period of the judges have been discovered both at Beersheba and at Arad. In both places settlements arose around an early cult place, connected with the traditional well in the case of Beersheba and with the Kenite family related to Moses in the case of Arad (Judg. 1:16). Both were new foundations in the thirteenth or twelfth century B.C.E. at sites not occupied in the Canaanite period. At Beersheba this unwalled city is the first settlement, founded on bedrock. At Arad an early city existed in the Early Bronze Age II between ca. 2900–2700 B.C.E. An interval of about 1,500 years separates the two periods; in fact, then, the settlement at Arad was founded on a desolate hill, exactly as Beersheba was.

If that is the case, what of the Canaanite king of Arad who appears in the conquest traditions? He definitely was not dwelling at Tel Arad; yet its identification with biblical Arad has been strengthened by the appearance of the name Arad on two of the Hebrew ostraca discovered during the excavations. Some scholars believe, therefore, that the king of Arad was essentially some kind of Bedouin sheikh and that Hormah was the only Canaanite city in the area. So far, however, no site of the late Canaanite period (sixteenth–thirteenth centuries) has been discovered in the whole region, and this result seems to be final. On the other hand, there do exist two sites of the Middle Bronze Age (ca. eighteenth–seventeenth centuries B.C.E.), which may fit the traditions about Arad and Hormah well. These are Tel Malhata and Tel Masos, located between Beersheba and Arad on the Beersheba dry river, about 6 kilometers from one another. But if the easternmost of these settlements was Canaanite Arad, what was its name during the Israelite period, and may we suppose that the name moved to another site, about 12 kilometers to the north? Fortunately, we possess a document of the Israelite period which may furnish an answer to these questions. In the Shishak list, commemorating his campaign five years after Solomon's death, there are two fortresses *(hagarim)* in the Negev called Arad: Arad-rabat (= the great) and Arad of the house of *y-r-h-m* (= Jerahmeel?). It seems, therefore, that the early Arad now became a city of the Jerahmeelites (cf. 1 Sam. 27:10, 30:29), while the new central fortress was erected on the commanding hill farther north.

With these problems in mind, we started excavations two years ago at Tel Masos from our base camp at Beersheba, working in collaboration with a German expedition. The preliminary archaeological survey had already revealed that this was a unique site. Instead of the usual high, artificial *tel* (hill) with many occupational levels, one above the other, we have here three neighboring sites erected on shallow hills near the ancient wells. South of the river bed is the first, a Middle Bronze Age enclosure surrounded by an artificial rampart of approximately the eighteenth century B.C.E. North of the river bed is the second, a large settlement of the Early Israelite period. Beside it there is another smaller settlement of a later phase of the monarchy, partly overbuilt by a Byzantine monastery; this is Khirbet Meshash, the Tel Masos indicated on the maps.

The most interesting for our purpose is the early Israelite settlement. It is an unwalled village, extending over an area of approximately 40 dunams (10 acres). One should remember that David's Jerusalem was smaller and that Beersheba was only about 10 dunams. Well-built houses were discovered wherever excavations were carried out, many of them typical Israelite "four-room houses" with rows of pillars, well known from other parts of the country. Three levels of occupation were found with pottery of the thirteenth to eleventh centuries B.C.E. Among the pottery appears not only Philistine ware but also bichrome-decorated and red-burnished ware, which is known mainly from northern sites, such as Megiddo and Tel Abu Hawam near Haifa, and which was doubtless imported from the northern coastal region. The finds also include a decorated ivory in the shape of a lion, similar to the Megiddo ivories of the twelfth century. The latest pottery dates to ca. 1000 B.C.E., and it is clear that the settlement was destroyed and abandoned before the construction of the strong fortresses at Arad and Beersheba.

It is obvious that this large and well-established settlement is one of the major cities of Simeon, which fits well the information about Hormah (cf. Judg. 1:17; 1 Sam. 30:30). Evidently, this period represents the heyday of this tribe and explains its place in the Israelite league before its integration into Judah. Moreover, the Book of Chronicles preserves a remarkable piece of evidence. After the enumeration of Simeon's cities comes the concluding passage: "These were their cities unto the reign of David" (1 Chron. 4:31). This information has now been confirmed most surprisingly by Tel Masos: the heyday of Simeon was before the reign of David!

These discoveries lead to several conclusions:

a) The eastern Negev had no sedentary settlement on the arrival of the Israelite tribes. The stories about Canaanite Arad and Hormah may refer, therefore, only to early traditions, which have nothing to do with the period of conquest and settlement.

b) The Israelite settlement in the Negev is a process of pastoral occupation of an unsettled region accompanied by all the difficulties to be expected in this semiarid region.

c) The period of settlement appears as one of relative peace and security, which permits the existence of large, unfortified settlements based on pasture and agriculture and also on small industries and trade. This general picture is again vividly drawn in the description of Simeon in the Book of Chronicles, though not Hormah but another city (Gedor or Gerar?) is mentioned: ". . . and they found fat pasture and good, and the land was wide and quiet and peaceable; for they of Ham *had dwelt there of old*."

This is a completely new picture of the process of conquest and settlement. Instead of the accepted view of a violent conquest followed by an apparently unending series of warlike acts, there is the hardly opposed infiltration into unoccupied areas followed by a long period of relatively peaceful conditions. We should be wary of idealizing: Tel Masos was twice destroyed during that period. Yet these were rather short-lived episodes, and the large and flourishing settlement evidently existed for more than two centuries without feeling the necessity for walls.

Is this picture true only for the Negev, or may we take it as an illuminating example for the whole country?

In reality this is the picture which becomes more and more patent in other regions of the country as well, and the Bible itself hints at it. The conquest story is fragmentary and legendary. Most Canaanite cities were strong and the Israelites could not overcome the Canaanite chariotry (cf., e.g., Josh. 13:1, 17:14 ff; Judg. 1:27 ff.). This forced them to settle first in unoccupied areas, like the wooded, hilly regions. It is the same process that is revealed now in the semiarid Negev.

Many early Israelite settlements have been discovered in all the hilly regions, in areas which were virtually unoccupied until that period. As a rule, they had no fortifications. Some survived up to the period of the monarchy, but many were deserted and never resettled before ca. 1000 B.C.E. (the end of the First Iron Age).

How long did these villages exist and what is the date of the beginning of Israelite settlement in these regions? Not all may be from exactly the same period, but evidence is growing that their beginnings go back to the fourteenth century B.C.E. That is probably the date of the arrival of the tribes of Joseph and with them of Joshua, and the battle of Gibeon (in which no cities were conquered!). Shiloh, the center of the Israelite "amphictyony" was founded in the fourteenth century and utterly destroyed in the middle of the eleventh century, according to the pottery found in the excavation. There is no reason to doubt that this settlement, which existed for approximately 300 years, was founded by the Israelite tribes (on a site briefly occupied in the beginning of the second millennium, and later deserted for approximately 500 years). The best dated object has been found recently at Khirbet Raddana, a typical early Israelite settlement on the border between

Ephraim and Benjamin. It is an inscribed jar handle and the pre-
served letters are of a distinct transition type between the proto-
Sinaitic script of the middle of the second millenium and the proto-
Canaanite inscriptions of the thirteenth century from Lachish.

After the Joseph traditions, we hear only about one large battle
during the period of the judges: the battle of Deborah. What is its
date? Various dates have been suggested, somewhere in the twelfth
century, but it seems today that all these were too late. The following considerations speak for a date in the late thirteenth century,
not later than 1200 B.C.E.:

a) Hazor was destroyed in the late thirteenth century according
to the excavations. A disconnection of this city from the battle of
Deborah demands a severe, unjustified correction of the text.

b) The death of Shamgar, the son of Anath, who killed 600
Philistines "and he too delivered Israel" (Judg. 3:31), precedes the
battle. Strangely, as a result, ". . . caravans ceased and travellers
kept to the byways. The peasantry ceased in Israel, they ceased
. . ." (Judg. 5:6 ff.). A possible suggestion for such a "delivery" may
be the destruction of the Egyptian garrison city Beth Shean (Stratum VII), which was at least partly manned by mercenaries of
Aegean stock. This was probably accepted with satisfaction both
by Canaanites and Israelites, but even with the temporary disappearance of the Egyptian overlord, the strife between them came
to an open clash. The destruction of Beth Shean VII is again dated
to the latter part of the thirteenth century.

c) The only two Canaanite cities mentioned in the Song of Deborah are Taanach and Megiddo: ". . . then fought the kings of
Canaan, at Taanach, by the waters of Megiddo" (Judg. 5:19). The
destruction of the last fortified Canaanite city at Megiddo (Stratum
VII A), ca. 1125 B.C.E., has been regarded by William F. Albright
as a *terminus post quem* for the battle, supposing that the Megiddo
springs were now in the territory of neighboring Taanach. However, recent excavations of Lapp at Taanach have shown that this
city was destroyed completely together with Megiddo VII A and
that the site remained unoccupied until the tenth century. The

termination of both Canaanite cities, ca. 1125 B.C.E., has thus become a *terminus ante quo* for the battle. Moreover, we know from various biblical passages that several generations passed between the battle of Deborah and the destruction of the two Canaanite cities. In the Song of Deborah, Issachar still occupies the Jezreel Valley and Machir the northern part of the central mountains. Later on we do find Machir in northern Transjordan and Manasseh in the central mountain region, and his families also penetrate the Jezreel Valley where we find them in the days of Gideon. Taanach and Megiddo are mentioned among the Canaanite cities which were not occupied by *Manasseh*(!) at a certain stage (Judg. 1:27, and cf. Josh. 17:11). The destruction of the two cities constitutes a *terminus ante quo* for all these traditions, and, again, the battle of Deborah must definitely be earlier.

The battle of Deborah is the only large encounter recorded in the Bible for the entire period of the judges, until the unfortunate battle with the Philistines at Eben ha-Ezer, ca. 1050 B.C.E. If the battle of Deborah occurred at the end of the thirteenth century, then at least 150 years passed between the two battles. What traditions of wars have been preserved in the Bible for this long period of six or seven generations? The repulsion of the Midianite invasion by Gideon, and the struggles with the neighboring Transjordanian kingdoms in the days of Ehud and Jephthah. All three encounters are episodic and marginal affairs, which left hardly any lasting traces. In general, then, this was a period of peace and security, in which no real enemy endangered the settlement of the tribes in their areas. The great powers disappeared from the area and the country was left to itself. Canaan was weak and retreating, and the Philistines did not settle down until the second half of the twelfth century. The various peoples of Transjordan settled simultaneously with the Israelites and clashes occurred mainly in the border regions. Thus we see a long period of basically quiet and undisturbed settlement, unchallenged by any dominating power.

Matters changed in the middle of the eleventh century, when the first strong rival endangered the existence of Israelite settlement and sovereignty: the Philistines. That meant the end of the many open villages which had been founded throughout the country. Tel Masos was at length abandoned; and in the days of the United Monarchy, strongly fortified fortresses and royal cities, like Beersheba and Arad, took the place of the open villages. The establishment of the monarchy was the answer of the Israelite population to the severe danger.

Israel reaches its highpoint in the United Kingdom, strategically, politically, economically, and culturally. The dynamism that produced these changes was a response to violence. However, the sudden strength of the young monarchy is the harvest of a long period of quiet and patient settlement during times when "there was no king in Israel; every man did what was right in his own eyes" (Judg. 21:25). This was possible because no major enemy endangered the existence of the people.

BIBLIOGRAPHY

Weippert, M. *Die Landnahme der israelitischen Stämme in der neueren wissenschaftlichen Diskussion.* Gottingen, 1967.

R. de Vaux. *Histoire ancienne d'Israël, Des origines a l'installation en Canaan.* Paris, 1971.

Y. Aharoni. *The Land of the Bible,* pp. 174–253. Philadelphia, 1967.

"New Aspects of the Israelite Occupation in the North." *Near Eastern Archaeology in the Twentieth Century* (N. Glueck vol.), edited by J.A. Sanders, pp. 254–67. New York, 1970.

"Khirbet Raddana and its Inscription," *Israel Exploration Journal* 21 (1971): 130–35.

EPHRAIM URBACH

4 Jewish Doctrines and Practices in the Hellenistic and Talmudic Periods

After generations of tragedy in Jewish history, culminating in the Nazi Holocaust of six million Jews in our own century, we may raise the question of whether we are able to speak at all about the problems of violence and defense in the past without taking into consideration the events described in contemporary memoirs, documents, and other relevant literature. On the other hand, we also may ask whether we are able to grasp the realities which lie behind the violence of our own days without looking into the events of the past. Some say that one should not unearth the past for the sake of reconciliation. "Dwell on the past and you will lose an eye," one proverb admonishes.

Aleksandr Solzhenitsyn, however, recalls that the same proverb continues, "forget the past and you will lose both eyes." We cannot know in advance which period in the past may hide the most illuminating and instructive information about a certain phenomenon. In considering the problems of violence and defense during the hellenistic and talmudic periods of Jewish history, we are dealing with an era that is very remote, poor in sources and historical writings, and sometimes completely lacking in reliable documents. Often we must look to halakhic or aggadic sources. We may be encouraged, however, by the saying of the French scholar and man of letters, Ernest Renan, that in history a document has more weight in proportion to its lack of historic form.

We shall have an opportunity to prove the correctness of Renan's observation not only when we come to make use of talmudic sources but, initially, when we deal with historical sources. Avigdor Tcherikover, for example, opens his *Hellenistic Civilization and the Jews* with the following sentences:

The war with Persia did not come as a sudden decision on the part of the young king Alexander the Great. Alexander's father, King Philip, had already made all necessary preparations for it and had even sent a small force to Asia under the leadership of Parmenio, one of his best generals. Philip would without doubt have attacked the Persians himself had he lived. Macedon, which under his rule had been transformed from an unimportant petty kingdom into a strong state, had become, thanks to the conquest to Thrace, a next-door neighbor of the lands of Asia Minor which were subject to Persia which had begun to be openly hostile to the sudden flowering of the new kingdom. The king of Macedon was compelled to defend the frontiers of his realm and to anticipate the danger that threatened him, but in the midst of the preparations for war, Philip fell by the sword of one of his courtiers and the task of carrying out his ideas passed to his son Alexander, a young man of twenty who succeeded him to the throne.[1]

Here we already have various aspects of violence and defense which opened a new era in Jewish history, as in human history, an era whose description actually repeats itself in different periods. The murder of Philip, an act of violence within a state, taking place in the context of the violence then spreading between states, sets the stage for the history of violence in the hellenistic period. Here is the account of J. B. Bury in his *History of Greece:*

The designs of Philip probably did not extend beyond the conquest of western Asia Minor, but it was not fated that he should achieve this himself. In the spring after the Congress, his preparations for war were nearly complete, and he sent forward an advance force under Parmenio. . . . The rest of the army was soon to follow under his own command. But Philip, as a frank Corinthian friend told him, had filled his own house with division and bitterness. A Macedonian king was not expected to be faithful to his wife; but the proud and stormy princess whom he had wedded was impatient with his open infidelities. . . . The crisis came when Philip fell in love with a Macedonian maiden of too high a station to become his concubine—Cleopatra, the niece of his general Attalus. Yielding to his passion, he put Olympias away and celebrated his second marriage. At the wedding feast, Attalus, bold with wine, invited the nobles to pray to the gods for a *legitimate* heir to the throne. Alexander flung his drinking-cup in the face of the man who had insulted his mother, and Philip started up, drawing his sword to transpierce his son. But he reeled and fell, and Alexander jeered: "Behold the man who would pass from Europe to Asia, and trips in passing from couch to couch!" Pella was no longer the place for Alexander. He took the divorced queen to Epirus, and withdrew himself to the hills of Lyncestis, until Philip invited him to return. But the restless intrigues of the injured mother soon created new debates, and when a son was born to Cleopatra, it was easy to arouse the fears of Alexander that his own succession to the throne was imperiled. Philip's most urgent desire was to avoid a breach with the powerful king of Epirus, the brother of the injured woman. To this end he offered him his daughter in wedlock, and the marriage was to be celebrated with great pomp in Pella, on the eve of Philip's departure for Asia. But it was decreed that he should not depart. Olympias was made of the stuff which does not hesitate at crime, and a tool was easily found to avenge the wrongs of the wife and assure the succession of the son. A certain Pausanias, an obscure man of no merit, had been grossly wronged by Attalus, and was madly incensed against the king, who refused to do him justice. On the wedding day, as Philip, in solemn procession, entered the theatre a little in advance of his guards, Pausanias rushed forward with a Celtic dagger and laid him a corpse at the gate. The assassin was caught and killed, but the true assassin was Olympias and it was Alexander who reaped the fruit of the crime. Willingly would we believe that he knew nothing of the plot and that a man of so generous a nature never stooped to thoughts of parricide. Beyond dark whispers there is no evidence against him; yet it would be rash to say that his innocence is certain.[2]

This is the verdict of Bury. The story reveals how acts of violence which occurred in the family of a ruler in ancient times were of the greatest influence upon the future of the world.

We do not know whether the great monarch Alexander knew

anything about the history of the tiny province called Yehud under the Persian government. But if there were men who heard descriptions of the event at the court of Philip, they could easily recall parallels in their own ancient history as described in the biblical books of Samuel and of Kings. Until the Greek translation of the Bible 150 years after Philip's death, readers of Greek could know little or nothing of the territorial expansion of the Jewish kingdom under the reign of David, who went to war in anticipation of the perils threatening his state, nor of rebellions such as those of Absalom, whose behavior so resembles that of Alexander. It is indeed doubtful that, in conversing with Alexander, the high priest (Simeon according to talmudic tradition, Jadua according to Josephus) dwelt on such parallels with the events which had brought the conqueror to power.

Still, it was a fact that when Alexander appeared tiny Judea already had a long and interesting history of both violence and defense, internal and external. It also had a spiritual legacy, however, in the laws of the Torah, the words of its prophets, and the wisdom of its sages. These contained moral standards whose transmission to the world of nations through the Greek translation would be no less influential than the conquest of the great king, who himself later became a legendary figure in Jewish lore.

As several documents have survived from the time of Antiochus III and the Roman period, in which the rulers pledged the Jews the right to live according to their ancestral law, a number of scholars are inclined to assume that Alexander himself was the first to publish a pronouncement to this effect when he entered Palestine in 332 B.C.E.; this was also his behavior in relation to other nations. Life according to ancestral law meant autonomy in religious affairs, and, accordingly, Alexander designated the people of Judea as an ethnos. This system prevailed during the Ptolemaic rule, which lasted for nearly a century, and later during the Seleucid period, which began in 198 B.C.E. with the conquest of Jerusalem by Antiochus III and lasted until the persecutions by Antiochus Epiphanes, who, with the aid of armed force, attacked the monotheistic cult and the practice of the Jewish religion in Jerusalem, substituting for them the cult of the Olympian Zeus and Greek religious practices.

Greek Culture Versus Jewish Monotheism

The decree and actions of Antiochus Epiphanes stand out in the history of the ancient world as the first policy of violence against a religion, a policy which aroused the first acts of martyrdom. These became an example for future generations—for the Maccabean revolt and for the establishment of the new independent Hasmonean state. Many attempts have been made to explain the reasons and motives for Antiochus's policy. Some historians have viewed his decrees as a reflection of his character—his nervousness, hysteria, or even madness (hence the nickname "Epimanes," meaning "stark raving mad"; Antiochus had taken for himself the name "Epiphanes," meaning "God revealed"). Others have painted a different picture of Antiochus. It would be enough to cite Eduard Meyer, who believed that the king was a true Seleucid, diversely talented, full of energy and drive, one of the most important personalities of the dynasty. According to this view, Antiochus was mainly interested in spreading Hellenistic culture.

In Palestine he encountered another deeply rooted tradition, Jewish monotheism, and the encounter resulted in a fierce clash, for the Jews did not show an inclination to live according to the customs of the Greeks. This view is supported by the First Book of Maccabees (1:41): "And the king wrote to all his kingdom that all should be one people and that each people should abandon its customs, and all people did as the king commanded." There are various theorists who, not satisfied with the explanation of forcible hellenization, try to find political motives connected with the situation of the Seleucid kingdom. However, even granting that there may have been such motives, these alone do not explain how a ruler who exhibited Greek skepticism in religious matters and broad-minded tolerance of every strange and curious cult came to order the execution of those Jews "who do not wish to go over to Greek ways of life." The resistance of the Jews called forth an intense reaction, even though there were Jewish hellenizers, such as Jason and Menelaus, who were ready to change Jerusalem according to the Greek policy of Antiochus by building a gymnasium and emphebeum.

To understand the reasons underlying Antiochus's severity toward the Jews it is necessary to recall an earlier episode when the people of Jerusalem rose in open revolt against the Syrian king, who had laid his hands on the treasures of the Temple. The suppression of the revolt by Apollonius brought about the settlement of the nation of a foreign god in Jerusalem itself. This meant confiscation of the agricultural property of the citizens, the infiltration of new settlers into their homes, acts of violence and rape upon their former inhabitants, and sometimes even expulsion from the town. Sources report a mass flight from the town, the fugitives having no other alternative but to organize themselves in bands and to live the life of guerrillas. This happened in the year 168–167 B.C.E., before the decrees of Antiochus. Because the population was not a Greek one, the police force of Antiochus at Jerusalem was partly Syrian, although they had adopted the Greek language and cult. Even the Temple was ruled by the Syrians, who made sacrifices to the God of Israel in the form of the Syrian Baal. Only hellenizers then could continue to perform the priestly function, but there was a small group among the fugitives, the Hasidim, who remained a dangerous element.

Once it became clear that the revolt had been led by people for whom devotion to their own Torah was the watchword of the uprising, the extirpation of that Torah was seen as the means to quell the rebellion. This is the explanation for Antiochus's decree. A religion could be regarded as a danger even by Greeks if it was considered to undermine the foundation of the state's political life; it then became a "barbaric superstition." Thus the events described resulted in Antiochus's decree to force the Jewish people to transgress the laws of their fathers and desecrate God's commandments. Although he may have had some initial sense of personal abhorrence for the Jews and their religion, that alone would not explain his policy. The intensified response to the initial display of Jewish resistance provides the explanation. But the promulgation of the decrees making religious persecution a law was itself an act of violence, and its purpose was the annihilation of the Jewish faith and of the Jewish people.

The Nuremberg Laws provide a modern parallel. Although published in September 1935, they were but the consummation of developments, events, and persecutions which preceded them. These laws not only provided official and legal sanction for earlier violent actions, but they also became the starting point for more radical and atrocious expressions of violence.

Similarly, in the case of the persecutions by Antiochus, violence appears not as an exigency, not as an action undertaken to face certain circumstances, but as a policy. That the results differed from what the Seleucid king expected was the outcome of the successful resistance of the Hasidim under the leadership of the Maccabees, as well as favorable developments in the general political situation of the Seleucid kingdom; and, after all, much still remained to be explained as a miraculous salvation.

The war for religious freedom became a war of liberation and eventually led to the establishment of the Hasmonean kingdom, thus freeing the nation from the great danger of outside violence. The new kingdom, however, continued to wage wars which were politically motivated. The Hasmoneans were interested in capturing an outlet to the sea, to secure the way to the coast and thus free the newly established state from the danger of sudden raids by not very friendly neighbors. A rivalry developed between Judea and the Greek cities which had supported Antiochus and his generals during the war of liberation and continued to be a threat to the new state. The Hasmoneans showed the Greek cities no mercy and destroyed several of them, expelling the inhabitants and forcing them to become converts.

The judaization of the Syrian population of the Greek cities was part of a political program of the Hasmoneans. To the population concerned, however, this was religious persecution; the same state that had emerged from a war against persecution was following in the footsteps of its former conquerors. The hostility of the hellenized Syrians of Palestine to the Hasmoneans is evidenced by a Greek inscription found in the excavations at Gezer: "May fire consume Simon's palace, says Pampas." This curse was incised on a block destined to be used for a building set up in Gezer by Simon's order, and its author was probably one of the laborers and a man of Gezer.

Violence and Counterviolence

During this period of conquests and conversions the Hasmonean kings became more and more like hellenistic rulers, thus arousing domestic strife and acts of violence and counterviolence which occupy a considerable span of time during their rule. When Josephus in *Antiquities of the Jews*[3] describes the kingdom of perhaps the most important Hasmonean king, Alexander Yannai, he must admit that Alexander maintained foreign troops as did other Greek rulers. He could not use Syrians and he could not rely completely upon the Jewish soldiers because his own people revolted against him. Josephus mentions one occasion when, standing beside the altar during a celebration of the Sukkot festival, the king was pelted with citrons *(etrogim)*. His revilers added insult to injury by saying that he was descended from captives and was unfit to hold office and to sacrifice. Enraged at this, he killed some 6,000 of them and also placed a wooden barrier about the altar and the Temple as far as the coping of the court, which the priests alone were permitted to enter. In this way he blocked the people's access to him. Of course, as Josephus recounts, the people committed countless insulting and abusive acts against him, but still he seems to have reacted with needless severity. As a result of his excessive cruelty, the Jews nicknamed him "Thracidas" (the Thracians were renowned for their savagery). Following Yannai's reprisals, his opponents, about 8,000 in all, fled by night and remained in exile as long as he lived. The Talmud's report is quite different, but it contains enough common elements to make Josephus's general picture an acceptable one. It relates the conquest of Alexander, the feast which followed it, the slander of his ancestry, and his advice as to the suppression of his opponents; all these are mentioned in a very ancient baraita, Kiddushin 66a, which is written in biblical style.

Josephus does exaggerate at times, and, like other historians of his time, he uses certain conventional narrative devices; but the basic veracity of his account cannot be denied. There seems to be no reason, beyond the tendency to exalt the personality of Alexander Yannai, to doubt these reports. It is noteworthy that some historians believe every word of Josephus about the conquests of Alexander, working hard to identify the various places he mentions (and he gives a very long list of towns and places conquered by Alexander), but at the same time doubt every unfavorable report. It is true that the end of Alexander Yannai is described by Josephus in a way which reminds us of the story of Alexander the Great. Perhaps for this reason his report about the advice given to his wife deserves our attention. In his *Antiquities of the Jews*[4] Josephus writes: "After all these conquests, King Alexander [Yannai] fell ill from heavy drinking and for three years he was afflicted with a fever, but still he did not give up campaigning until being exhausted from his labors. He met death in the territory of Gerasa while besieging Rabaga, a fortress across the Jordan." This description reminds us exactly of the description of the death of Alexander the Great, who also engaged in heavy drinking and feasting but still continued to conduct the war and the battle in the east of Persia, etc. Josephus writes in the same vein as many other historians. But then comes a report which is quite different. When Queen Salome, or Shlom-Zion as she is called in Hebrew, saw that Yannai was on the point of death and no longer held any hope of recovery, she said to him: "To whom are you leaving me and your children who are in need of help from others." Thereupon he advised her to follow his suggestion to keep the throne secure for herself and her children and to conceal his death from the soldiers until she had captured the fortress. On her return to Jerusalem, as from a splendid victory, she should give a certain amount of power to the Pharisees, for if they praised her in return for this sign of regard, they would dispose the nation favorably to her:

"When you come to Jerusalem, send for the Pharisees and showing them my dead body, permit them with every sign of sincerity to treat me as they please, whether they wish to dishonor me by leaving it unburied because of the many injuries they have suffered at my hands or in their anger wish to offer my dead body any other form of indignity. Promise them also that you will not take any action while you are on the throne without their consent. If you speak to them in this manner, I shall receive from them a more splendid burial than I should from you. For once they have the power to do so, they will not choose to treat my corpse badly and at the same time you will reign securely." With this exhortation to his wife, he died at the age of forty-nine, after reigning twenty-seven years. Alexandra [Salome] acted according to his advice and they [the Pharisees], in turn, went to the people and made public speeches in which they recounted the deeds of Alexander. They said that in him they had lost a just king, and by their eulogies, they so greatly moved the people to mourn and lament that they gave him a more splendid burial than had been given any of the kings before him.[5]

True, Josephus is exaggerating here and the "testament" of Alexander Yannai is no more than a *topos*. But the change in the prevailing conditions during the rule of Salome seems to be a well-established fact. Although the talmudic sources are less explicit and are very brief, the picture we get of the reign of Salome, the wife of Alexander, is recorded in talmudic literature as one of tranquillity, freedom, and conciliation. It was a period of great fertility in the country, as idyllically pictured in the tanaitic midrash to the third book of Moses.

The problem we are concerned with is not so much the struggle between the sects and the differences between them as the fact that for only short times during the Hasmonean and Herodian periods were affairs revolved in such a way that the internal struggles were kept from breaching public order and from unlawful exercise of physical force. Of course, one should recognize that times free of the unlawful exercise of force have not occurred very frequently throughout history. Even the British and the French have been among the most ungovernable of people, habituated to violence as a national pastime, and it took them a long time to settle down.

Reprieve from Conflict

Possibly a longer period of political independence and a peaceful situation might also have brought about a more ideal inner relationship between the various parties and social strata of the population. This reflection is based upon a short episode in the history of Judea, the years of the rule of Agrippa I. This period is to be understood against the background of the policy of the Roman Empire, which used the local kings as tools and made them more or less vassals of the emperors and under the supervision of the consuls of the various provinces. In the case of Agrippa there were also friendly personal relations with both Gaius Caligula and Claudius. Agrippa, as king of the whole of Palestine and not only of Judea, faced many difficult problems in dealing with the various populations of the countries and the different factions among the Jews. He confronted these problems in a way quite different from that of the first Hasmoneans, as indicated by Josephus's report on Agrippa's dealings with the people of Dura.

Dura was actually a Greek town, and as such it had to have an image of Caesar in its houses of worship and temples. Thus some of the young people set up an image of Caesar in the synagogue of the Jews. This action provoked Agrippa exceedingly, for he understood that it was tantamount to an overthrow of the laws of his fathers. Without delay he went to see Publius Petronius, the governor of Syria, and denounced the people of Dura. His intervention was successful. Petronius, legate of Tiberius Claudius Caesar Augustus Germanicus, issued a letter to the people of Dura explaining that it was against the will and the decree of the emperor to have his own image in a Jewish synagogue, which would be a violation of Jewish law. In his letter he writes: "For both King Agrippa, my most honored friend, and I have no greater interest than that the Jews should not seize any occasion under the pretext of self-defense to gather in one place and proceed to desperate measures."[6] Petronius knew very well that violence or actions of violence brought about counterviolence; he had not written his letter only out of friendship for the Jews, but because he was afraid that something resembling revolution or rebellion would occur. He concludes his letter with very significant words: "For the future, therefore, I charge you to seek no pretext for sedition or disturbance, but to practice separately each his own religion."

This, of course, was the achievement of Agrippa's policy, which he also followed in his own relations with the Greek population. In light of the subject of violence and defense, it is interesting to consider the contrast between Agrippa and his grandfather Herod, described by Josephus: "Now King Agrippa was by nature generous in his gifts and made it a point of honor to be high-minded toward Gentiles, and by expending massive sums he raised himself to high fame."[7] Agrippa took pleasure in conferring favors and enjoyed popularity, thus being in no way similar in character to Herod, who was king before him. The latter had an evil nature, was relentless in punishment and unsparing in action against the object of his hatred. It was generally admitted that he was on more friendly terms with Greeks than with Jews. For instance, by giving them money, he adorned the cities of foreigners, building baths and theaters, erecting temples and porticos. By contrast, there was not a single city of the Jews on which he deigned to bestow any gift worth mentioning or to carry out even minor restorations.[8] Here Josephus does Herod injustice, failing to report what Herod did for the restoration of the Temple in Jerusalem; in the Talmud, however, you find a saying that a man who has not seen the Herodian Temple has never seen a great and beautiful building (Bava Batra 4a).

Josephus is like other historians of his time. He exaggerates in his negative description of Herod in order to justify his praise of Agrippa, whom he describes as a man of gentle disposition and a benefactor to people of other nations as well as his own. To his compatriots, however, he was proportionately more generous and compassionate. He enjoyed residing in Jerusalem and did so continuously, scrupulously observing the traditions of his people. He neglected no rite of purification and no day passed for him without the prescribed sacrifice.

Without mentioning it explicitly, Josephus also provides a comparison between the personalities of Agrippa and Alexander Yannai in the following story. A native of Jerusalem, named Simon, who had a reputation for religious scrupulousness, assembled the people in a public meeting at a time when the king was absent in Caesarea and had the audacity to denounce him as "unclean" (a term that refers to matters of ritual purity). The commanding officer in the city reported Simon's action to the king by letter. The king thereupon sent for him and, since he was sitting in the theater at the time, bade Simon sit down beside him. "Tell me," he then said quietly and gently, "what is contrary to the law in what is going on here that disqualifies me from entering the Temple?" Simon, having nothing to say, begged pardon. Thereupon the king was reconciled to him more quickly than one would have expected, for he considered mildness a more royal trait than passion and was convinced that considerate behavior was more becoming in the great than wrath. He therefore even presented a gift to Simon before dismissing him.[9]

The description of Agrippa by Josephus is confirmed by talmudic sources with less verbosity, but not with less meaning. The Mishnah (Bikkurim 3:4) reports on the bringing of the first fruits to the Temple and describes this celebration as follows: "The flute was played before them until they reached the Temple Mount.

When they reached the Temple Mount, even King Agrippa would take a basket, place it on his shoulder, and walk as far as the Temple Court." King Agrippa behaved during the festival like everybody else, carrying on his shoulder the basket with the first fruits. More is said about him elsewhere in the Mishnah (Sota 6:8). According to the Bible, the close of the first festival day of the Feast of Tabernacles in the eighth year after the going forth of the seventh year, was celebrated in Jerusalem, and they used "to prepare for the king in the Temple court a wooden platform on which he sat, for it is written: 'at the end of every seven years and the set time'. . . . The minister of the synagogue used to take a scroll of the Law and give it to the chief of the synagogue. The chief of the synagogue gave it to the prefect, the prefect to the high priest, and the high priest gave it to the king. The king received it standing and read it sitting. King Agrippa received it standing and read it standing, and for this the sages praised him, and when he reached the verse: 'They may not put the foreigner over thee which is not thy brother,' his eyes flowed with tears because he was a descendant of Herod, who was an Edomite. But they called to him: 'Our brother art thou.' He read from the beginning, and then the paragraph of the king and the blessing until the end." Here we have a man who was not only a political leader but also a great personality.

Of certain interest is a remark transmitted in the Babylonian Talmud, in the Tosefta, and in the Palestinian Talmud by a Babylonian, Rabbi Nathan, who lived toward the end of the second century. His comment about the behavior of the sages at the time of Agrippa was: "The people of Israel made themselves worthy of punishment by annihilation, because they flattered King Agrippa."[10] But in this Rabbi Nathan was less concerned with the times of Agrippa than with his own time, because he was in opposition to the patriarch of his own time and used the case of Agrippa as the pretext for stating his own uncompromising stand.

N O T E S

1. A. Tcherikover, *Hellenistic Civilization and the Jews* (Philadelphia, 1959), p. 1.

2. J. B. Bury, *A History of Greece,* 1900, 2nd. rev. ed. 1913, or numerous reprints, 1927, 1959, etc. (In one popular "modernized" edition of Bury the editor has tampered with this expression of the historian's judgement.)

3. *Antiquities of the Jews*, XIII, xiii, p. 5.

4. Ibid., XII, xv, p. 5.

5. Ibid., XIII, xv, p. 5.

6. Ibid., XIX, vi, p. 3; cf. *The Jewish War,* II, x, pp. 4–5.

7. *Antiquities of the Jews,* XIX.

8. Ibid., XIX, vii, p. 3.

9. Ibid., XIX, vii, p. 4.

10. Babylonian Talmud, Sota 41b; Palestinian Talmud, Sota 8:7; Tosefta, Sota 7:16.

EPHRAIM URBACH

5 Jewish Doctrines and Practices in Halakhic and Aggadic Literature

For Rabbi Johanan ben Zakkai, the last of the tannaim who was still active during the time of the Temple and the first of those who were to be active after its destruction, the altar symbolized "making peace between man and his fellow, between man and his wife, between city and city, nation and nation, government and government, family and family."

This quotation, which appears in the Mekhilta of Rabbi Ishmael,[1] reflects a lofty ideal retained even after a long experience of differences, struggles, and upheavals. Sometimes even the altar itself was the reason for such quarrels and struggles. The road the sages took during these stormy events was not a smooth one, for they were compelled to maneuver through treacherous times. The principle of hereditary succession, based on purity of lineage as proved by official archives, prevailed both in pre-Hasmonean and Hasmonean times, and the rules of succession applied also to offices of authority. So we learn from Josephus[2] that wars and quarrels were occasion for the destruction of archives and genealogical records. He does not mention that this occurred during the times of Herod, but from a relatively late source it appears that Herod was interested in their destruction because his family could not prove a legal right of succession. In the Babylonian Talmud, too, the slaying of the sages by Herod is linked with the question of Herod's descent. As we have already mentioned, this question was the focal point of violent actions both by the king and by his opponents during the time of Alexander Yannai. According to another report, even Agrippa prevented such troubles only by the wisdom of his actions.

In such struggles as these the position and security of well-known families had been undermined, and attempts to establish genealogical facts by force were not wanting. It seems, then, that to this period must be assigned the anonymous tradition in the Mishnah (Eduyot 8:7) which reads: "The family of Beth Zerepha was in the land beyond Jordan and Ben Zion removed it afar by force. And yet another [family] was there, and Ben Zion brought it nigh by force." This means that force was used to elevate certain families to offices and make them fit to be vested with those offices. Others were removed from office or deprived of office by force.

In the struggle between the old aristocracy and Herod and his men, the sages took a reserved or neutral position. On the one hand, Shemaiah, who was probably the expert of the Sanhedrin, took a stand against the insolence of the young Herod toward the high court, condemned the cowardice of his colleagues, and prophesied a bitter end for them at the hands of the Edomites. On the other hand, the sages did not support Antigonus when Herod besieged Jerusalem, but neither did Herod succeed in securing their cooperation. Two sages who stood at the head of the Pharisees— Josephus called them Polion and Samayas—refused to swear allegiance to Herod.

I am inclined to accept the view of scholars who identify the two sages with Shemaiah and Abtalion.[3] For those who acted subversively Herod's practice was, we know, to sentence them to banishment abroad or to work in the mines. Because the sages preferred to remain with their people, they endeavored to hold aloof from politics and government business. Their estrangement from the government and the cautious policy they adopted helped them continue their work among the people. The extent of their popularity was definitely related to their negative attitude toward the man in authority and toward the aristocracy. In this respect, considerable significance is attached to the story recounted in the following baraita:

Our rabbis taught that it once happened that a certain high priest went forth from the sanctuary and all the people followed him, but on seeing Shemaiah and Abtalion, they left him and followed Shemaiah and Abtalion. Finally, Shemaiah and Abtalion came to take their leave of the high priest [they took a difficult middle course between outright rejection and open endorsement of the official institutions, and even when the high priest was not of their preference, even if they were opposed to him, they continued to recognize him as a high priest], whereupon the high priest, who was of another spirit, said to them: "May the descendants of Gentiles come in peace" [alluding to the descent of Shemaiah and Abtalion from families of proselytes]. They replied: "May the descendants of Gentiles who act as Aaron did, come in peace, but let no one who is a descendant of Aaron, who does not act like him, come in peace." [Babylonian Talmud, Yoma 91b]

The version, reported by Rabbenu Hananel, one of the great commentators of the Talmud, is of special interest. According to him, Shemaiah and Abtalion came to pay their respects to the high priest saying: "May the scion of Aaron come in peace." He replied: "May the descendants of the Gentiles come in peace," etc.

We do not know who this high priest was, and it is not essential in this context that we should know. But whether it was Aristobulus, the Hasmonean, or perhaps the high priest appointed after the destruction of the Hasmoneans by Herod, the rabbis regarded both as not acting like Aaron, although they recognized their priesthood and paid them the honor due to their office. This incident enables us to explain the dictum of Hillel in Avot (1:12): "Be of the disciples of Aaron, loving peace and pursuing peace, loving mankind and bringing them nigh to the Laws." And this is to point out the expression "Be of the disciples of Aaron", which means not of the descendants of Aaron, that is, not priests. Why were the disciples of Aaron chosen as ideal, and not the disciples of Abraham, the father of the Jewish nation, or the disciples of Moses, the giver of the Torah? Obviously, the aggadic observations on Aaron's pursuit of peace flow from Hillel's saying but do not serve to elucidate it. The explanation is simple: the *disciples* of Aaron stand here against the *sons* of Aaron, as against the descendants of high priests stand those who pursue peace and bring people nigh to the Torah, namely the sages.

In summing up our findings concerning the class constituted by the sages until the end of the Second Temple period, we must say that it comprised a group of men who regarded study and instruction as well as works of charity and loving kindness as their primary task. They were men who lived among the masses and were close to them and their troubles, men who esteemed and honored the national institutions of the people, the religious institutions, the sanctuary, the Sanhedrin, and the priesthood, and protested against the wrongdoings of those in charge of the administration and government. As individuals they also participated in the work of the institutions and endeavored to influence them—not as an elite seeking power and leadership but as one that served as an example.

It was precisely the existence of the Hasmonean monarchy, and subsequently the monarchy of the house of Herod with its institutionalization, that provided the framework in which the sages found their sphere of activity. In the world of the sages during the Temple period you find no bureaucratic organization—no system whatsoever of appointment, no promotion, no remuneration, nor even any real arrangements for training or definition of functions. Likewise, there were, of course, no titles; simply the personal name of the sage was used. The titles of "rabban" or "rabbi" are of a later time.

Dissension Among the Sages

The weakening of the official institutions, the strengthening of the position of the sages, and their growing involvement in the affairs of the Sanhedrin and of the priests in the Temple, created difficulties and problems that they could no longer avoid. The influence of the sages was probably strengthened in the days of Hillel, both on account of his distinguished personality, which enabled him to overcome hostility, and also because of the prevailing conditions, which undermined the position of the old aristocracy and elevated a new ruling class who aimed at securing a certain measure of legality and recognition among the masses. But here, in the time of Hillel and shortly after it, we are already confronted by some quarrels and differences which are not to be explained only as differences of opinion and of scholarly approaches.

The dynastic principle that had become crystallized in the school of Hillel gave rise to dissent. Although Rabban Gamaliel, the son or grandson of Hillel, and Gamaliel's son Simeon were no patriarchs, they nevertheless held important positions in the Sanhedrin and carried out central functions. The fact that the school of Shammai insisted on the investigation of the genealogy of disciples does not in itself give approval to the principle of bequeathing offices, and is even consistent with the dictum of Akabya ben Mehalaleel: "Your own deeds will bring you near, and your own deeds will remove you far." But at the end of the Temple period the disciples of the school of Shammai still submitted to the authority of Rabban Gamaliel, as we learn from the evidence of the Mishnah (Orlah 2:12), which reads: "Joezer, Master of the Temple, was a disciple of the school of Shammai, and he said: I asked Rabban Gamaliel the Elder, when he was standing at the Eastern Gate. . . ." Here is a fine example of the great value of the rabbinic texts as historiographic resources; although we do not receive much expressly historical data from talmudic literature, brief passages such as this sometimes display much more than a long account of Josephus. We learn quite a lot from these two lines of Hebrew: first, that a disciple of the school of Shammai had an official standing in the Temple; second, that Rabban Gamaliel the Elder already had a central position. Third, that a disciple of Shammai felt himself to be subordinated to the decisions of Rabban Gamaliel.

Another piece of evidence from a baraita (Tosefta Sukkah 2:3) clearly states: "Johanan Hahorani, although he was a disciple of Shammai, acted only according to the views of the school of Hillel." But the relations between the two schools became sharply exacerbated in the days of the "great rebellion," when we find evidence of interaction between political and religious affairs. Rabban Simeon ben Gamaliel supported the freedom fighters but opposed the extremist Zealots. They nonetheless joined the followers of the school of Shammai and, armed with swords and spears, slew disciples of the school of Hillel, forcing them, as reported both in the Palestinian Talmud and in the Babylonian Talmud, to accept their edicts. Here we have an act of violence touching not only on political affairs, but on questions of Halakhah. Legal decisions at that point were being made by force. The Talmud adds in a later comment: "And that day was as grievous for Israel as the day on which the golden calf was made."[4]

The "eighteen decrees" were not enacted in the Temple or on the stairs of the Temple Mount but in an upper chamber of Elazar ben Hananiah ben Hizkiya ben Garon. He was one of the disciples of Shammai—and probably the descendant of a distinguished family —who held the position of commander of the army in the land of Edom, according to Josephus's *The Jewish War,* II. In a fragment of the *Sifre Zuttah,* discovered by Jacob Nahum Epstein, we read: "There were Edomite disciples in the school of Shammai at that time," which means there is a connection between the Zealots, the Edomites who supported them, and the disciples of Shammai. Political factiousness and civil strife invaded the world of the sages, and the decisions taken in the halakhic sphere went according to the powers of the schools. But it appears that through these disputes there were also sages who pursued an independent course in an endeavor to reach a consensus.

The patriarchate, which developed after the destruction of the Temple, became the highest political, juridical, and administrative authority of the people. But the patriarchs, descendants of Hillel, especially from the time of Rabban Gamaliel II in Javneh, had to face the problem of enforcing enactments, rules and procedures, and policies of nominations and appointments. Above all, they faced the difficult problem of the financial maintenance of the institutions. They were forced by circumstances to maintain close relations with the upper and richer classes, who supported these institutions; and these relations again caused tension between the patriarch and the *am ha-aretz,* the simple man. The hierarchy and protocol which developed during the centuries of the patriarchate also became the focal points of tensions and bad feelings among the sages themselves.

I have mentioned a saying, or comment, of Rabbi Nathan, who censured the old sages for their partiality to King Agrippa. Rabbi Nathan's criticism was not directed so much against the sages of the times of Agrippa as against some sages of his own time who flattered the patriarch Rabban Simeon ben Gamaliel, to whom he himself was in sharp opposition. He even acted together with Rabbi Meir in a manner designed to bring about his removal, an action which actually was taken in the case of Rabban Gamaliel, who was deposed from the patriarchate for a certain period.

The greatest of the patriarchs, Rabbi Judah Ha-Nasi, enjoined his son, Rabban Gamaliel: "Conduct your patriarchate with men of high standing, and throw bile among the disciples, i.e., insist on strict discipline" (Ketubot 103b).

His grandson, Rabbi Judah Nessiya, had some guards of Gothic origin, and he sent such a guard to arrest Resh Lakish, who had said something not very complimentary about the patriarch and criticized him in public. Rabbi Johanan, the most important scholar at the time, intervened, and the patriarch agreed to go with him to the place to which Resh Lakish had fled. But this stubborn amora added only new criticism to his previous remarks. The only defense he offered for his behavior was to say: "He," meaning the patriarch, "has no right to withhold the teaching of the Torah" (Palestinian Talmud, Sanhedrin 2:1). This answer changed everything because all questions of honor and status perforce fell away wherever there was any danger of *hillul ha-Shem* (of desecrating the Divine Name), which was considered to be the gravest sin. The rule that "wherever desecration of the Divine Name is involved, no deference is shown to a rabbi" is reported in the name of Rav and Samuel, and in the name of Rav Ashi. It thus spans the entire period of the amoraim and is also reported anonymously in the Talmud.

Strict insistence on the upright conduct of the individual sage served to prevent any decline of the honor in which the class of the sages and their institutions—and, in the final analysis, the Torah itself—was held. If an associate, a *haver,* is detected in a transgression, he is disgraced because he mingles pure with impure things; he holds in contempt the Torah, which ought to be precious to him. However, the sage was not permitted to be satisfied with his own personal perfection. Since he was required to lead, instruct, and guide his community, he was guarantor of the whole congregation of Israel. Although this feeling of being surety was required of every Jew—*kol Yisrael arevin zeh ba-zeh*—it had a special significance where the sage was concerned.

Rabbi Nehemiah, one of the tannaim, interpreted the verse "My son, if thou art become surety for thy neighbor, if thou hast struck thy hand for a stranger" (Prov. 6:1) thus: "This refers to *haverim* [ordinary scholars]. As long as a man is a *haver* he need not be concerned with the community and he is not punished on account of it. But once a man is placed at the head, and has donned the *tallit* [the cloak of office], he may not say, 'I look after my own welfare. I care not for the community.' The whole burden of communal affairs rests upon him. If he sees a man doing violence to his fellow-man [the text uses the Greek word for violence, *bia*] or committing a transgression and does not seek to prevent him, he is to be punished on account of it. And the Holy Spirit cries out: 'My son, if thou art become surety for thy neighbor, thou art responsible for him. And thou hast struck thy hands for a stranger [*zar*].' The Holy One, blessed be He, says to him: 'Thou hast entered the arena [*zirah*], and he who enters the arena must either win or be defeated."[5]

Self-Defense for the Patriarchs

The patriarchs and others who bore official responsibilities had numerous opponents and probably often answered their detractors with interpretations of biblical passages where they could easily find principles by which to justify their actions, or at least perhaps to convince their critics that it is easier to criticize than to assume responsibility. We have an example in Leviticus Rabbah (12:5), which deals with the criticism of Jeroboam against Solomon. It is reported that King Solomon, after constructing the Temple, spent the night with his Egyptian wife, and she caused him to sleep too late to open the gates of the Temple. But the gates of the Temple had to be opened at a certain hour, before it was too late to bring the offerings. Jeroboam came at the head of the people of Jerusalem and said to them: "Look at your king, see what he is doing." But the Midrash comments in terms of a passage in Hosea (13:1), which reads "When Ephraim spoke trembling [*retat*] he was exalted [*nasa*] in Israel, but he incurred guilt through Baal and died." They took Ephraim to be Jeroboam since he came from the tribe of Ephraim; and they understood *nasa,* he was exalted, to imply that he became a prince *(nasi)* in Israel. The choice of term was significant, for the same word, *nasi,* was the title of the patriarchs. It remained then to explain the prince's downfall, and the sages drew their explanation from a play on the word *retat:* "When Jeroboam spoke of the failing *(r'titon)* of Solomon, the Holy One, blessed be He, said, 'Why do you reproach him? He is a *nasi* of Israel. By your life I shall give you but a little taste of his authority and you will not be able to stand the test.' As soon as he became king he forthwith incurred guilt through Baal and he died."

This midrashic interpretation with the leading word *nasi,* is a kind of self-defense of the *nesi'im,* the patriarchs, against criticism made by some of the scholars. The violent policy of Rehoboam was not justified, but did Jeroboam prove to be better? Was his counter-violence justified? Interestingly enough, by an addition to the biblical story Josephus holds a more definitely antirevolutionary position. Josephus gives the report of the Book of Kings, but he adds one sentence which does not appear in the Bible. The Bible says only, very briefly, that "King Rehoboam sent Adoram, who was over the levy, and all Israel stoned him with stones, so that he died . . . " (1 Kings 12:18). Josephus adds here: "So bitter did they feel toward him and so great was the anger they nourished that, when he sent Adoramos, who was in charge of the levies, to appease them and soften their mood by persuading them to forgive what he had said if there had been in it anything rash or ill-tempered owing to his youth, they did not let him speak, but threw stones at him and killed him" (*Antiquities of the Jews,* VIII, v, 220). Nothing of this is related in the Bible. Josephus tries to place the rebellious behavior of the people in a worse light than the Bible does.

The attitude of the tannaim and amoraim toward violence and defense finds its expression both in the interpretation of the biblical stories in which violence is dominant, and in their comments and rulings concerned with certain biblical laws and commandments. A comparison of their interpretation and tradition with those of Philo and Josephus and with other systems of law proves to be of great assistance in understanding the underlying ideas of the rabbis.

The Cities of Refuge

The Book of Exodus (32:27) contains an order given by Moses to the sons of Levi: ". . . Each of you put sword on thigh, go back and forth from gate to gate throughout the camp, and slay brother, neighbor, and kin." Philo dedicated his attention to this verse in three different works. In two of them he deals with the law, which opens the cities of the Levites to the fugitives from vengeance. These cities became the *arei miklat,* places of asylum which were for men who committed homicide but were not considered to have done so purposely. The action taken by the Levites, upon the order of Moses, and the right granted to people who committed unintentional homicide to flee to some of the cities allotted to this tribe, leads Philo not only to the conclusion that not every kind of homicide is culpable, but to the discovery of an inner nexus between the two incidents and to an apologetic justification of the order of Moses. In his book on the sacrifices of Abel and Cain he writes:

And here we may turn to another matter which deserves more than a passing consideration. Why did he throw open the cities of the Levites to the fugitives from vengeance and deem fit that there the holy should live side by side with men reckoned unholy, namely those who had committed involuntary homicide? The first answer is one that follows from what has been already said. We showed that the good are a ransom for the bad. Therefore it is with good reason that the sinners come to the consecrated to get purification.

Secondly, as they whom the Levites receive are exiles, so too the Levites themselves are virtually exiles. For as the homicides are expelled from the home of their nativity, so too the Levites have left children, parents, brothers, their nearest and dearest, to win an undying portion in place of that which perishes. The two differ in that the flight of these is not of their own desire, but for an involuntary deed, while those have fled of their own free will in loving quest of the highest. Again, the homicides find their refuge in the Levites, the Levites in him who is the Ruler of all.[6]

Here we have a theological interpretation, which utterly trans-
forms the command of Moses.

"And once more"—continues Philo—"they who slew involun-
tarily were granted the right of living in the same cities as the
Levites, because they too were privileged as a reward for slaying
in a righteous cause. We find that when the soul fell and honored
the god of Egypt, the body, as gold, with an honor which was not
its due, the holy thoughts with one accord of their own motion
rushed to the defense in arms. These arms were the proofs and
arguments which knowledge gives."[7] Here we have an extreme
allegorical interpretation. Philo intends that the arms used were
actually arguments which knowledge gives. "And they set before
them, as their captain and leader, the High Priest and prophet, and
friend of God, Moses."[8]

Philo returns to the same theme again in *De Specialibus Legibus*
("On Special Laws"), and again he finds an excuse, saying that
"this campaign, waged spontaneously and instinctively on behalf
of piety and holiness toward the existing God, and fraught with
much danger to those who undertook it, was approved by none
other than the Father of all, Who took it upon Himself to judge
the cause of those who wrought the slaughter, declared them pure
from any curse of bloodguiltiness, and gave them the priesthood
as a reward for their gallantry."[9] Thus Philo stresses the fact that
the Levites have acted not upon their own will, not even upon the
command of Moses, but upon the direct command of the Lord. In
conclusion, he also notes that not every kind of homicide is culpable but only that which entails injustice. Every other form of
homicide, if done from "an ardent yearning for virtue," is laudable
and, if unintentional, is free from blame.

In Philo's book *On Drunkenness,* both the Levites, whose action
was caused by an ardent yearning for virtue, and the unintentional
murderers are servants of justice and providence. According to this
theological justification of violence, the involuntary homicide unwittingly has a part to play in the rectification of some past injustice. Similarly, Rashi explains the treatment of the unintentional

murderer, according to midrashic tradition, in such a way that the man who is murdered is thought to have probably committed a comparable crime himself and to have escaped detection. Thus his death is his punishment. Philo apparently was familiar with such a midrash.

But these explanations, given by Philo, were not quite satisfying, perhaps not to himself and certainly not to all of his listeners. So he went on, as was his custom, to a more radically allegorical level of meaning, according to which not human beings but the senses and false opinions were killed. In *On Drunkenness* he explains that the story about the action of the Levites represents the exceedingly strange paradox "that these people who were homicides, fratricides, slayers of the bodies which are nearest and dearest to them, though they should have come to their office pure in themselves and in their lineage, having had no contact with any pollution, even involuntary, far less voluntary," should be entrusted with the work of the Temple. Philo resolves the paradox as he sees it by making the following interpretation: "Not living, reasoning animals, composed of soul and body, were slain by the Levites. No, they are cutting away from their own hearts and minds all that is near and dear to the flesh. They hold that it befits those who are to be ministers to the only Wise Being, to estrange themselves from all that belongs to the world of creation. . . . Therefore we shall kill our brother—not a man—but the soul's brother, the body."[10] This allegorical interpretation rises to a level of sublimity far removed from the narrative of the text. But for that very reason it plays an important role in the subject we are considering. On the one hand, Philo's allegorization may seem to soften the apparent brutality of the Levites' act. On the other hand, however, the same approach could be used, with allegories sufficiently sublime, as justification of violence in the name of religion and other ideologies.

These lofty and highly spiritual interpretations of Philo are not to be found in the Talmud or in the midrashim. As far as they touch at all on the question of the order of Moses to the Levites, they turn it into an ordinary trial and say: "Executed by the sword were only those against whom there were witnesses, and who were the previously warned." It was a legal action. People who commit the sin of idolatry can be sentenced if there were two witnesses against them, and if they were warned beforehand. "Those who were not warned, underwent the ordeal of the faithless wife. And those against whom there were no witnesses, perished during a pestilence" (Palestinian Talmud, Sotah 3:4). Here we have an absolutely different approach to these acts of extraordinary violence.

A later midrash goes even a step further. While Philo stressed the point that the order given to the Levites was the order of the Lord himself, this midrash dares to say that it was the act of Moses, who hoped to divert the wrath of God from the people as a whole. He proclaimed the order in the name of the Lord because he was afraid that if he gave the order in his own name the Levites might ask him: "Have you not taught us that a Sanhedrin which executes one man in seven years is called ruinous [*mehablanit,* destructive]? So how can you order the simultaneous execution of so many people?" (Seder Eliyahu Rabbah, chap. 4). It is a very daring midrash because it contradicts the explicit text of the Torah, but it stems from a conviction that a court, a Sanhedrin, which executes many people is ruinous and that the actions of a leader must have their own rationale. The action of the Levites is considered as a polical act with a religious background. The blame for the backsliding is put upon a part of the people, and the exemplary punishment is intended to save the rest.

There is no attempt to connect the story with the Levitic cities for refuge from the avenger. The right of asylum was well-known in the ancient world in nearly all systems of laws, both in the East and in the West, in Near Eastern countries, and in Greece itself. Temples served as places of asylum. This was in essence a method of mitigating the abuse of private vengeance, which not only preceded the establishment of a regular judicature but continued to prevail—and still continues to some extent—in the Middle East. In principle the right of revenge was recognized both in biblical law and in Halakhah, The cities of refuge existed in Palestine during the period of the Second Temple.

Self-Help in the Face of Violence

Closely connected with the right of revenge is the problem of self-help in order to repel violence or danger.[11] In accordance with the Book of Exodus (22:1), the Mishnah (Sanhedrin 8:6) teaches: "Who burrows his way in, is judged on account of its probable outcome." This statement refers to a burglar who is burgling his way into a house. (The expression in the Torah is *ba-mahteret.*) The Talmud comments: "What is the reason for the law of breaking in? The reason is that it is certain that no man is inactive where his property is concerned. Therefore, this one, the thief, must have reasoned: If I go there, the owner will oppose me and prevent me. But if he does, I will kill him. Hence the Torah decreed, If he come to slay thee, forestall by slaying him *(haba le-horgekha hashkem le-hargo)."*

This right of self-help has been expanded in the Mishnah to include the defense of others; unlike Roman law, Jewish law actually makes it a duty for a third person to come to the rescue of an attacked fellow man. The Mishnah teaches: "The following *must be saved* from sinning, even at the cost of their lives: He that pursues after his neighbor to slay him, or after a male (for pederasty), or after a betrothed maiden (to dishonor her). . . ." But it is not allowed as a means of combating idolatry (Sanhedrin 8:7), only in cases in which it is connected with a personal attack upon a third person. Thus the command of Moses to the Levites is clearly ruled unlawful.

But this right, and obligation, of saving a victim from a pursuer has its limitations. The pursuer's life should not be taken if there is another way to save the pursued. This is the view of Rabbi Jonathan ben Shaul, and it has been generally accepted, as is proved by the interpretation of the story of Joab. The sentence of Rabbi Jonathan ben Shaul (Sanhedrin 74a) says: "For it is taught —if one was pursuing his fellow to slay him, and he could have been saved by maiming a limb of the pursuer, but did not thus save him [killing him instead], he is executed on his account." It means he has got to be very careful to do only what is needed to save the pursued man, and he has got to be very cautious in his actions.

This ruling has been generally accepted because the Mekhilta already contains this teaching to a certain degree, and the Talmud itself includes it in the story of Joab. When Joab, David's general, was brought before the court and Solomon the Just asked him: "Why did you kill Abner?" he answered: "I was Asahel's avenger of blood." Asahel was the brother of Joab, and Abner had killed him. "But Asahel was a pursuer," remonstrated Solomon, "Abner killed him in self-help." "Even so," answered Joab, "but he [Abner] should have saved himself at the cost of one of his [Asahel's] limbs." The Mekhilta assesses the problem thus: just as if the girl has someone to protect her from the attack of the pursuer and she nevertheless kills him, she is guilty of murder; so also here, if the owner of the house had someone to protect him from an attack by the burglar and the owner nevertheless kills him, he is guilty.

The Talmud (Sanhedrin 74a) has it in the name of Rabbah, but treats it as a matter of common sense, that a man should not save himself by killing a third person. Rabbah told of a man who came to him asking: "The governor of my town has ordered me: go and kill so and so, if not I will slay thee." Rabbah answered: "Let him rather slay you, than that you should commit murder. Who knows that your blood is redder? Perhaps his blood is redder." One cannot save himself by killing a third person. Defense, in such cases, tends to become violence. The problem of defense and self-help becomes more complicated if we come to deal not with a direct act of violence but with behavior in cases of conflict arising in situations when the saving of the life of one man constitutes a threat to the safety of a whole community—a problem that many people had to face during the Holocaust.

The Tosefta (Terumot 7:20)[12] states a controversial principle of Halakhah: "If a company of Jews walking on the road is threatened by Gentiles, who say—give us one of you that we may kill him, otherwise we shall kill you all, they must rather all be killed. However, if the demand is for a named individual, like Sheba son of Bichri, then in order to avoid wholesale slaughter, he should be surrendered."[13]

The conflict presented here is a dilemma that many people have had to face, and we are still facing it today. Jewish law is unambiguous on this issue: if a certain person is not singled out, there is to be no giving in, not even to save a town. But there were people who were even more radical, and when a named person was claimed they took a more strict view. The more lenient view probably reasoned that if a named person is claimed, compliance does not involve the guilt of selection, which is a very difficult thing. The Palestinian Talmud (Terumot 8) presents the more extreme view in its account of Ulla bar Koshev (Genesis Rabbah, in the parallel text, reads "Kosher," which probably means a rebel in this case), who was wanted by the Roman government. He fled to Rabbi Joshua ben Levi, who dwelled in Lydda. The Roman troops came, surrounded the city, and said to the leaders: "If you do not hand him over to us, we shall destroy the city." Rabbi Joshua ben Levi went to Ulla's hiding place, reconciled him, and handed him over to them. The story continues that Elijah, blessed be his memory, who appeared often to Rabbi Joshua ben Levi, stopped doing so. Rabbi Joshua ben Levi fasted many fasts, and Elijah finally appeared in order to say: "Shall I reveal myself to informers?" Rabbi Joshua protested: "Have I not acted according to the Mishnah?" This man was named, and according to the Halakhah he was allowed to hand him over. But the prophet retorted: "Is this a Mishnah of *hasidim,* of pious men?"—for pious men are expected to act otherwise; they are expected to be more strict.

No definite indication is given here as to what Elijah expected Rabbi Joshua ben Levi to do. But the man who told the story probably was of the same opinion as Rabbi Shimon ben Lakish, which is mentioned in the Palestinian Talmud, that even in the event of such a threat, no one is allowed to hand over a man who is not clearly guilty to be punished by death. If a man is named and his guilt has not been proved, he should not be handed over. This was also the attitude of Rabbi Simeon ben Johai. Under the prevailing conditions of foreign rule, which was considered both by Rabbi Simeon ben Johai and Rabbi Simeon ben Lakish to be the source of violence and injustice, the principle was that in no circumstances should a fugitive be handed over to the Roman authorities. People considered by the Roman authorities to be guilty of capital crimes were not considered guilty by the Jewish sages. Rabbi Judah and Rabbi Johanan took a less strict view. Of course, one has to take into account that informers were considered outlaws in nearly all societies, and the Halakhah ruled *moridim v'ein ma'alim,* which means they may be killed offhand and nobody should save them if they are in danger.[14]

The Limits of Violent Punishment

We have touched upon the limitations of self-help as a contribution to diminishing violence, and we shall now have to consider the Mishnah (Sanhedrin 9:6) which contains a regulation stating that "if a man stole a sacred vessel or cursed by *kossem* [the meaning here is not very clear], or made an Aramean woman his mistress, the Zealots *(kannaim)* may fall upon him." This ruling most probably belongs to the times of the first Hasmoneans, or perhaps even to the time of the war and struggle against the hellenizers. It reminds one of the actions of Phinehas in Numbers (25:6).

However, there is a baraita that censures the action of the Zealots and designates it as not being in accordance with the opinion of the sages. Rabbi Judah ben Pazi, one of the amoraim, transfers this stricture even to the person of Phinehas himself—here again we have an example of a daring interpretation. The claim is made that Moses and the elders intended to pronounce a ban against Phinehas, were it not for the intervention of the Holy Spirit.

From the standpoint of human justice, the action of Phinehas was illegal. We again find an absolutely different attitude in the comments of Philo, who remarks that if any members of the nation betray the honor due to God they should suffer the utmost penalties. They have abandoned their most vital duty, their service in the ranks of piety and religion; they have chosen darkness in preference to the brightest light. And it is well that all who have a zeal for virtue should be permitted to exact the penalties offhand and with no delay, without bringing the offender before jury and council or any kind of magistrate at all; they should be permitted to give full scope to the feelings which possess them—that hatred of evil and love of God which urge them to inflict punishment without mercy on the impious. F. H. Colson rightly thinks that Philo is extracting a general law from the case of Phinehas, and that this interpretation is against the midrash and the sages.[15]

Close to the opinion of Philo is again the more radical tanna, Rabbi Simeon ben Johai, who extends the permission to kill a pursuer so as to prevent murder, sexual violence, or idolatry. His arguments are that if we are saving him by taking his life, "because of the honor of human beings, should we not act likewise when the Eternal is concerned?" (Babylonian Talmud, Sanhedrin 74a. In the Palestinian Talmud, it is reported in the name of his son Rabbi Elazar.) Simeon ben Johai's view has not been the accepted one, but it probably represents an older stratum in the history of Halakhah and was not only the outcome of his own character.

There is yet another Mishnah that preserves forms of punishment which are not based upon the biblical prescription and which by their cruelty caused some embarrassment to the teachers of later generations, who took the trouble to interpret them so as to make them more lenient. The Mishnah (Sanhedrin 9:5) reads: "He who was twice flagellated [for two transgressions and then sinned again] is placed by the beth din in a cell and fed with barley until his belly bursts". There is no such punishment mentioned in the Bible itself. The Mishnah continues: "One who commits murder without witnesses, he is placed in a cell and [forcibly] fed with the bread of adversity and the water of affliction." Bread of adversity and water of affliction are mentioned in the Book of Isaiah (30:20), but not as a punishment. However, the Talmud comments: "Because he has been twice flagellated the beth din places him in a cell?"

Rabbi Jeremiah answered in the name of Resh Lakish: the reference is to flagellation for an offense punishable by extinction. It means not just flagellation but *karet*, Divine punishment by premature or sudden death. Thus he is already liable to death at the hands of God, but the time of his death has not yet come. Since, however, he abandoned himself to sin by transgressing a third time, you hasten his death. Rabbi Jacob said to Rabbi Jeremiah ben Tahlifa: "Come, I will interpret it for you. This treats of flagellation for one sin involving extinction, which was twice repeated, but if he committed two or three different sins, each involving extinction, it may merely be his desire to experience sin, and not a complete abandonment thereto." This is a very interesting and a very fine distinction. Unlike a man who makes himself accustomed to a certain definite sin, if a man commits a number of different sins, he may be doing it only in an attempt to undergo several different experiences, and his crimes must be treated independently in sentencing. This line of interpretation proves that the amoraim did seek exceptions to these ancient mishnayoth.

To the second part there is also a question: how do we know that a man committed murder if there were no witnesses? Rav said that we know by disjointed evidence, which means evidence witnessed by two persons who were not standing together. According to Jewish law, if the witnesses were together he cannot be proved guilty, but there were nevertheless two witnesses. So in such a case they deal with him in the way prescribed by the Mishnah. Samuel said: "without a warning." This means there were witnesses, but there was no warning. Rabbi Hisda said: "through witnesses who were disproved as to the minor circumstances of the crime, but not on the vital points" (Sanhedrin 81b). In a case such as this it may be proven that the accused is a murderer, but because of legal technicalities the evidence is not entirely acceptable; therefore, the Mishnah introduced these punishments.

One fact must be stressed: these punishments, or any others, were not to be used to extract a confession from the accused. Although in a civil case the admission of fault or liability had the power of one hundred witnesses *(hoda'at ba'al din keme'ah edim)* —the suspect's confession as an item of evidence in capital cases was completely rejected, and the rule of *ein adam mesim atzmo ra'a* (a defendant may in no way contribute to his own conviction)— has prevailed since ancient times and remained absolute. This is completely different from other legal systems where the confession of the man himself is considered full proof, which we know can lead to acts of violence to force the accused to confess. Some scholars have put forward theories that this rule was a late one and that older Halakhah recognized confession as evidence, but these theories never really were proven, as has been shown by A. Kirschenbaum.[16] This rule guaranteed a great measure of defense against violence by the state and its judicial authorities. The use of torture to extract a confession from the reluctant lips of suspects creates the climate for making violence the basis of authority, be it the Spanish Inquisition, the Nazi rule, or the developed Soviet system described by Solzhenitsyn.

Thanks to the above mentioned principle, the judicial system of Israel was far removed from these acts of violence, even at times when it was not exempt from cruelty. Of the same Simeon ben Shetah, who acted in the times of Alexander Yannai and Queen Salome, and who executed eighty women sorcerers in Ashkelon, it is reported that he said: "May I see consolation if I have not seen one man pursuing another into a deserted building, and I ran after him, and saw a sword in his hand, and the blood was dripping, and the mouth moving convulsively, and I told him: 'Evil-doer [*rasha*], who killed this man? Either I or you, but what can I do? Your blood is not delivered into my hands, because the Torah declared: "according to two witnesses shall a man be punished by death." He who knows men's thoughts may punish this man who killed his fellow' " (Sanhedrin 37b). The great teacher could probably have found means to extract a confession, and he himself might have served as one witness; but against all this stood the basic principle: no capital punishment without two witnesses and no confession.

No less instructive in this regard is Philo's interpretation of Deuteronomy 24:16, which also contains an example of stress to inflict violence upon one set of persons in substitution for another in order to reach the culprits. In his *De Specialibus Legibus* Philo calls it an excellent ordinance that fathers should not die for their sons, nor sons for their parents, but each person who has committed deeds worthy of death should suffer for it alone, and in his own person. There are those, he says, cruel of heart and bestial of nature who are of a different view:

I mean those who are either secretly and craftily, or boldly and openly threaten to inflict the most grievous sufferings on one set of persons in substitution for another, and seek the destruction of those who have done no wrong on the pretext of their friendship or kinship, or partnership, or some similar connection with the culprits. And they sometimes do this without having suffered any grievous harm, but merely through covetousness and rapine. An example of this was given a little time ago in our own district by a person who was appointed to serve as the Collector of Taxes. When some of the debtors, whose default was clearly due to poverty, took flight in fear of the fatal consequences of his vengeance, he carried off by force their womenfolk [this is a description which is very similar to what we read in Solzhenitsyn] and children and parents and their other relatives and subjected them to every kind of outrage and contumely in order to make them either tell him the whereabouts of the fugitive, or discharge his debts themselves. As they could do neither—the first for want of knowledge, nor the second because they were as penniless as the fugitive—he continued this treatment, until while wringing their bodies with racks and instruments of torture, he finally dispatched them by newly-invented methods of execution. He filled a large basket with sand, and having hung this enormous weight by ropes round their necks, set them in the middle of the marketplace, in the open air, in order that while they themselves sank under the cruel stress of the accumulated punishments, the wind, the sun, the shame of being seen by passers-by, and the weights upon them, the spectators of their punishments might suffer by anticipation.

Some of these, whose souls saw facts more vividly than did their eyes, feeling themselves maltreated in the bodies of others, hastened to take leave of their lives with the aid of the sword or poison or halter, thinking that in their ill plight it was a great piece of luck to die without suffering torture. The others, who had no such opportunity to dispatch themselves, were brought out in a row, as is done in the awarding of inheritances, first those who stood in the first degrees of kinship, after them the second and the third and so on till the last. And when there were no kinsmen left, the maltreatment was passed on to their neighbors, and sometimes even to villages and cities, which quickly became desolate and stripped of inhabitants, who left their homes and dispersed to places where they expected to remain unobserved.[17]

Here is an example of a method which has been applied through the ages. Of course, we may say that the attitude of Simeon ben Shetah and the principle of two witnesses does not do justice and leaves convicts unpunished. But it seems that the sages were not ready to accept in such cases the principle that *vim vi repellere licet,* force is permitted to repel force. Only in civil cases are there examples in which no judicial decision could be reached and the rule of *kol d'alim gever,* let the stronger prevail, was applied. Only in civil cases is it said: "Seeing that the law has not determined one way or the other, each must fend for himself" (Gittin 60b).

In capital cases there was no room for "let the stronger prevail," or even for a judge to do away with the strict demands of procedure. One might argue that public security also must be considered. In fact, in unusual times special provisions were made for a *hora 'at sha'ah,* a temporary dispensation, not to be taken as precedent. This involved the virtual abolition of all ordinary regulations of procedure. Rabbi Eliezer ben Jacob taught: "I heard that we are allowed to punish not according to the Halakhah and not according to the Torah" (Palestinian Talmud, Hagigah 2:3; Babylonian Talmud, Yevamot 90b). There were prerogatives conceded to the high court or to a king, but they were limited to a certain period and made dependent upon many conditions in order to guard against lawlessness and violence. The problem facing any authority is how to find the proper relationship between the interests and necessities of the community, the group, or the society, the rights of the individual, and the value of human life. Both those who view themselves as representing the interests of the community and those who are concerned with the rights of the individual can try to achieve their ends by brute physical force, which continuously endeavors to expand and leads to violence and counterviolence.

To the biblical verse, "a man who is his neighbor's enemy lies in wait for him . . ." (Deut. 19:11), the sages added: "If a man transgresses a light transgression, he is to finish with a heavy one. Hatred in the heart, striving to avenge, bearing a grudge, not caring if your brother may find his living with you, leads to bloodshed and to the necessity of the intervention of the governmental authorities" (*Sifre* on Deuteronomy).

The warning of Shemaiah—"hate lordship and make not thyself known to the government"—was repeated more explicitly three hundred years later by Rabban Gamaliel the Patriarch, the son of Rabbi Judah Ha-Nasi: "Be cautious with those in authority, for they let not a man approach them but for their own purposes" (Avot 1:12). But this caution does not contradict the warning of Rabbi Hanania, the prefect of the priests, who said: "Pray for the peace of the kingdom, since but for thereof we had swallowed up each his neighbor alive." It is the peace of the kingdom which justifies its authority. The fear of the government *(mora'ah shel malkhut)* is needed to preserve human life. The guiding principle in using force or defense, both for the individual and the state, remains the absolute value of human life, "for in the image of God made He man" (Gen. 9:6). Shedding human blood includes all ways of taking human life, even suicide. In modern life the observance of this principle applies not only to the relationship of an individual to the state and of the state to an individual, it also presents a challenge to modern science and modern medicine. Combating illness and promoting health is a sacred task, but it involves in our times questions of ethics and morality, as it is connected with the problem of finding the limit between treatment and experiment on human beings.[18] In a certain sense our sages dealt with these problems.

In an old mishnah, in Oholot 7:6, the sages laid down a rule: "One does not push away a life for a life." Accordingly, so long as the child is in the womb of the mother, embryotomy is permitted; but once the greater part of the child has passed through the birth canal, it is not. Modern medicine faces the danger of sliding into a breach of the Hippocratic oath when patients are subjected to physical procedures without choice. These problems, like many others, can be partly solved if the society is not a passive one, provided that it acts not through violence but in defense of its rights.

The sages recognized that in the existing order of the world there was no possibility of attaining the realization of administrative and social ideals in their purity. Things will change, they said, only when the Holy One renews the world. We have had very bad experiences with all attempts to renew the world by men. But, these experiences notwithstanding, we are responsible for the existing system. Thus we have an obligation to be unflagging in our efforts to improve it and to do so in the spirit of the affirmation of Genesis "that man is created in the image of God."

NOTES

1. *Ba-Hodesh,* chap. 1.
2. *Against Apion,* I, 17; cf. Eusebius, *Historia Ecclesiastica,* IX, 1–3.
3. See my "Class Status and Leadership in the World of the Palestinian Sages," *Proceedings of the National Academy in Jerusalem,* 1968.
4. Babylonian Talmud, Shabbat 17a; Palestinian Talmud, Shabbat I,4.
5. This is an ancient tradition cited in a later midrash, Exodus Rabbah 27:9. Rabbi Nehemiah's exegesis turns on a play on words: those who have entered the arena *(zirah)* are those whom the verse speaks of as having "struck their hands for a stranger" *(zar),* and it is they, therefore, who are held responsible for the actions and the welfare of the community at large.

The analogy is between the commitment made by the gladiator on entering the ring and the responsibility assumed by a leader on donning the mantle of office—for at that point neither can stand aside; both must either win or lose.

6. *De Sacrificiis Abelis et Caini* IV, xxxviii, pp. 128–29, trans. after F.H. Colson and G.H. Whitaker, Loeb ed., vol. II, 1929 (reprinted 1968), p. 187.

7. *De Sacrificiis,* IV, p. 130.

8. *Loc. cit.*

9. *De Specialibus Legibus,* I, ix, pp. 51–57, trans. by F.H. Colson, Loeb ed., vol. VII, 1937 (reprinted 1958), pp. 127 ff.

10. *De Ebrietate,* xv–xvi, pp. 66–70, trans. by F.H. Colson and G.H. Whitaker, Loeb ed., vol. III, 1930 (reprinted 1960), p. 351.

11. See Boaz Cohen, "Self-Help in Jewish and Roman Law," in *Jewish and Roman Law,* vol. II (New York, 1966), pp. 624–50. Samuel Klein's treatment of the cities of refuge is found in *Kobetz ha-Hevra le-Hakirat Eretz Yisrael* (Jerusalem, 1935), pp. 81–102.

12. See the commentary of S. Lieberman, *Tosefta ki-Fshuta,* pp. 420 ff., and D. Daube, *Collaboration with Tyranny in Rabbinic Law* (London, 1965).

13. This refers to 2 Sam. 20, in which the delivery of the rebel Sheba, as decided by Joab, saved the city of Abel.

14. The term *moridim* may refer to the Roman punishment of sacking, which was praised by Cicero but known to the Mishnah only as a crime *(kavash alav letoch ha-mayim)* by which the victim was "forcibly submerged in water" and not allowed to surface.

15. *De Specialibus Legibus,* I, pp. 54–55, and Colson's note *ad loc.* in the Loeb ed., VII, pp. 617–18.

16. A. Kirschenbaum, *Self-Incrimination in Jewish Law* (New York, 1970), pp. 41–49.

17. *De Specialibus Legibus,* III, xxix, pp. 153–68, trans. after F.H. Colson, Loeb ed., vol. VII, 1937 (reprinted 1958), p. 573 ff.

18. See A. Barram, *Modern Trends of Violence* (London and Cambridge, Mass., 1973).

6   Violence and the Value of Life: The Halakhic View

Let me begin by saying that I approach our subject as a political scientist and not as a professional historian. As a political scientist I begin as Plato and Aristotle did, with a discussion of human nature. Moreover, I plan to deal with the subject conceptually and analytically rather than chronologically.

Perhaps by way of introduction I might also add a point about myself, and the best way to explain this would be with a story. A man had been prevailed upon by his wife, after much importuning, to clean their attic. After he had cleared everything out of the attic, he realized that among the things he had burned was an old family Bible, and he began to have misgivings about having destroyed this family treasure. He turned to a friend of his and said, "I'm beginning to worry; perhaps it wasn't a nice thing to do, to burn the old family Bible. What's more, I seem to recall that on the frontispiece of that Bible there were large letters, G U T E N." Whereupon the friend said, "You idiot, you probably burned a Gutenberg Bible. The last copy sold for about $40,000." "Oh, no," said the husband. "Mine wouldn't have brought a cent. Some nincompoop by the name of Martin Luther wrote all over the margins."

My prejudice, I might say, is that I am loath to discard any part of the Bible or any of the glosses that the rabbis have written on the Bible through the millennia. While I do not always agree with rabbis and have on many occasions expressed considerable dissent, by the same token I have altogether too much respect for the integrity and sincerity of my forebears not to try to understand, empathetically at least, that which they tried to create and contribute to Jewish thought and survival.

That is a prejudice of mine and I must record it in advance. However, starting with human nature, as I promised, I think we must posit in advance that to act violently, to act with aggression, is human. This is recognized, for example, by Konrad Lorenz, who discusses aggression and violence in the animal kingdom and in the human kingdom. Jewish law, or Halakhah, recognized this. There is a tendency to violence in human nature, but as with all instincts, whether the instinct is for food, for sex, or for recognition, Jewish law seeks never totally to repress, only to control, to regulate, to make constructive, to dignify, even to sanctify, every instinct that human beings have, including the instinct for violence and aggression. For this reason generally it must be conceded that Judaism is not committed to pacifism. It may be, as Reuven Kimmelman suggests, that there were rabbis in the third or fourth century who opposed violence as a means of ensuring Jewish survival, but theirs was decidedly a minority point of view.[1] On the other hand, Maurice Lamm, in his essay "Red or Dead," shows that the sources would well establish that pacifism is not a Jewish ideal.[2] If pacifism is the pursuit of peace at any and all cost, then it was never an authoritative Jewish teaching. Tolstoy rejected all violent resistance to evil in the social order, regardless of cause and circumstance, because an active revolution must fight evil with another evil, namely violence. He believed in passive, individual resistance and derived it from the New Testament, from Matthew: "Resist not evil." Gandhi also made it a strategy of politics and later attempted to make it a policy of state. Gandhi's proposal for Jews during the Holocaust was also passive resistance. It was counsel given after the tragedy and thus untenable. Gandhi's passive resistance might have been effective against an England which had a conscience, but it would not have accomplished anything vis-à-vis Hitler. Quite the contrary, it was precisely what Hitler would have wanted.

But even in situations in which humans less beastly than Hitler are the enemy, passive resistance often has serious limitations. It either cannot be consistently maintained, or it results in the loss of the best manpower that a cause can possibly mobilize. One such situation in modern times is that of the Student Non-Violent Coordinating Committee, which played an important role in the black revolution in the United States during the sixties. Howard Zinn's *The New Abolitionists* questions how nonviolent nonviolent direct action can be, and he proves, for example, that in 1964 the group had to concede that it would not stop a Negro farmer in Mississippi from arming himself to defend his home against attack.

Judaism, therefore, is more concerned with regulating the circumstances which would permit the exercise of violence—by individuals, by groups, and by states—than it is with the elimination of violence at all costs. Violence is at one and the same time an important way both to destroy and to conserve one of the most important values in the value system of Judaism—human life. Violent action usually endangers the life of the aggressor as well as the lives of those against whom the violence is directed. Generally one's own life is regarded as having the highest priority, but if one is to engage in violence it must be in accord with Jewish law and in behalf of the value of life or a value even higher than the value of life. Never is one to lose sight of the ultimate value to be achieved. Thus, war for war's sake, which in Judaism is represented by Amalek, is the essence of evil. There can be no compromise in the opposition to such a policy. Duels to vindicate one's honor are heinously sinful. Sadism and masochism are not to be tolerated. Even asceticism is frowned upon in that it is held to be a form of violence against the self, except in the very special cases where nothing less will help one to overcome physically or spiritually self-destructive behavior.

Violence Against the Self

It is in the light of this brief statement on the approach of Judaism to violence that we can proceed to analyze many different kinds of violence. Some I shall discuss briefly, others at greater length. My first category is violence against oneself. The first instance of that is suicide, which is prohibited. If the Halakhah had a prohibition against self-incrimination and the confession of a criminal was of no value in a criminal prosecution, then this form of violence against one's self was regarded by Maimonides as unacceptable because there are people who want to destroy themselves and may seek to do so by confessing to the commission of crimes.[3]

It is remarkable that in the thirteenth century Maimonides should have been concerned with the death impulse emphasized by Sigmund Freud centuries later, and this is the very reason that Maimonides gives for outlawing confessions in a criminal prosecution. Still another form of violence against the self is heroism, risking one's life to save another. This, too, is a form of violence against one's self, entering upon what in Halakhah is called *safek sakana*. I enter upon a course of conduct which might lead to my end, but I am hoping to save someone who is in a *vadai sakana*, definitely in danger of losing his life. This problem is discussed in commentaries on the Rambam, especially the *Kesef Mishnah* and the *Shulhan Arukh*.

During the months immediately following the Yom Kippur War, a case arose in the Israeli army with regard to this legal issue. Israeli soldiers had been given an order not to bathe in the Suez Canal because of the danger; yet, because of the heat, many soldiers did violate the command and bathed in the Canal. Certain Orthodox soldiers raised the question whether soldiers who obeyed the command might lawfully risk their lives to save those who seemed ready to forfeit their lives by violating the command and bathing in the waters of the Suez in order to refresh themselves. The Israeli rabbinate resolved the question in the affirmative. The soldiers were permitted to enter a *safek sakana,* a possibility of danger, in order to save those soldiers who were in a *vadai sakana,* a certainty of danger. What is especially interesting is the rationale set forth in a responsum by Rabbi Yehuda Gershuni, the great talmudic scholar.[4] Gershuni's rationale was simply that the mere fact that someone recklessly endangers his own life does not mean that he has forfeited God's interest in him. His body does not belong to him. It is God's. Therefore, it is the duty of bystanders not to suppose that it "serves him right" if he were killed.

The same principle, that one's body is not his to forfeit, applies also to organ transplants. Halakhah does not accept the notion that irreversible brain damage constitutes death. May a man leave a will to the effect that should he suffer irreversible brain damage his heart should be donated to another? Unfortunately, according to Halakhah, he is not the proprietor of his organs and therefore cannot make a decision with regard to their disposition. The Jewish principle is that the body does not belong to the individual, and if the body does not belong to the individual, then the mere fact that one risks it does not relieve a bystander from entering into *safek sakana* in order to save the person.[5]

This principle also relates to the problem of abortion, which may be regarded as violence against the person. Generally speaking, abortion is prohibited according to Jewish law unless there is danger to the mother. At that time the foetus is in the category of a *rodef*: it is threatening the life of the mother and therefore can be removed. However, in this connection too there is a tremendous literature debating this subject, and as far back as two centuries ago, one of the great talmudic scholars wrote that an abortion should be permitted where the child would be a *mamzer* (a bastard) and consequently would suffer immeasurably.[6] The criterion here is not physical suffering. This opinion is not concerned with abortions to save children who would have been diseased or physically handicapped, but abortions to spare a child the emotional hurt of being treated as an outcast in a society which frowned upon bastards and did not give them the right to marry as they chose. In a case such as this violence against life was permitted because life without a certain quality was not regarded as sufficiently sacred to warrant the avoidance of violence.

This brings us to the most problematic of all situations involving violence against the self—martyrdom. While the concept of martyrdom may have been a psychological means for Jews to confront their situation, from the point of view of the halakhic value system of Judaism, it is not a *mitzvah* of the first order. It is a much greater *mitzvah* to save one's life, and we are placing things in the wrong perspective when we put the emphasis on martyrdom instead of on self-help and self-preservation. Zionist activism is therefore not a new position, for this was the position of Judaism throughout the ages. It was possible in the nineteenth and twentieth centuries to do more about self-preservation than one was able to do before, but at no time in Jewish history was martyrdom thought of as preferable to self-preservation. This is an important point in understanding the Jewish situation.

Thus, to begin with martyrdom is to be avoided if at all possible. No place in the Torah, no place in the written law, is it a *mitzvah* to sacrifice one's life for God. However, you will find in the Torah the command to preserve one's life. When we seek sources concerning martyrdom in talmudic literature, we find only three situations in which one is expected to submit to being killed: if one is asked to murder another, to commit illicit intercourse, or to commit idolatry. Therefore, when we think of the martyrs who heroically declared that they would rather die than be captured at Masada, it would be very difficult in halakhic terms to say that they performed the *mitzvah* of dying *al kiddush ha-Shem,* for the sanctity of God's name. It is a misreading of Jewish law to give primacy to martyrdom.

The term *kiddush ha-Shem* is used in talmudic literature not only in connection with death but also in connection with life.[7] In talmudic discourse *kiddush ha-Shem* means the following: so deport yourself that anyone seeing your behavior will say, "Blessed is that man's God." When I return a trove to a non-Jew, or when a non-Jew gives me change in excess of that to which I am entitled and I return the change and he says, "That is an honest man; blessed is the God that inspires that man to perform good deeds" —that is *kiddush ha-Shem.* This is the only talmudic definition we have of *kiddush ha-Shem:* to prompt someone to acknowledge that the Jewish God must be great to inspire the kind of behavior that is observed in the Jew.

It has been suggested that Jews at one period substituted martyr-dom for actual resistance, and in the modern age we have reverted again to active resistance. This thesis is difficult to accept, however, since Jews have always engaged in every type of defense that was possible. There were four types of response behavior that were possible when Jews were subject to violence: they could engage in self-defense and always did; they could submit to martyrdom; they could engage in flight; or they could accommodate, as the Mar-ranos did.

Halakhah prefers self-defense, but many of us, under the influ-ence of modern theorists such as Hannah Arendt, unfortunately think that *kiddush ha-Shem* was preferred to the preservation of life. But Jews, we must remember, during the Holocaust and prior to it as well, were under an enormous disadvantage when self-help or self-preservation was involved. At least four or five points must be considered by us. First, there were many instances of self-defense in Jewish history, but Jews too often found themselves defenseless in the face of the superior numbers, training, and weap-onry of their attackers. As early as 1096 at Bishop Square, Mainz, the Jews fought valiantly against the Crusaders. Salo Baron has written that although in 1648 Polish Jews defended many cities against besieging Cossacks, they never had sufficient arms and hardly ever any military training. Furthermore, Jews were always widely scattered and easily exposed to the wrath of their neighbors. The Jews were not notorious cowards—this is an unfortunate ca-nard. As Israel Abraham writes:

The Spanish armies contained a large number of Jewish soldiers who fought both under the Cross and the Crescent in the great wars that raged between the Christians and the Moors. The martial spirit of the Jews of Spain showed itself in their constant claim of the right to wear arms and engage in knightly pastimes. Spanish mobs did not attack the Jewish quarters with impunity, but elsewhere in Europe and in the East, the Jews occasionally displayed a courage and a proficiency in self-help which, had it been more frequently exercised, would have put an entirely different complexion on the relations between the governments of many states and their Jewish subjects in later centuries.[8]

A curious sidelight on the courage of Jews is cast by the fact that the royal lion-tamers in Spain were Jews. One Jew was also a famous pirate who prepared a strong fleet to meet the Spanish galleys, as the English state papers of the year 1521 bear witness. Yet, and this is my second point, as always, the Jewish situation was unique. It was not only that Jews were defenseless. A Muslim minority in a Christian country could always threaten the assailants with reprisals against the Christian minorities in other lands, but Jews, even when they were in a position to deal a strong blow, found that they had to subordinate the destiny of their particular community to the welfare of the whole people. They had a strong sense of solidarity with their coreligionists everywhere, and thus, for example, the Jews of Tulczyn in 1648 refrained from attacking treacherous fellow combatants among the noblemen. They chose to die instead when their leaders exhorted them: "We are in exile among the nations. If you lay hands upon the nobles, then all the kings of Christianity will hear of it and take revenge on all our brethren in the dispersion, God forbid."

In our own century we have a tragic but eloquent example of what the Jews always dreaded. I refer to the bullet fired in 1938 by Herschel Grynzpan, whose story is beautifully told by Abram Sachar in *Sufferance Is the Badge.*[9] At that time Poland was calling back all of her citizens, and Herschel Grynzpan's parents were caught in a vise. After receiving a letter from his parents describing their distress, he decided to take revenge by destroying some great Nazi officials, made his way into an embassy in Paris, and killed a third-rate bureaucrat of Nazidom. That shot was the pretext for the dreadful pogrom of November 1938, which precipitated a reprisal against all the Jews in Germany.

Is the situation so different today? Self-defense may sometimes be helpful to one Jewish community, but Jews must always be terribly concerned about how it will affect Jewish communities elsewhere. Thus Jews in South Africa are concerned when the State of Israel exercises its sovereign right to vote in the United Nations in accordance with the dictates of its conscience against South Africa. And the Jews of the Soviet Union are hostages in order to force Jews in the United States not to be too militant in support of the Jackson Amendment. Thus, the uniqueness of the Jewish situation has a very important impact on the use of self-defense by Jews in any part of the world, whether in 1648 or 1938 or 1974. The problem of our dispersion and our sense of responsibility for each other prompts us to be more circumspect before we resort to tactics that may avail in one place but can cause irreparable damage in another.

Thus, when Jews were able to engage in self-defense they did, but not always was this, the halakhic desideratum, available to them. Not always was it possible; sometimes for logistical reasons it was impossible. After Germany's defeat in World War I, havoc broke loose in Germany. Rosa Luxemburg was done to death as she was being carried to prison, and there was fear in Berlin that the Jewish quarter would be attacked. Jewish front-line veterans formed a unit for self-defense and the catastrophe was averted. In Germany this was possible, but in Poland there was a different situation to confront. Poles sought to expel the Ukrainians from eastern Galicia. They stormed Lemberg on November 22, 1918, and promised their troops, in good Cossack manner, that as a reward they would receive permission to plunder the Jews for forty-eight hours. The Jewish self-defense was disarmed; bars and bolts were removed from the Jewish quarter by squads of engineers with their equipment; and a pogrom ensued in which seventy-three were killed on the spot, while many died later of their wounds.

In addition to these two external problems, the might of the enemy and the dispersion of the Jews, there were also internal problems. Jews were always a thinking people and were always plagued by ideology. Even when they agreed among themselves on self-defense they could not always agree on methods because of ideological differences. Thus, for example, the horrors of Kishinev in 1903 prompted Hayyim Nahman Bialik and Simon Dubnow to complain that Jews permit themselves to go to slaughter. And when the pogroms of 1905 came around the Jews prepared themselves. They were going to resist and fight for self-preservation. But alas, by the time the pogrom epidemic of 1905 broke out, every tiny faction among the Jews was stuck fast in an ideological web and the attainment of unity proved impossible. Israel Zangwill derided the numerous factions within Jewish self-defense organizations in his "Ghetto Comedies," and Milton Konvitz, in his essay "From Jewish Rights to Human Rights," bears out this analysis. Konvitz gives the details of the events of 1905 and shows how the effectiveness of these groups was sapped by class and party divisions. In Zhitomir, for instance, there were three separate defense groups: a Bund defense unit, a Poalei Zion self-defense unit, and a nonlabor Zionist defense unit. The result was that coordinated self-defense proved impossible. Similar was the experience of the Jewish Defense League. It started off simply as a self-defense organization, but soon it became political with the result that its effectiveness was virtually destroyed. This involvement in ideology is one of the problems we constantly face, for war requires regimentation, the galvanization of a force.

A further point is prompted by the kabbalists in the Middle Ages, who tried to rush the advent of the Messiah. There were speculative kabbalists who were interested in theory, but there were also operative kabbalists who sought to accomplish practical results—to twist God's arm, so to speak, and hasten the coming of the Messiah. The whole concept of the making of a Golem indicates the extent to which Jews were always interested in self-help rather than in martyrdom. They did not rely on God alone. They wanted to push God, to force Him to act. As in many other instances in the past, they did not have the right formula; they did not have atomic weapons, but they never preferred slaughter to survival.

This brings me to the last point, a point which is developed very fully in the Holocaust literature, particularly by a young writer named Michael Shazar, who points to the fact that even during the Holocaust, in addition to self-defense, there was a manner of resistance which is a form of survival. Jews who did not survive physically at least tried to show the Nazis that they could not crush them spiritually. Out of the Holocaust came a responsum about one Jew in the concentration camps who insisted on putting his phylacteries on his head no matter what the Nazis did to him. Work started very early in the morning, so he could not do this secretly; it was done openly, as an act of defiance. Shazar talks extensively about the act of defiance as a way of saying, "You can break my back, but you are not going to crush my spirit; I shall continue to live, and even if I don't live physically, I am going to live, my people are going to live, my traditions are going to continue to live." Finally the Nazis decided to brand a swastika into the forehead of this Jew who put his *tefillin* on his forehead every day. The Jew then felt that he could not put the *tefillin* over a swastika since by Jewish law nothing can intervene between the skin and the *tefillin*. But he wanted to know whether under those circumstances he would be permitted to put a bandage on the swastika so the *tefillin* would not rest on an unholy symbol. This was a unique kind of resistance, and the emphasis was not on dying for the sake of getting some share of the world to come. It was not martyrdom to be assured of immortal life, as in Islam, or to atone for the sins of others, as in Christianity. It was a way of struggling to ensure the survival of the Jewish people and their tradition in whatever way possible.

In Germany in 1946, immediately after the Holocaust, I saw a *siddur* that had been handwritten from memory by a Jew who was afraid that the Jewish prayer book would disappear from the face of the earth. This point can perhaps best be summed up with a beautiful insight by Yitzhak Nissenbaum, one of the martyrs of the Holocaust. Nissenbaum, in an unenviable position, had to preach to the inmates of the concentration camp on the Day of Atonement. *Kiddush ha-Shem* may be a *mitzvah,* he told them, it may be a *mitzvah* to sanctify God's name, but the circumstances vary from time to time and from place to place. In the Middle Ages, he said, Jews may have felt that they were performing the commandment of *kiddush ha-Shem* by committing suicide because at that time the Christians wanted to conquer the souls of Jews and convert them to Christianity. Therefore, the only way to frustrate Christians was by making it impossible for them to win Jewish souls; if a Jew died, then Christianity lost a target for baptism. Today, Nissenbaum told the other inmates, what the Nazi wants is not the soul but the body of the Jew. He wants Jews to perish. Therefore, the greatest *mitzvah* is to survive, to frustrate the Nazis by preserving Jewish lives. Therefore, he urged them, escape, hide in the forest, join the underground, do whatever you must to live. Nissenbaum was being consistent with the Jewish tradition when he placed the greatest emphasis on self-preservation.

Violence Against Others

Now I come to the second category, violence against other human beings, and the best I can do as a political scientist is to classify the material and offer several illustrations of each type. There are many forms of this type of violence. First, there is violence against one's attacker, which is permitted. Halakhah allows one to engage in self-defense against the attacker, who is called a *rodef.* It is licit for me to kill anyone who wants to murder me or sexually abuse me, but this is the only justification that the Talmud gives for the exercise of violence other than by constituted authority, as in war or by sentence of a court. (Sol Roth's article on the "Morality of Revolution" discusses this in great detail.[10]) The concept of *rodef* was extended to include informers. Jews were allowed to kill an informer, even try him and execute him, because he was attacking the Jewish community. If he could no longer perform his nefarious deeds—if, for example, there was a way to make certain that he would never inform against the Jews again—then the death penalty was not allowed. Thus, execution was permitted as a preventive measure, not a punitive one.[11]

In our day it has been suggested by Aharon Lichtenstein that when a person threatens the Jewish community not only by informing but also by adversely affecting the entire social, economic, or health structure of a community, he is in the category of a *rodef,* and violence against such a person would be permitted. A threat to poison the water or sabotage the communications or power systems of a country would come under this classification.

Third, one may engage in violence to redeem captives because captives are in danger of losing their lives, and thus one would be acting to save other people. Jews always have assumed that anyone taken into captivity might suffer the fate of those Israeli prisoners who were taken by Syria in the Yom Kippur War. This may help us to understand why the patriarch Jacob did not object to the plan of his sons Simeon and Levi to weaken the inhabitants of Shechem by making them undergo circumcision. The Bible clearly indicates that their sister Dinah, after her rape, was still in captivity. Simeon and Levi wanted to save her from the house of her captor, and for that purpose the use of violence is permitted. This, however, did involve approval of the massacre of the weakened Shechemites, for which Jacob bitterly censured his sons prior to his death.[12]

Fourth, one is allowed to engage in violence in defense of property, but that is a limited license; for even then, in the final analysis, one may engage in violence only to preserve life. If I may kill to defend my property it is, says the Talmud, because there is a presumption that the burglar knows that it is human nature for a proprietor or the owner of a house to do everything to defend his family. Therefore, the burglar knows that he may be killed, and when he comes to burglarize the property he is assuming that he himself may have to kill in self-defense. Consequently, the proprietor may kill on the presumption that the attacker is going to kill. Again, resort to violence from a halakhic point of view revolves around the central value of the sanctity of life, and these are the only circumstances under which I can defend my property at the risk of someone else's life.

Fifth, one may sometimes resort to force in defense of one's religious convictions, but not to the point of killing. Thus, I have a right to expel from my house a slave who has been emancipated and now may no longer cohabit with a non-Jewish slave. If I injure him in the process of expelling him, I might not have to pay, but I may not kill him except in self-defense (Babylonian Talmud, Baba Kama 28a).

Outside my home do I have a right to engage in violence in order to uphold God's honor, to champion God's law? May I kill one who desecrates the Sabbath, or a man and woman engaged in illicit intercourse? In the Bible we are told that Aaron's grandson Phinehas did precisely that. But God's response to him, says Rabbi Naftali Zevi Judah Berlin, was that he was given "a covenant of peace," to calm him and restore his peace of mind. God does not want vindictiveness in His behalf, although the zealous saints sometimes forget this. Vindictiveness brings guilt and guilt feelings in its train.

A distinguished commentator on the Talmud, known as the Ha-Makne, provides us with an interesting insight with regard to one of the best known laws of the Bible. In the Book of Deuteronomy we have the laws of war, which direct that if in the course of a war a soldier should fall in love with one of his captives she will enjoy a great measure of humanitarian consideration (Deut. 21:10). If he seeks to marry her he must take a number of steps designed to prevent hasty action and, should marriage follow, to assure the dignity of her person. Many have asked why the Bible is so indulgent as to grant the right to cohabit with a captive and ultimately marry her. However, Ha-Makne tells us that in time of war it is to be expected that moral standards will be lowered. This might prompt a zealot to try to defend God's honor as Phinehas did. He might kill the soldier and his beloved. Therefore, by being permissive, the Torah protected the soldier and the "beautiful woman" with whom he was infatuated and made any interference by the zealot a capital offense if the zealot should become so exercised over the breach of the moral law that he kills in consequence thereof. In time of war Jewish law does not expect superhuman conduct from those engaged in it.

Another category is violence to avenge wrongs. Under no circumstances are Jews permitted to engage in violence for the sake of vengeance. Such acts of revenge are prohibited by the Bible. Samuel Belkin makes a beautiful point on this subject in his book *In His Image.*[13] Belkin tells us that even though in the ethical literature of Judaism one finds the doctrine of *imitatio Dei*—just as God is merciful we must be merciful, and just as God is kind we must be kind, and just as God is compassionate we must be compassionate—nonetheless one will never find in Jewish literature, either halakhic or aggadic, a statement to the effect that just as God is zealous so must we be zealous, or just as God is vengeful so must we be vengeful.

One exception regarding vengeance begs for explanation, the case of the *goel ha-dam*. If a man commits an accidental murder he is not subject to the death penalty but has the privilege of fleeing to seek asylum in a "city of refuge." A relative of the victim is allowed to pursue him and kill him; the assassin is at the mercy of the blood avenger, the *goel ha-dam,* until he reaches the city of refuge. This would indicate that we do have one situation in which it is permitted to commit violence in order to avenge a wrong. However, this must be understood properly. There is a difference of opinion in the Talmud as to whether this is permissive or mandatory. The prevailing view is that it is permissive—pursuit by the *goel ha-dam* is allowed but is not a *mitzvah.* It is a greater *mitzvah* not to engage in violence. Yet the *goel ha-dam* serves an important purpose within the context of Jewish law in primitive or semiprimitive times.

How, then, in a society with no investigative agencies, did one apprehend a killer? There simply was not the law enforcement machinery that is available in modern societies, and what the Torah conceived of was a method of making the law self-operative. When a man killed accidentally the first thing he did was to flee. Instead of trying to hide, he fled immediately to a city of refuge, where he declared himself and received protection from any avenger. In that way it was possible to determine who committed the crime. He was then told that if he had committed the crime intentionally he would be tried for a capital offense. He was brought back in safe custody to the city where the crime was committed and tried there. If he committed the crime with malice or forethought he was executed. If, on the other hand, he committed the crime unintentionally he was brought back to the city of refuge, where he stayed until the high priest died. There he was to atone for his sin.

In other words, according to most authorities, the institution of the *goel ha-dam* was certainly not a *mitzvah;* it was a way of setting the law enforcement machinery in motion by having criminals present themselves for trial. This form of violence was indulged so that society could apprehend those who committed homicides, and from that point on the judicial machinery took its course through trials to determine whether the killing was intentional or unintentional.

Thus we conclude our discussion of the instances of violence by individuals against individuals and move on to violence by the state against individuals, individuals against the state, and violence between states.

Violence Against Constituted Authority

Let us first consider violence against constituted authority. There is a dearth of materials with regard to violence against the Jewish state because Jews have not had a state for such a long time. Yet it would be a mistake to assume that because there was no Jewish state there was no kind of constituted authority with virtual sovereignty in the Jewish community. Jews in their own communities have enjoyed legal autonomy over the centuries; they wanted it and even paid for the right to enjoy it. They taxed themselves in order to have control of their own courts, and very often the king, or feudal lord, entered into an agreement with a Jewish community for a quid pro quo to grant them legal autonomy.

This was the situation in Muslim countries, where all religious minorities enjoyed legal autonomy. Thus, one can visualize violence against constituted authority in a Jewish community which had legal autonomy; but, generally speaking, the commission of such acts was not permitted. The legal term was *mored be-malkhut,* rebellion against the king or against kingship, punishable by death.

The source for this doctrine is not in the Pentateuch but in the Book of Joshua. The Jews, so to speak, delegated the power of enforcement to Joshua and his successors. Very similar to the covenant of Hobbes and Locke was the covenant between the Jews and their king, and one of the provisions of that covenant was that they would give the king obedience. Anyone who did *not* do so could be punished for committing a crime mentioned in the Bible. There is nothing in the Bible about treason, but a man who challenged God's authority or any authority delegated by Him was considered a *rodef,* a pursuer. He was undermining the fabric that kept the community together. Thus Jews developed through the years this notion of a contract between the constituted authority and themselves. There were obligations on both sides, and for the breach of these obligations there were sanctions.

This does not mean that because Jews were not permitted to rebel or practice violence against constituted authority they had to be submissive. There is a respectable body of literature sanctioning nonviolent protest and an enormous amount of writing about the ethics of protest against constituted authority. Jews had an obligation to make even kings do the right thing, and certainly those who were responsible for the welfare of the Jewish community. Making them aware of their duties and penitent with regard to their evil was in the best prophetic tradition. The prophets were rebels against constituted authority; but even Elijah, who was the greatest rebel of all and so often in flight from the wrath of Queen Jezebel and King Ahab, paid deference to the king he denounced because it was necessary to respect the king and maintain his authority. Violence was not sanctioned, but there was an ethic of protest.

There is also a Jewish tradition of civil disobedience, and a classic example is to be found in the Talmud itself. The rabbis legislated against the use of wine made by non-Jews and tried to do the same with respect to oil. The Jews accepted the former but not the latter, and the rabbis had to abolish the prohibition. As a result, there is a classic maxim of Jewish law that no court with legislative power can ever legislate anything that the majority of people cannot or will not accept. This is one of the great democratic aspects of Jewish law.

Just as in the United States one can challenge the constitutionality of the president, of Congress, or even of a judge if their actions appear to violate the basic law of the country, so in antiquity Jews were able to challenge the mandate of a king. One was not allowed to rebel, but if one disobeyed on the basis that the command given was in violation of the law of the Torah, one was not punished. A Sanhedrin would hear the case, and there was no punishment if it was found that the king had given an unconstitutional command. This kind of judicial review was also a form of resistance.

In Jewish law there is one additional form of resistance to constituted authority often overlooked—the law of *zaken mamreh*. In this case a high court ruled that an elder or judge had been in error, reversed him, and sent the case back to him. It then became his duty to apply the law as it had been decided by a majority in the high court. If he refused to do so, if he defied the Sanhedrin, he committed an unpardonable offense and a capital crime. However, said the Talmud, while he could be deemed a criminal for breaking the very fabric of the social order and the judicial system, that did not preclude him from going up and down the countryside to preach that the court in Jerusalem had erred. He was guaranteed the right to continue his dissent, not in action but in speech. There would of course be anarchy and bedlam if lower courts did not obey higher courts, but in the talmudic system anyone could proclaim his dissent. Thus the right of protest against constituted authority is deeply rooted in the Jewish tradition.

Generally, one ought to take note of the importance of dissent in Jewish law and in Jewish communal life. The Talmud recorded all dissenting opinions, and there was always the possibility that what was the dissenting view in one century might become the majority view in another, precisely as has happened in the history of the United States. Child labor laws, for example, were held unconstitutional by two courts in succession until a third court finally held them to be constitutional.

However, the major problem in revolts against constituted authority involves not the courts but the underprivileged, those who are disadvantaged by the constituted authority. George Sorel, in *Reflections on Violence* (1961), says that nothing good was ever accomplished except through violence. However, Jewish law holds that violence is not permitted unless life is at stake. Was there, then, any way in which the poor could unshackle the yoke of those who were oppressing them? First, there was the right to strike, which is as ancient as the Talmud itself. Second, the right of the poor was a right against the community, a legal right: the poor did not have to rebel because they could sue the community for subsistence. They did not sue for compassion or empathy but sought enforcement of what was their legal right to live.

The poor could also benefit from the fact that the community had the right to fix wages and prices. The fixing of the price of wheat, for example, was in the hands of the seven elders of the city, who were democratically elected and had the power to adjust the economy in order to cope with crises, with drought, or with agreements in restraint of trade.

In effect, then, what the community had were means to make

unnecessary what Herbert Marcuse has called the "counterviolence of the poor." There were built-in techniques to prevent exploitation by the affluent, which, according to Marcuse, constitutes
violence against the poor. One such means that deserves special
consideration is the closest equivalent that Jewish law has to the
modern ombudsman. The Talmud tells us that a group of butchers
made an agreement among themselves to control the supply of
meat and thus perhaps increase the price. For breach of the agreement the offending party would suffer the destruction of the hides
of the cattle he had slaughtered. One butcher committed this
offense, and his colleagues destroyed his hides; he sued for damages
and won his case. The agreement was nullified because it did not
have the approval of the "important man" in town who, so to
speak, was the defender of the public interest. Indeed, in labor
disputes in the United States it would be advantageous for the
public if settlement agreements required not only the approval of
employers and employees but also of someone who was designated
to see to it that the interest of consumers and the public at large
is not placed in jeopardy.

What about violence by Jews not against constituted Jewish
authority but against the state in which they live? This has been
a basic problem for Jews who live in a country that is not their own.
To what extent must they avoid rebellion? First, there is doubt as
to whether Judaism would permit a revolution for political freedom, or what we call political sovereignty. This question goes back
to the time of the Maccabees, when there was a controversy as to
whether the war against the Greeks would have been justified for
any goal other than the right to worship God in accordance with
their beliefs. Political sovereignty in itself was not deemed very
consequential.

Even today, Joseph Schultz takes the position that fighting for
political sovereignty may be the undoing of the Jewish people,[14] a
view that is certainly consistent with that of the Hasidim in the
time of the Maccabees. He maintains that Jews, because of their
messianic complex, frequently box themselves in at the risk of their

survival, as they did in the years 70–71. He is critical of Chief Rabbi Mordecai Goren and others for encouraging the Jewish people in that complex, for he believes that Jews may not be able to retreat if they become obsessed with the idea that this is the messianic era and that therefore we must not relinquish one inch of Israeli soil. This was the controversy of Rabbi Johanan ben Zakkai, and it may adversely affect present chances for survival as it did in the years 70–71. With regard to rebelling against non-Jewish states, Jews must be cautious, and there are fewer legal ways available to them than when they challenge authority within the Jewish community.

The opposite point of view is represented by Albert Memmi, who holds that what really counts is political sovereignty. According to Memmi, all of Jewish history up until now has been a mistake; the whole Jewish tradition is simply evidence of Jews having been colonialized, developing in the process a rationale and a philosophy of Judaism that made it possible to live as colonials. Now, Memmi says, Jews must determine their own destiny, but the revolution is not yet complete because Jews have not yet substituted a new tradition to provide the ideology appropriate for the new era. What matters, he believes, is for Jews to be completely free and independent.

On the question of whether Jews may engage in violence for the state in which they live, one also finds a difference of opinion. The Hofetz Hayyim, who lived only a generation ago and was one of the most respected of all halakhic authorities in the twentieth century, takes the position that Jews should fight for the country in which they live because, according to Halakhah, all rules pertaining to kingship, all laws applicable to Jewish kings, are applicable to non-Jewish kings. Jewish kings are responsible for the maintenance of law and order, and so are non-Jewish kings. We owe them our obedience. Therefore, whatever privileges a Jewish king would have to mobilize, to conscript, and to tax, non-Jewish kings also have; Jews must obey, even to fight in the army of the country in which they live. Others have taken the opposite position. One nineteenth-century authority, for example, felt that one may not risk one's life in the wars of non-Jews. Certainly a Jew may not be a mercenary.

State Violence Against Individuals

What does the Halakhah have to say about violence by states against individuals? The first form, of course, is punishment and corporal punishment, which in Jewish law meant either capital punishment or lashes. We have very little proof of punishment by imprisonment until the Middle Ages. Certainly one of the greatest achievements of Jewish law is the fact that imprisonment for debt was not authorized either by the Bible or the Talmud. We derive this from a verse in the Bible which speaks of a Hebrew being sold into bondage for theft but not for having borrowed money and being unable to repay. Thus there was no imprisonment for debt, and ancient Jewish society was spared the scourge of sixteenth-, seventeenth-, and eighteenth-century England until the days of Charles Dickens and his protests against imprisonment for debt. The Talmud expanded upon this and it protected the debtor not only against slavery or imprisonment but also against search and seizure. According to biblical and talmudic law, one could not enter his house to see what he had.

Unfortunately, both of these rules for the protection of the debtor were relaxed in the Middle Ages. It is a rather sad chapter in Jewish history that imprisonment for debt was then introduced.[15] Apparently there were too many Jews who owed money while living in luxury, and Rabbenu Tam held that it was necessary to enter their homes and make searches and seizures.

When Jews in the Middle Ages got into the moneylending business some biblical and talmudic prohibitions were relaxed and some rights were expanded. For example, the right to privacy, which dates back to the earliest days of Jews in the desert, was expanded in the Talmud in a magnificient way. Jews had the right to privacy some three to four thousand years before Justice Louis D. Brandeis recognized that it was emerging in American constitutional law. In the Middle Ages the right to privacy was expanded. The French talmudist Menahem ben Solomon of Perpignan, known as the Meiri, even talked about "bugging"; although electronic eavesdropping was then unknown, he wrote about the right to privacy with regard to speech. This is another example of the ways in which Jewish law was very protective of the accused.

With regard to self-incrimination, I already indicated that the prohibition against it was based upon the fact that Jews did not want to give any scope to the death impulse. However, what is generally not well known is that the Jewish right against self-incrimination is still broader than any such right elsewhere. In the United States one has a right not to confess, and if a confession is coerced one can plead so. This is a constitutional privilege rather than a right. Moreover, if one refuses to take the stand in one's own defense, the judge will tell the jury to remember that the mere fact that the defendant did not take the stand in his defense is not to be held against him. His failure to testify is not to be regarded as consequential, even though it is often difficult for the jury to ignore his refusal. During the 1950s, for example, many individuals lost their jobs not because they were proved to be Communists but because they failed to indicate whether or not they were. In effect, they had no protection whatever from the self-incrimination clauses of the Constitution of the United States or the Constitution of the State of New York. In Jewish law, however, it is not a privilege against self-incrimination—it is an absolute immunity. I can come into court and say I killed so-and-so, but by Jewish law such a statement must be held of no consequence. This is the extent to which Halakhah protects the individual against one form of violence by the state, forced confessions.

What is Judaism's position on religious coercion? One cannot gainsay that according to Judaism the state can coerce individuals to perform God's commandments. There are many rationalizations in the apologetic literature for this point of view—none very satisfying. Karl Lewellyn used to say that in every society there are individuals who resist while most people are "drifters," conformists who go along with the stream. Maimonides seemed to feel that only some kind of emotional block would prompt an individual to exercise his will against God's will and that coercion, or the threat of it, would make him identify once again with the majority. It restores his sanity, so to speak, his emotional balance, his real free will. In modern times the problem is a very serious one—especially for the leaders of religious Zionism in the State of Israel. Would they exercise coercion against the minority if they were in the majority? Replies have been made in this century by Chief Rabbis Abraham Kook and Yitzhak Herzog, who were deeply committed to the establishment of a Jewish state, and by the distinguished halakhic authority known as the Hazon Ish, who was opposed to the establishment of the State of Israel: they all agreed that there should be no coercion whatever.

There is one exception in the halakhic tradition to the rule that dissenters can be coerced. If a Jewish child has been taken captive in infancy, has been raised among non-Jews and then restored to the Jewish community, there is no right to coerce him. He cannot be accused of disobeying God's will because of some emotional or intellectual failure. Rabbis Kook and Herzog, as well as the Hazon Ish, argue that everyone today is in the category of such a captive Jewish infant. Because of the environment in which we live and the winds of doctrine blowing everywhere, most of us are the captives of mores and outlooks to which we succumb unwittingly. In this sense, all are comparable to the infants against whom no religious coercion is to be exercised. Indeed, this is a legal fiction. The early pioneers of Israel, and even its most distinguished leaders, were raised in environments in which there was total commitment to all of Judaism. Their rebellion came much after their infancy, and it is nonsense to regard them as Jews who in infancy were taken captive by non-Jews. But legal fictions are a very much respected manner of updating legal systems, including the Halakhah.

Violence Among States

With regard to violence by states against other states, there is a rich halakhic literature distinguishing between obligatory wars and permissive wars. Much has been written about this subject, notably Maurice Lamm's essay "Red or Dead" and Solomon Zevin's essay in *L'Or ha-Halakhah.* Let me also make but a few points here.

In the halakhic view an obligatory war—to conquer the Land of Israel and to defend it—was mandated by God. A permissive war —to expand one's territory or to improve the economy—required the combined consent of the king and the Sanhedrin of seventy-one, the group which had supreme legislative and judicial authority. Thus the executive, legislative, and judicial authorities of the Jewish state had to agree. In the United States the pattern is very similar, except that the Supreme Court has no share in the decision.

When the Sanhedrin and the king agreed, however, could their declaration of war ever be regarded as unjust? Maimonides would not so hold. Yet centuries later Samuel David Luzatto took the position that there is no biblical or talmudic justification for a war against anyone who is not an enemy and offers no threat to your safety. The fact that the Bible speaks of war against *oyveikhem*— your foe—means that wars may be waged only against those who present a danger. In any other circumstance the waging of war is not permitted.

As for serving in the armies of states in which Jews lived, we have already seen that this was permitted by most halakhic authorities. When Jews began to enjoy the blessings of democratic countries they even fought for the right so to serve. Asser Levy in New Amsterdam insisted on the privilege and refused to pay a tax in lieu of military duty. Dubnow cites many other such instances. We ought to remember, moreover, that Asser Levy was no assimilationist Jew: he also fought for the right to have a kosher abbatoir in New Amsterdam.

The final point one might make with regard to the exercise of violence is that it is unlikely that it will accomplish its objective. I have already indicated that one may exercise violence for the loftiest value, which is the sanctity of life itself. But if there is little likelihood that this value will be conserved, and if, on the other hand, it will be placed in greater jeopardy, then one must be very hesitant about exercising violence.

This point is especially relevant to Israel's present problem of the return of the conquered territories. On the one hand, you have in Israel a very respectable group of halakhic authorities who argue that Jews may not give back an inch of sacred soil on obvious halakhic grounds. This land is ours, they say, given to us by God. God ordered us to take it and to hold it by risking our lives for it. We were told to engage in war—in violence—for that purpose, and war ipso facto means the loss of life. Therefore, Chief Rabbi Yitzhak Nissim, and Rabbi Zevi Yehuda Kook, the son of the former chief rabbi, are unequivocally opposed to the return of any part of the land.

The "doves," on the other side, include Rabbi Joseph B. Soloveitchik, whose public statements and essays on the subject have received attention all over the world. To him the issue is whether the sanctity of life is not so great that if Jews can buy peace with the return of some of the soil it is not more important to save life. Yet how do these authorities answer the question of Rabbi Nissim, which on its face is such a logical one. The answer is simple: Jews were told to go to war only when victory was something that was likely. It is a halakhic requirement that one does not engage in violence or war unless victory is probable. When God told the Jews to conquer the Holy Land He was on their side. Today victory is not necessarily something of which Israel can be assured, and thus the problem is whether on the basis of the present situation Halakhah would dictate the return of the territories.

In this connection Rabbi Yehuda Gershuni makes a fine point. Gershuni cites the story of Johanan ben Zakkai, who in the year 70 C.E. held that Judea could not win against the Romans. Victory was impossible. The Zealots had said they could win, and this was the issue of their day. When Johanan ben Zakkai was about to die he was agitated, and when his students asked him why he trembled he said, "Why should I not tremble! If I were about to face a human sovereign, I would tremble. Now, when I am about to face the King of Kings, should I not tremble?" Perhaps, said Rabbi Gershuni, his speech revealed his feeling of guilt. Perhaps he had done wrong. Perhaps he capitulated to the Romans when he should have stood by the side of his own kin who wanted to resist. Rabbi Gershuni based his insight on the fact that Ben Zakkai committed a "Freudian slip" when he told his students, "Prepare a chair for King Hezekiah." Why did Hezekiah come to his mind? Simply because that king had had the same challenge in his day. Sennacherib was outside the gates of Jerusalem. King Hezekiah did not know whether to fight the head of the great empire of Assyria. Could little Judea stand up against that lion? He decided to fight and a miracle occured: the enemy was stricken with a plague and Jerusalem was liberated from siege. On his deathbed Rabbi Johanan ben Zakkai thought of him and wondered whether perhaps he too could have relied on a miracle. Or perhaps the situation was then different and one should not have relied on miracles thereafter.

Israel's present situation raises still other problems. Even if one were to disagree with the Hasidim of the Maccabean period and hold that political sovereignty is a cause for which war and violence are justified according to Halakhah, one must ponder whether in the modern age any small state can ever achieve it—at any sacrifice. Israel is now totally dependent for survival upon the United States, and to wage suicidal warfare in defiance of the will of the United States may be to engage in a war in which victory is virtually impossible. Could this be a just war?

The Talmud, in connection with a slave who is only half-slave but half-free—as in the case of a slave who had been owned by partners, one of whom emancipated him while the other retained his ownership—suggests that no one is free unless he has but one master, God. Even the Exilarch in Babylon was not a free agent; he had a human and foreign master other than God. Can Israel delude itself into believing that it is free, autonomous, and sovereign?

Perhaps Israel's destiny now—even as a state—is to play its historic role, which, in the view of Jacob Talmon, is ever to question the legitimacy of human authority over other humans. Those imposing authority resort to violence; so do those resisting authority. The question always is not whether there shall be violence but when and how. This is the authentic halakhic approach, and it will still bear further analysis and development.

In a statement made after the Yom Kippur War, André Schwarz-Bart said: "We [Jews] are human beings like everyone else. We have hardly any illusions on the subject and any time we had a national history it was as bloody as any other. Nevertheless, it seems to me that it is not because of our injustices, but because of our insistence upon absolute justice, even when we were unfaithful to it, that we have come to experience our particular fate among the nations."

The truth is that we Jews have had a tremendous amount of violence in our history. Yet we never lost sight of what was absolute justice, and we tried at least to curb, to regulate, and in some way to make a contribution to human dignity and sanctity in the unique way that was ours.

NOTES

1. Reuven Kimmelman, "Non-Violence in the Talmud," *Judaism,* 17, no. 3 (Summer 1968), 316–34.

2. Maurice Lamm, "Red or Dead," *Tradition,* 4, no. 2 (Spring 1962), 165–97.

3. Mishneh Torah, XIV, *Judges,* Hilkhot Sanhedrin 28:6.

4. Yehuda Gershuni, "Or ha-Mizrach," *World Zionist Organization,* 21, no. 1 (Tishre 5732, 1972), 3–8.

5. J. Emden, *She'elat* Yavetz (Altona, c. 1740), Responsum 43.

6. *Mamzerut* (technical bastardy), according to Jewish law, applies only to the offspring of adulterous or incestuous sexual relationships, not to children born out of wedlock, and proof of *mamzerut* is most difficult. See my *One Man's Judaism* (New York, 1970), pp. 212–16.

7. Louis Jacobs, *Jewish Values* (London, 1960), chap. 5, pp. 74–85.

8. Israel Abrahams, *Jewish Life in the Middle Ages,* ed. by C. Roth (London, 1932), p. 253.

9. A. L. Sachar, *Sufferance Is the Badge* (New York, 1939), pp. 60–68.

10. Sol Roth, "The Morality of Revolution," *Judaism,* 20, no. 4 (Fall 1971), 431–42.

11. I. A. Agus, *Rabbi Meir of Rothenburg* (Philadelphia, 1947), II, pp. 665–66.

12. See N. Levovitz, *Iyunim be-Sefer Bereshit* (Jerusalem, 1967), pp. 264–65. Haamek Davar on Numbers 25:12.

13. S. Belkin, *In His Image* (New York, 1960), pp. 29–30.

14. J. Schultz, "Jewish Militarism and Jewish Survival," *Judaism,* 22, no. 4 (Fall 1973), 468–74.

15. M. Elon, "Le-Ma'asar be-Mishpat la-Ivri," *Jubilee Volume for Pinhas Rosen* (Jerusalem, 1962), pp. 171–201.

JOEL L. KRAEMER

7   War, Conquest, and the Treatment of Religious Minorities in Medieval Islam

This discussion shall attempt to cover certain salient Islamic attitudes on questions of war and treatment of religious minorities, particularly the Jews. As we shall observe, the Jews in medieval Islam did not by themselves constitute an independent class, but they were included, along with Christians and others, in a special category, the status of which was governed by Islamic law and determined to a considerable extent by extralegal practice.

Attitudes to War and Conquest

The Islamic attitude to war is epitomized in a key passage in *The Mukaddimah* of Ibn Khaldun (1322–1406): "Wars and different kinds of fighting have always occurred in the world since God created it. . . . It is something natural among human beings. No nation and no race [generation] is free from it."[1] Thus, according to Ibn Khaldun, war is natural, permanent, and universal. The cause of war, he suggests, is revenge. The roots of revenge are envy, hostility, and zeal for religion or for political success. Elsewhere he states that injustice and mutual aggression are innate in human and animal nature. Men, he says, are driven by a love of power and a need to dominate others. They seek victory and domination for the sake of honor and pride. The ceaseless competition for domination creates discord and war. Consequently, people require a strong ruler to restrain them and to prevent anarchy and mutual annihilation.[2]

Not every struggle for power and domination is evil according to Ibn Khaldun. Wars among neighboring tribes and competing families and wars caused by hostility among savage desert nations are unjust and lawless. But there are wars which Ibn Khaldun says are deemed holy and just, namely the *jihad* and war against seceders and those who are disobedient.[3]

The *jihad* is the "just war" of Islam. Repression of rebels (war against dissension, secession, and civil strife) is considered by Ibn Khaldun and by early Muslim jurists as a type of *jihad.* There is a deep-seated aversion to rebellion and civil strife in the Islamic political scheme. Constituted authority in the Islamic state is viewed as divinely sanctioned, and rebellion is thus tantamount to an act of heresy. *Jihad,* on the other hand, is holy; it is an act of piety and fulfills a religious obligation as it seeks to spread the message of Islam to the non-Muslim world, which is the *dar al-harb* (domain of war).[4] In considering *jihad* as a religious obligation, one may compare the *milhemet mitzvah (hovah),* or obligatory war, in Jewish history. Obligatory wars were directed against the Amalekites and the like during the Israelite conquest under Joshua. Wars of territorial expansion are called *milhemet reshut,* or permissable war.[5] What Jewish law considers permissable war is considered obligatory in the Islamic system.

In the Islamic view, until their religion is realized in a universal state by the conversion of *dar al-harb* to *dar al-Islam,* a state of permanent belligerency exists between the two domains. It has been suggested by some that this permanent belligerency between the world of Islam and the non-Muslim world represents a kind of sublimation of the permanent state of hostility that prevailed among the desert tribes in the pre-Islamic period. Muhammad created in Medina a supertribal confederation or community *(umma)*, consolidated by the belief in Allah and His Apostle. Henceforth, warfare among the believing Muslims became outlawed. Tribal and family feuds and the ancient practice of raiding and vendetta were in principle set aside. Instead, the *jihad* became a communal obligation, directed against the enemy, who was not of the *umma:* the Meccan pagans, the Jews, and eventually the Byzantine and Persian empires. The theory is that in this manner the so-called "natural aggressiveness" of the desert Arabs was channeled to the outside and put into the service of a higher cause, or at least a more far-reaching vision than was involved in the familiar patterns of tribal raiding.

The holy war should not be viewed simply as a violent expression of hostility; it is first and foremost a striving for Islamic domination. This domination may be attained in a variety of ways: by the sword and by the word; by coercion and by preaching and persuasion. Indeed, the latter means are regarded as preferable, if possible.

If the aim of holy war is to convert the domain of war into the domain of Islam, what constitutes the domain of Islam? Essentially the domain of Islam may be defined as territory which has accepted Islamic sovereignty and is ruled by Islamic law. Geopolitically this includes the community of believers (Muslims) and members of the tolerated religious communities who have submitted to Islamic domination. These religious minorities are accorded protection and autonomy in the religious and personal spheres.

The domain of war is territory which has not acceded to Islamic domination. In theory, it cannot have relations with the domain of Islam on an equal basis. The domain of war has no legitimate status. In modern terms one may say that it is not the object of recognition. The state of belligerency with the domain of war will last, in the Islamic view, "until the day of the Resurrection." During this period of permanent holy war, whether active or dormant, negotiations may be conducted with parties of the domain of war, but the status of such parties is not accepted *de jure,* and treaties with them may not be established on a fully reciprocal or permanent basis.

The holy war is a collective duty of the Muslim community. It may be declared only by the leader of the Islamic state, who summons the believers by the call to *jihad* when he deems conditions favorable. The obligation to pursue the holy war actively is predicated upon chances of success; that is, the leader of the community is not obligated to declare active hostilities when the odds are against victory.

Participation in the holy war is an act of religious devotion. "The holy war is the monasticism of Islam," says a venerable tradition. Whosoever dies "for the sake of God" is assured the supreme pleasures of Paradise. He is a *shahid,* or martyr. The word, like its Greek counterpart, means witness; the *shahid* gives witness to the true faith by his self-sacrifice. W. Cantwell Smith has contrasted the Muslim with the Christian martyr, indicating that the *shahid* of Islam died fighting "with history," i.e., on the side of history, on the path of Allah, in a battle to extend the territory of Islam. The Christian martyr sacrificed his life fighting "against history"; his victory was spiritual or transcendental, not of this world. In this connection, Cantwell Smith describes Islam as "a religion of triumph in success, of salvation through victory and achievement and power."[6]

The career of Islam was launched in a flurry of conquest and success. It is crucial to bear this in mind. The fundamental orientation of Islam toward history is one of optimism regarding ultimate success. The use of power is not shunned, and one is hard put to find anything resembling the western (Judeo-Christian) soul-searching and pangs of conscience concerning the application of violence. Still it should be stressed that Islam's victory need not be military. Indeed, capitulation of the enemy prior to hostilities is preferable to bloodshed, and Islamic law obligates Muslim armies to invite the enemy to accept Islam before an attack is unleashed. The "people of the Book," or possessors of a "Revelation" (Jews,

Christians, "Sabaeans," Zoroastrians) were given the opportunity to surrender while retaining their religion. In exchange for acceptance of Islamic sovereignty and payment of tribute, they were accorded protection and autonomy in infracommunal religious matters. If they refused submission, the alternative was war. Pagans were given the narrower choice of Islam or the sword, although certain legal schools permitted non-Arab pagans to evade conversion by submitting to Islamic rule and paying tribute.

In the Islamic view, war was the penalty the enemy paid for refusal to accept Islamic terms. This is reminiscent of the biblical rule of warfare expressed in Deuteronomy 20:10–12. There the enemy is offered "terms of peace" which are in fact terms of surrender. Indeed, the Hebrew words *hishlim* and *shalom* in the Deuteronomy passage do not mean "make peace" and "peace," as commonly understood, but rather "surrender" and "submission." In both the biblical rule and in the Islamic system, making peace and surrendering are equivalent.[7] The difference, of course, is that the biblical rule lapsed with the completion of the conquest of the land, while the Muslim version extends to the end of time and the furthest boundaries of the world.

Contemporary Muslim writers stress that peace is an ideal which ranks high in the Islamic scale of values. One may concur with this view, with the qualification that the nature of peace presupposes Islamic domination and supremacy, a *pax Islamica.* The peaceful coexistence of divergent systems, the world of Islam and the non-Muslim world, on a basis of mutual recognition and reciprocity is not an Islamic ideal. The modus vivendi established between the two spheres in the course of history is not an ideal but rather a concession to reality, an adjustment to temporary setbacks in the prosecution of the holy war.

Interestingly enough, the holy war is considered by contemporary Muslim writers to be defensive in essence, for the very existence of the domain of war is regarded as an implicit threat to the integrity of Islam. The great Islamic conquests are now often viewed by Muslim scholars as a crusade for religious freedom and as wars of liberation from persecution and ignorance. Underlying this view is the conception of Islam as the natural religion of mankind. Accordingly, Muslim arms simply permitted this true faith to be expressed. Conversely, wars against Islamic countries are viewed as offensive and aggressive.

For non-Muslims who dwell within Islamic domains, the acceptance of Islamic sovereignty is sufficient, along with payment of tribute, to guarantee the "people of the Book" safety and communal autonomy. Here there is a fundamental difference between the status of Jews in the world of medieval Islam and that of their confreres in Christian Europe. The Church had no rationale for continued Jewish survival, save as a symbol in their degradation of the truth of Christianity. In the Islamic system the Jews are accorded a status of legitimacy, albeit a degraded one.

Muhammad, it must be remembered, did not claim to bring a new faith but to repristinate the ancient religion of Abraham, which in his view had become corrupted. According to Islamic belief, the celestial book or heavenly archetype descended to mankind in parts, and the Jews received as their share a portion of the Revelation. But they proceeded to misunderstand and even corrupt "the Word," and thus their Scriptures represent a distorted picture of "the Truth." Moreover, they rejected the Apostle of Allah and hence must be fought until they surrender. But their acknowledgement of God and possession of the revelation distinguishes them (along with other "peoples of the Book") from pagans. Their existence in the Islamic state as a separate body, a religious minority, is accepted.

This does not mean that medieval Islam had a favorable attitude toward the Jews. In fact, the dominant tone of the Koran is, if anything, hostile. It seems that Muhammad initially hoped that the Jews of Medina would be convinced of the authenticity of his mission and message. When he failed to persuade them he adopted a vehement tone against them, regarding them as enemies. We cannot enter into the circumstances of this fateful encounter and the ensuing rupture and hostility between the Jews and the Muslim prophet. What is crucial is that the Jews of Medina rejected Muhammad's claims to prophecy. (Prophecy had ceased after Malachi, according to normative Judaism.) Moreover, Muhammad impressed his Jewish contemporaries as rather ignorant of the Bible, and he seems to have borne the brunt of their ridicule. His violent reaction, along with the economic needs of the burgeoning Muslim community, were causes of the conflict which led to the banishment or liquidation of the Jewish tribes of Medina.

According to the Koran, the Jews must remain humbled and debased for all time. This attitude is reminiscent of the early Christian conception of the Jews as a people rejected by God: "And humiliation and wretchedness were stamped upon them and they were visited with wrath from Allah" (II, 61 and elsewhere). The "policy of degradation" applied by Muslim authorities to the Jews in medieval times stems from the attitude enshrined in this text.

Treatment of Religious Minorities

In the course of the Muslim conquests, populations that capitulated to Muslim armies were granted a guarantee of security, called *aman, ahd,* or *dhimma.* Treaties with conquered cities guaranteed safety of life and property and the inviolability of religious edifices in exchange for submission and tribute. Those who benefited from these contracts were called *dhimmis* or *ahl al-dhimma,* which may be understood in the sense of protected people, i.e., those accorded the hospitality and protection of Islam in return for their allegiance.

The precedent for this kind of agreement may well have been the submission of settled oasis areas in the desert to bedouin tribal groups powerful enough to exact tribute. Some scholars, as well as modern Muslim reformers, have found in this arrangement with the protected peoples elements of the *protection tutélaire,* the sacred hospitality and right of asylum found in pre-Islamic Arab society. Accordingly, the Jews and other minorities were, so to speak, the guests of the Islamic state.[8]

In the Koran, however, the tribute offered by the people of the Book is associated with their degraded station. "Fight those who believe not in God and the Last Day and do not forbid what God and His messenger have forbidden—such men as practice not the religion of truth, being of those who have been given the Book— until they pay the tribute *(jizya)* out of hand *(an yadin)* and have been humbled" (IX, 29). The final phrase is an exegetical crux that has received treatment in at least four scholarly articles—by M. Bravmann, Cl. Cahen, M. J. Kister, and F. Rosenthal. Kister, for example, takes the phrase to mean "until they pay the *jizya* out of ability and sufficient means, they [nevertheless] being inferior." In any case, the historical (if not philological) significance of the verse depended upon its interpretation by Muslim exegetes and jurists and its practical application by administrators. It was interpreted quite literally in the regulation which stipulated that a member of the people of the Book must publicly offer the tribute on his open palm to the *amir,* who from his high distinguished seat cuffed the subject's neck and had him driven off by a guard, thus literally humbling him.

The guiding principles in the treatment of the protected minorities were the predominance of Islam ("Islam dominates and is not dominated") and the "policy of degradation." The tributary taxation was also, to be sure, a vital source of income for the Islamic state. As early as the defeat of the Khaybar Jews at the hands of Muhammad and his followers (628), the decision was made to permit the defeated inhabitants of the town to retain their land on payment of an annual tribute. Thus, in addition to the booty secured in battle, a fixed income was assured for the future. This kind of arrangement became a model for the later policy of the caliphs.

In addition to the *jizya,* which at first seems to have been a kind of tribute based upon the population of a town and was then a poll tax, a special land tax called *kharaj* was also imposed upon the

Jews and other *dhimmis.*[9] This land tax was considerably higher than the tithe *(ushr)* paid by Muslim landowners,[10] and the disparity naturally encouraged conversions. This trend deprived the treasury of income, however, and the loss impelled the hardbitten governor of Iraq, al-Hajjaj, to discourage conversions. The caliph Umar II (717–20) provided a partial solution by fixing the *kharaj* on the land itself, regardless of ownership, and thus converts to Islam continued to pay the heavier tax even after conversion.

Treatment of Jews and other "protected" minorities in medieval Islam is generally considered tolerant.[11] Such a generalization can be made only if one compares the situation of Jews under Islam with that of Jews in medieval Europe. What typified the situation of the Jews who lived under Islam was the quotidian character of the discrimination. It was not generally a question of inquisitions, expulsions, or massacres (in short, what European Jews suffered); it was the quality of life, the daily reminders of inferiority, that rankled. Even the philosophers and poets of the famous Golden Age in Spain, when the Arabo-Muslim and Jewish "symbiosis" reached its peak, reflect the common daily harassment and taunting of members of "the despised religion." Jews were not the objects of officially sponsored superstitious fear and hatred, as in medieval Europe, but they were victims of officially instituted contempt.

Discriminatory practices were imposed in order to set the protected minorities apart and to assure their inferior status. It should be noted from the start, however, that the discriminatory rules were often more honored in the breach than observed to the letter. If the legislation affecting the Jews had been consistently applied, life would have been grim indeed. It is unsound to deduce actual social conditions by inference from legislation. Nevertheless, with this caveat in mind, it must be said that laws did have an impact upon life. They were on the books and available to the more fanatically minded ruler bent upon persecution, and they also contributed to the molding of public opinion.

Much depended upon the whims and caprices of rulers and the

volcanic emotions of the mob. Consequently, the Jew lived in constant insecurity and vulnerability. For example, when the fanatical Fatimid ruler al-Hakim (996–1021) went on a rampage of persecution, he had thousands of non-Muslim religious edifices destroyed, forced Jews and Christians to convert, and otherwise embittered their lives, thus causing a mass exodus from his realm. In an example of mob action, on December 31, 1011, an agitated crowd of Muslims in Fustat (Old Cairo) assaulted a group of Jews returning from a funeral, accusing them of deprecating Muhammad. Twenty-three Jewish elders were imprisoned as a result of the assault.

In general, political, economic, and military reverses and tensions with the Christian world exacerbated anti-*dhimmi* sentiment and intensified persecution. The situation of the Jews varied from place to place and from one time to another; but if a trend can be discerned over the centuries, it was toward greater discrimination. The political and socioeconomic decline of the Arab countries (the heartlands of Islam) in the later Middle Ages adversely affected the Jews.

The first caliph to impose discriminatory restrictions systematically was Umar II, a devout monarch of the Umayyad dynasty. Umar adhered to the Koranic precept of humbling the non-Muslim people of the Book and encouraged conversions to Islam. Many discriminatory regulations are incorporated in a document known as the "Covenant of Umar." Though attributed to the time of Umar I, it contains rules which in fact evolved gradually and were eventually systematized and applied by Umar II.[12]

It is related that Umar II issued his discriminatory rulings after having mistaken a group of Arab (Taghlibite) Christians for Muslims and having saluted them. The story conveys the primary motive for the legislation, which was to discriminate in two senses: to differentiate in terms of identity and in terms of favor. It was during the reign of Umar II that the last great Arab offensive against Constantinople terminated in catastrophic failure, and the consequent frustration may also have been a factor in the caliph's ardor. Among the discriminatory rules enforced by Umar II were ordinances requiring *dhimmis* to wear clothing which would set them apart from Muslims, forbidding them to use saddles on horses, ordering them to shear the hair on their forehead short.

The famous Abbasid caliph, Harun al-Rashid (786–809), prescribed that the people of the Book must wear a distinctive belt *(zunnar)* and a tall conical cap *(kalansawa)*. Like Umar II, Harun was often occupied with the holy war against the infidel Byzantines. The distinctive signs he imposed upon the *dhimmis* may indeed have served purposes of military security. Such considerations are alleged to explain Harun's destruction of churches along the frontier.

During the reign of al-Mutawakkil (847–61), when the Abbasid Empire underwent a religious reaction and efforts were made to expunge foreign influence in Islamic theology, the religious minorities again became victims of discriminatory persecution, this time even more degrading. Among other things, they were forced to wear the *zunnar* belt and the conical cap of a distinctive color, with two buttons on it, along with a honey-colored hood. Al-Hakim, during his rampage, imposed the *zunnar* belt and a special sign or badge *(ghiyar)* and forbade the use of riding horses. The fanatical Almohad dynasty of North Africa and Spain (1130–1269) also imposed such restrictions, although sumptuary regulations pale into insignificance alongside the atrocities which marked the rise of the Almohads. It is interesting to note that the use of special dress and a distinctive badge, officially sanctioned by the Fourth Lateran Council in medieval Europe, was of Islamic origin.[13]

It has been observed that these restrictions were not uniformly imposed. Outbursts of strict application of the rules occurred when the minorities forgot their lowly station and imprudently displayed symbols of prosperity. When a Maghreb vizier stopped off in Egypt on his way to Mecca (in 1301) he was struck with dismay at the affluence of local Jews and Christians and duly registered a protest with the authorities. They imposed colored turbans, blue for Christians and yellow for Jews, and prohibited the use of horses or mules. Many *dhimmis* converted to Islam in preference to the self-abasement entailed by wearing the turbans and riding upon asses.

In the Islamic legal system the Jew did not enjoy equal status with the Muslim; his life was worth less from the point of view of Islamic criminal law. According to a tradition, "A believer may not be put to death because of an infidel." Majority legal opinion interpreted this to mean that the life of a Muslim may not be taken in punishment for killing a member of the protected people. Only one legal school, the Hanafite, demanded a life for a life, interpreting the word "infidel" in the tradition as denoting a member of the domain of war and not a *dhimmi;* but this interpretation was impractical and of very limited application in ordinary life. The blood-wit, demanded by Islamic law in cases of homicide, was set at a lower rate for the life of a Jew or Christian than for that of a Muslim. Again, only the Hanafite school required equal payment in all cases. The Malikites required one-half the normal blood-wit for the life of a non-Muslim; the Shafi'ites, one-third; and the Hanbalites, one-half or, in cases of involuntary homicide, one-third.

Unequal treatment expresses itself in Islamic family law also. A Muslim may marry a woman of the people of the Book (excluding Zoroastrians), but a non-Muslim is not permitted to marry a Muslim woman. The guiding principle that Islam dominates and is not dominated is invoked here. The Malikite school goes so far as to permit taking the life of a non-Muslim who dares marry a Muslim woman, since he has thereby violated the pact *(dhimma)* between himself and the Muslims. The punishment of non-Muslims who had intimate relations with Muslim women, especially if adulterous, was so severe that offenders elected to convert rather than suffer it.

The principle of hierarchy was also applied to the sphere of economic activity. Non-Muslims were not permitted to own Muslim slaves. Their houses were not to be higher than those of Muslims. Non-Muslims were permitted to make commercial agreements, but the religious difference made partnership with Muslims difficult. Such partnerships were permitted in certain circumstances, though with disapproval, and the Muslim partner was obligated to supervise transactions in order to assure that Islamic law was not transgressed. In the sphere of economic activity principles tended to be bent for practical reasons. The intensive economic activity of Jews as traders and bankers in the world of medieval Islam is well known, and restrictions seem not to have hampered them appreciably. Indeed, the fiscal talents of *dhimmis,* both Jews and Christians, were often employed by the government, especially in the field of taxation. This naturally embittered the Muslim populace in certain cases.[14]

Civil and political rights of non-Muslims were limited. The military profession was reserved for Muslims, though jurists made exceptions if the protected peoples were employed in an auxiliary corps or in menial capacities ("as one uses dogs," it was said) without sharing in booty. Though the military remained the province of the Muslim elite, Jews and Christians were sometimes used as soldiers, despite prejudices against this. In the Muslim conquest of Spain, for example, both Jews and Muslims manned garrisons left behind the line of attack of the Muslim army.

The protected people were officially excluded from public service. Again, in fact, they often were employed and even preferred by Muslim rulers, since as outsiders they could be trusted to refrain from intrigues. The Umayyads were particularly liberal in employing the services of the people of the Book. Al-Hajjaj, the Umayyad governor of Iraq, placed a Jew named Sumayr over the mint, but such policies often produced a backlash. Umar II, for example, disturbed by the authority exercised by non-Muslims over Muslims, forbade their employment in official capacities. Often the Muslim populace brought pressure to bear upon the ruler to dismiss his *dhimmi* officials, or religious authorities protested infringement of the rules. Thus we find a flowing and then ebbing of *dhimmi* activity in the public domain. Umar II's measures seem to have had only a temporary effect, for dismissals from service of non-Muslims were reenacted by al-Mutawakkil and again during the reign of al-Muktadir (908–32).

Some *dhimmis* found themselves close to the court, especially in the capacity of physicians and scientists. They were relied upon in this sphere of activity for practical and, it would seem, partly for superstitious reasons.

Occasionally prominent Jews converted to Islam for reasons of convenience, ambition, or fear. Access to the highest ranks of Islamic society was smoothed by conversion. The talented Jew Yakub Ibn Killis converted to Islam in order to become a vizier of the Fatimids. The physician-philosopher Abu al-Barakat Hibat Allah al-Baghdadi (d. ca. 1164–65), who served caliphs and sultans, converted to Islam late in life "out of wounded pride or out of fear," according to rumors contained in biographical reports. The great historian Rashid al-Din, who wrote a famous universal history of the Mongol Ghazan Khan, was a convert from Judaism.

Conversions of this sort were infrequent, and they were not readily approved since the convert was not believed to be a sincere Muslim. Umar I reportedly had a Christian slave to whom he promised advancement upon conversion. When the slave refused the caliph cited the Koranic verse, "There is no compulsion in religion" (II, 256). Even if apocryphal, the story reflects a dominant attitude, for by ascribing an act of this sort to the revered Umar the restraint it shows is held up as meritorious. This Koranic verse is interpreted by Muslim exegetes as applicable to the people of the Book (though not to polytheists) and is a locus classicus for Islamic tolerance and acceptance of a mode of what may be called "religious pluralism."

Forced conversions did occasionally occur, however, even in the case of Jews and Christians, who were accorded "freedom of religion" by Islamic law. The persecution of religious minorities by al-Hakim has already been mentioned. He compelled Jews and Christians to embrace Islam, and many migrated from Egypt and Palestine before he relented and withdrew his illegal order. One of the founders of the Almohad dynasty addressed the Jews and

Christians in Fez in 1146, offering them the choice between Islam and death. Their large-scale persecution is known from the career of Maimonides, who fled Spain to avoid the bitter alternative. It has been suggested that Maimonides had to enact the role of a Muslim to escape persecution, but there seems to be no sound basis for this suspicion. In any event, his legal ruling regarding conversion out of duress in these circumstances tended to the side of leniency.

In general, it may be observed that forced conversions were rare in the medieval Islamic world. When such persecutions occurred they were usually associated with general oppression in Muslim society, from which even the Muslim populace also suffered, as in the case of the Almohads.

In concluding this brief survey of some aspects of the Islamic attitude to questions of war and the treatment of religious minorities, it should be stressed that the period under consideration cannot be judged fairly by alien or by modern liberal standards. True religious tolerance, freedom of thought and expression, and the right of self-determination were not values actively promoted by any major society at this time. Much of what we find in Muslim practice regarding religious minorities can be traced to Byzantine precedent, and the policy of degradation was certainly more acute in medieval Christendom. What is significant is that to a certain extent a kind of community of faith of the possessors of the old and new Revelations existed, within which a degree of religious pluralism was realized, albeit in a hierachical system of Muslim domination and non-Muslim inferiority.

Understandably, the Muslim regards the sovereignty of Islam as a noble ideal and the tolerance of the other faiths as an act of generosity and liberalism. Like the southern white in America, who argues that he was always good to his "nigras" and cannot comprehend their ingratitude, the Muslim proudly points to his patronism and hospitality without fully appreciating the feelings of his clients and guests.

With the establishment of a sovereign Jewish state in this century, a rupture occurred in the traditional relationship between the

Muslim patrons and the Jewish protected minority. Like the disruption of other traditional relationships in modern times (employer-worker, male-female, West-East), this transformation has been traumatic. In its long and glorious career Islam has been amazingly flexible in adjusting ideology and attitude to reality and behavior. Withal, the degree to which fundamental ideological outlook has remained immune to change is impressive.

NOTES

1. *The Mukaddimah,* trans. by F. Rosenthal (New York, 1958), II, pp. 73–74.

2. *The Mukaddimah,* I, pp. 262, 313, 380–81.

3. According to Muslim jurists and writers on public policy, holy war was directed internally against apostates, dissenters, seceders, rebels, and brigands. The word rendered in the Ibn Khaldun passage as "seceders" *(kharijun)* is sometimes translated as "rebels."

4. On *jihad* as both *justum* and *pium,* see M. Khadduri, *War and Peace in the Law of Islam* (Baltimore and London, 1955), p. 57; and idem, *The Islamic Law of Nations: Shaybani's Siyar* (Baltimore, 1966), p. 16. In my discussion of *jihad* I draw upon Khadduri and the article "Djihad," by E. Tyan, in *The Encyclopaedia of Islam,* New Edition.

5. See Maimonides, *Mishneh Torah, Melakhim* V–VII.

6. Wilfred Cantwell Smith, *Islam in Modern History* (New York, 1959), pp. 37, 39. On the meaning of the Deuteronomy passage, see H. L. Ginsberg, *Encyclopaedia Judaica* (Jerusalem, 1971), XIII, p. 196; and Jewish Publication Society translation (Philadelphia, 1962), p. 361.

7. A good statement of the somewhat idealized contemporary Muslim view of *jihad,* is found in 'Abd-al-Rahman 'Azzam, *The Eternal Message of Muhammad,* trans. by Caesar E. Farah (New York, 1965), Part V.

8. On the possible bedouin precedent, see C. Cahen, "Dhimma," in *The Encyclopaedia of Islam,* New Edition. Louis Gardet stresses the aspect of hospitality, citing Louis Massignon and the modern reformers Rashid Rida and Hasan al-Banna' in *La cité musulmane, vie sociale et politique,* (Paris, 1961), Etudes Musulmanes, I pp. 58–59.

9. The problems relating to the terms *jizya* and *kharaj* are complex. For details, see Daniel C. Dennett, Jr., *Conversion and the Poll Tax in Early Islam,* Harvard Historical Monographs, XXII (Cambridge, Mass., 1950); Frede Løkkegaard, *Islamic Taxation in the Classic Period* (Copenhagen, 1950); and C. Cahen, "Djizya," in *The Encyclopaedia of Islam,* New Edition. In a sense the *jizya* was compensation (Muslim scholars derive the word from a root with this meaning) for nonadoption of Islam and nonparticipation in the holy war. A system of poll and land taxes existed in the Byzantine and Persian territories overrun by the Muslims, so that the inhabitants would have regarded the Islamic taxation system as, in a sense, a continuation of local practice.

10. The taxes were burdensome, and collection, it appears, was not always simple. A. S. Tritton quotes a saying, "A Jew will never pay his taxes till he has had his head smacked." *The Caliphs and Their Non-Muslim Subjects* (Oxford 1930) p. 95.

11. On treatment of the protected peoples, see Salo Wittmayer Baron, *A Social and Religious History of the Jews,* vol. III (New York and Philadelphia, 1957), chap. 18; Antoine Fattal, *Le statut légal des non-musulmans en pays d'Islam*, L'Institut des Lettres Orientales de Beyrouth, X, (Beirut, 1958); S. D. Goitein, *Jew and Arabs, Their Contacts Through the Ages* (New York, 1955); Khadduri, *War and Peace in the Law of Islam,* chap. 17; Tritton, *The Caliphs and Their Non-Muslim Subjects;* G. Vajda, *"Ahl al-Kitab,"* in *The Encyclopaedia of Islam,* New Edition.

12. On the famous "Covenant of Umar," see Fattal, pp. 60–69; and Tritton, chap. 1. Both authors cite the reasons for rejecting the traditional ascription of the covenant to Umar I, but these persuasive arguments should not preclude the assignment of parts of the covenant to him.

13. On the use of the badge and distinctive attire in medieval Europe and the Muslim precedent for this practice, see Solomon Grayzel, *The Church and the Jews in the XIIIth Century* (Philadelphia, 1933), p. 61.

14. See Walter J. Fischel, *Jews in the Economic and Political Life of Medieval Islam* (New York, 1969).

Part Two

The Modern and Contemporary Periods

SALO W. BARON

8 The Modern and Contemporary Periods: Review of the History

The span of the modern period in Jewish history varies according to country and subject matter. On the whole, the Jewish emancipation period began in the West in the sixteenth century; it progressed to Central Europe during the eighteenth and nineteenth centuries and finally reached Eastern Europe in the twentieth century. In colonial America, however, Jews were to a large extent emancipated soon after their arrival.[1]

One outstanding feature of Jewish life in the Dispersion was that the people lived in a divided world. In ancient times one segment lived under the Roman Empire and another under the rule of Parthia or Sassanian Persia. Later on many Jews lived under Christendom; but, at least until the twelfth century, the majority resided in the countries of Islam. Today the Jewish people are divided between East and West, between the Communist world and the democratic United States, Israel, and Western Europe. Only a relatively small minority inhabits the so-called Third World. It is not a mere accident of history, perhaps, that the largest agglomeration of Jews is to be found in the United States and that until recently the second largest group lived in the Soviet Union. It is only in the last several years that the Jewish population of Israel has exceeded that of the Soviet Union, which has been steadily declining, according to the official statistics.

This position between countries of different ideologies, whether political or religious, has been the source of both dangers and challenges. Because Jews maintained a certain solidarity with coreligionists in an alien world, they could, and often did, appear suspect to their immediate neighbors. From time immemorial Jews have been accused of betraying state secrets to some enemy country where other Jews resided. In the perennial struggle between Rome and Parthia-Persia, according to an obscure talmudic allusion, Babylonian Jews seem at one time to have been forbidden to make pilgrimages to Palestine because Sassanian rulers were afraid that such pilgrims might furnish information useful to the Roman generals in the intermittent wars between the two empires.[2]

When the Moors invaded Spain in 711–712, the Jews of Visigothic Spain were accused by their Christian neighbors of having hailed the invaders as liberators. This was by no means mere invention by Jew baiters. Like some disgruntled aristocrats and burghers, but with much greater justification, the Spanish Jews had grievances against the Visigothic regime, which in the course of the preceding century had twice outlawed Judaism completely, forcing Jews to adopt Christianity; when these measures proved ineffective the Visigoths tried slow economic strangulation of their Jewish subjects. It is not surprising, therefore, that after occupying Toledo, the Spanish capital, the Moorish troops rushed ahead in their conquest and left the city in the hands of a Jewish garrison. So convinced were the Western Christians that the Jews had become the allies of the invaders, that chronicler after chronicler repeated the story of the Jews opening the gates of Toulouse to the onrushing Saracen troops. The only difficulty with that story was that the Moors never entered Toulouse.

Similar accusations were repeated time and again during the crusading era and in early modern times when Europe was confronted with the so-called "Turkish menace." The rapidly expanding Ottoman Empire of the sixteenth century was indeed a threat to Central and even Western Europe; and the Jews, who were treated much more favorably by the Ottoman rulers than by their Christian counterparts, appeared doubly suspect. One anti-Jewish writer in early seventeenth-century Poland, Sebastian Miczynski (to whom Jewish historians are otherwise greatly indebted for detailed information about Polish Jewry's occupational activities), devoted an entire chapter of his sharply critical *Mirror of the Polish Crown* to incidents illustrating how the Jews allegedly transmitted secrets of the Crown to the neighboring enemy, the Turks.[3] Occasionally such suspicions, even in the twentieth century, assumed almost ridiculous dimensions.

I myself recall an incident during World War I when the Austrian authorities discovered that some Galician Jews were using prayer books printed in Russia. Understandably, in reproducing the standard prayer for the welfare of the country and its rulers, these books contained the names of the czars then reigning in Russia, Alexander III or Nicholas II. Because Russia at that time was the principal enemy of the Austro-Hungarian Empire, any prayer for a czar appeared seditious. My father, who served at that time as the head of a large Jewish community, was immediately summoned by the district governor and ordered to help in the confiscation of all these supposedly subversive prayer books. Finally a compromise was reached: after the names of the czars were expunged or pasted over, permission was granted for the books to circulate again in the Jewish community.

This was a fanciful case of disloyalty, but it is a matter of record that some former Marranos, resentful of their maltreatment by the Inquisition in their Iberian homelands, after settling in Constantinople and quickly rising to positions of power and affluence, often tried to aid the Ottoman rulers in their struggle with Western Europe, especially against Spain, which was at that time at the height of her power and glory. Suffice it to mention the names of Don Joseph Nasi (formerly known in Portugal and the Netherlands as a New Christian João Miques) and later Don Solomon Ibn Ya'ish (known previously as a New Christian under the Portuguese name Alvaro Mendes). Both these men became influential advisers to the sultans and were elevated to the ranks of dukes of Naxos and Mytilene, respectively. In this capacity they persuaded the Turks to attack Spain at crucial moments.[4]

The case of Alvaro Mendes is especially striking. While still living in Paris and London as a New Christian, he was in direct contact with Henry III of France and Elizabeth of England. The Queen continued writing him friendly letters even after he settled in Constantinople and became known as a professing Jew. In 1588, when Spain's "invincible armada" was approaching the English shores, he was particularly helpful to England in her hour of peril. On the other hand, the distinguished physician Solomon Ashkenazi, a native of Udine in the Venetian Republic, opposed Don Joseph's policy; in 1573 he was instrumental in bringing about the conclusion of a peace treaty between the Ottoman Empire and Venice, where a year later he appeared as the ambassador of the Porte. Ashkenazi's intervention contributed to the Venetian senate's vote on July 7, 1573, to revoke the decree of expulsion of the Jews from the republic, enacted in December 1571. The physician-diplomat was also quite helpful to Henry de Valois in his candidacy for the throne of Poland in 1573. However, soon after being elected king of Poland and grand duke of Lithuania, Henry learned of the death of his brother, King Charles IX, surreptitiously left Poland, and assumed the throne of France as King Henry III.

Diplomatic interventions such as those just cited mark a new chapter in the history of the Jews as a political factor in international affairs. Yet these were relatively minor episodes in the long and more enduring evolution of Jews as intermediaries between East and West in international trade and intellectual exchange. Because Jews lived under both Christendom and Islam they were not only able to travel freely from one area to the other, but they were also certain of a brotherly reception on either side of the wall separating the two civilizations. A Jew from France or Germany arriving in Cairo or Baghdad was able to communicate with his brethren through a common language, Hebrew. In the ninth century, it is said, Hebrew was the only international language in the Mediterranean world. In contrast, Muslims were generally unable to communicate with Christians in Latin and only few Christians had any familiarity with Arabic. Equally significant was the mutual advantage of Jews of all countries that they could readily do business with one another on the basis of the same law. Even Muslims often encountered mercantile difficulties because of the legal diversities among the four schools of Muslim jurisprudence, while Christians from various lands often lived by sharply divergent customary laws prevailing in particular regions or of such disparate legal systems as were represented by the Syriac, Greek, Roman, and other written codes of law. The capability of the Jews as cultural intermediaries was highlighted as early as 797 by the famous embassy sent by Charlemagne to the caliph Harun al-Rashid, which consisted of two noblemen and their Jewish interpreter, Isaac. As it happened, the two aristocrats died during the journey, and Isaac, the survivor, became the sole intermediary between the two most powerful monarchs of East and West. As a paralled in the intellectual sphere we need but refer to the great services rendered by Jews to the Western world by helping transmit the fruits of Greco-Arabic philosophy and science to the Western European savants.

The divisions in the outside world often proved particularly helpful to Jews in their recurrent emergencies. From the seventh century on the Christian lands frequently yielded to outbursts of total intolerance. Between 613 and 661 Byzantium, Spain, Gaul, and Langobard, Italy, tried to suppress Judaism altogether. With the rise of Islamic society, many Jews were to find havens of refuge from such persecutions in the Muslim world. Conversely, when the Almohades tried to overcome the religious heterogeneity of their Moroccan and Iberian possessions and outlawed both Judaism and Christianity, many Jewish and Christian refugees found new homes in northern Spain, which was then under Christian domination. Some individuals, like the poet Moses Ibn Ezra, felt unhappy in their new environment,[5] but the fact was that they were able to continue living as Jews, which was in itself a great blessing. Thus it was not a serious misreading of history when the anonymous author of the *Seder Eliyahu Rabbah* claimed that God divided the world "in order to preserve Israel." The observation held equally true in the third, sixth, or ninth century when, according to different modern scholars, that particular midrash was written. In a more apocalyptic vein, the fourth-century Palestinian homilist, Eleazar bar Abina, predicted: "When you see empires in combat with one another, watch for the footsteps of the King Messiah."[6]

The same factors which operated to open escape valves for Jews facing governmental or mass assaults also contributed to their insecurity. Since Jews resided in so many countries that were frequently engaged in fighting one another, they were exposed to the attacks of foreign invaders or raiders from either side. Not surprisingly, therefore, the Jews of the late Middle Ages and early modern times increasingly became devotees of international peace. As loyal citizens of their respective countries, they not only recited the weekly blessings upon their rulers but also hoped for their *shalom* in its double meaning of well-being and peace. Only exceptionally did some rabbis pray for the victory of their particular country. One such penitential prayer *(selihah)* was composed, for example, by a leading sixteenth-century preacher, Eliezer ben Elijah Ashkenazi.

It is quite understandable, therefore, that Azariah Rossi, the sixteenth-century pioneer of Jewish critical historiography, could declare:

All the peoples of the world should know that, as long as we, the remnant of Israel, live as strangers and sojourners in a land which is not ours, we are obliged, in accordance with the words of the prophets and the custom of our fathers which is law, to pray for the peace of the kingdom which rules over us. Especially at a time like this, when our sins have caused our dispersion to the [four] corners of the world, we must also invoke Heaven to grant peace to the whole universe, that no people should raise arms against another.[7]

This was a widely prevalent sentiment among Jews, despite the fact that in some cases Jewish individuals may have benefited from warfare as contractors or financiers.

On rare occasions Jewish communities may have suffered less from military hostilities than their neighbors. Such seems to have been the case of the Thirty Years' War, when Protestants mercilessly slew Catholic civilians and Catholics did the same to the Protestants while the belligerent armies in both camps often felt induced to spare Jews as a neutral third force needed for maintaining some continuity in the production and availability of goods. Moreover, the very fact of this division between the various Christian sects indirectly afforded some relief from the animosities directed toward Jews. Jews certainly were no longer the sole religious minority whose elimination might appear desirable to unfriendly, bigoted, or self-seeking neighbors.[8]

At the same time, however, the growing fanaticism of the ever sharper interdenominational conflicts which culminated in the Thirty Years' War affected the Jews adversely in most Catholic countries. It contributed greatly to the intensification of the inquisitorial persecution of Marranos. First begun in the Albigensian War of thirteenth-century southern France, which affected Jews more indirectly, the attempted eradication of all religious dissent in fifteenth-century Castile and Aragon assumed dangerous proportions and threatened the very survival of Spanish and Portuguese Jewry. Although aimed mainly at the conversos, the Inquisition contributed greatly to the expulsion of the Jews from Spain in 1492 because of the feeling that as long as professing Jews remained in the country, the New Christians would never be completely absorbed by the majority.

Four years later the Spanish expulsion was followed by a parallel act of intolerance in Portugal. Unwilling to lose her Jews, Portugal put into effect an enforced conversion, which did not allow for the alternative of expatriation. Despite these drastic measures, Jews were by no means eliminated from Iberia, and both the Spanish and Portuguese Holy Offices were busy for centuries thereafter extirpating the vestiges of what they called the "judaizing" heresy. Even the offspring of converted Jews lived under a cloud of suspicion for many generations. With an increasing emphasis upon the *limpieza de sangre* (purity of blood), even great-grandchildren of former Jews, many of whom were undoubtedly pious Catholics, lived a more or less segregated life and, on the slightest provocation, were subject to prosecution for secret judaizing. Sometimes a simple denunciation by an enemy sufficed to bring about the arrest and investigation of any suspect.

The harsh procedure of the Inquisition, keeping suspects in dungeons for years without trial, have often been denounced both by contemporaries and by modern historians. Particularly the use of torture to secure confessions from the accused (which was, ironically, motivated in part by the consideration that no defendant should be condemned to death on the basis of circumstantial evidence alone), the subsequent public autos-da-fé, in which thousands of victims were burned at the stake, made the name of Spain a symbol of intolerance among nations. To be sure, this was a violent age and the judicial proceedings in many criminal courts were not much more humane. It suffices to recall the provisions of the contemporary Constitutio Criminalis Carolina enacted by Charles V for the Holy Roman Empire, which were no less cruel. The religious zeal of the inquisitors, however, heightened by the prospect of confiscating a culprit's property for the benefit of the Holy Office, and the long duration of the series of the inquisitorial trials, which, after a temporary interruption during the French Revolution, were continued until 1828, kept the *leyenda negra* (black legend) very much alive, especially among Spain's enemies and in the progressively "enlightened" European public opinion.

From the Jewish point of view, the Inquisition generated an upsurge of Jewish feeling among some of those who were able to escape their home countries, and it brought forth a number of martyrs who sacrificed their lives "for the sanctification of the name of the Lord." It also resulted in a vast Marrano dispersion. As in other celebrated cases of religious persecution—those of the

Huguenots in France, the dissenters of England, the Polish emigrés in the nineteenth century—this dispersion had a tremendous impact on the host countries. Since the Marrano migrations lasted much longer and extended over a much vaster geographic area, the historic impact of the Iberian violence was that much greater. It led directly to the resettlement of Jews in Western Europe, especially in Holland, England, and France; and this in turn brought about a great increase in the local as well as interterritorial influence of Jews.

The pioneering services performed by the Marranos in these countries significantly contributed to the rise of modern capitalism and enlightenment. Similarly, the relatively few New Christians who settled in the American colonies of Spain and Portugal—beginning with the expedition of Columbus, whose ships carried five Marranos among their eighty-eight voyagers—helped to lay the foundation for the Latin American civilizations of the modern period. Like its old world counterpart, the American Marrano Diaspora also brought forth a number of martyred witnesses to the Jewish faith, beginning with Hernando Alonso in 1521. The much larger number of Iberian Jewish exiles who settled in Muslim countries, particularly in the rising Ottoman Empire, greatly strengthened Eastern Jewry, for Jewish communal life in the eastern Mediterranean had declined severely in the last centuries of Byzantine rule prior to the Iberian expulsion. It was Marranos like Abraham Cardoso who also contributed much to some of the newer religious trends in Judaism, especially in connection with the Sabbatian movement. Here the violence of the Holy Office found its counterpart in the militant defense of an important segment of the Jewish people, which was one of several factors serving to stir up a strong revitalizing ferment in modern Jewish life.[9]

Most Protestant sects were as hostile to the Jewish people as the Catholics had been. Although striving to discard the Catholic traditions accumulated from the time of the Church Fathers to that of the medieval scholastics, the first leaders of the Reformation were too deeply imbued with the medieval spirit to assume a totally new stance on the Jewish question. In a recent paper, published by UNESCO in three languages,[10] I have tried to point out that the Protestant revolution, like most other victorious revolutionary movements in history, achieved a major transformation in the accustomed ways of life and thought only in those specific areas that it set out to change. It removed the dominance of the Catholic ecclesiastical establishment, including priestly celibacy and the monastic system, and repudiated the papacy as the controlling organ of religious life. It established its appeal to individual conscience rather than to mediation by a priesthood endowed with the sacrament of ordination, and it made good its general claim to return to Scriptures as the only source of information as to the revealed will of God. In all other matters, however, including some scholastic interpretations of the Bible and many institutional forms, it adhered to the existing conditions with only minor modifications. Regarding the Jewish question, the majority of Protestant teachers still harbored the old anti-Jewish prejudices of medieval Catholicism.

Most outspoken along these lines was Martin Luther. A man of violent temperament and accustomed to using earthy, even crude, language, he let loose a barrage of invective against the Jewish people which surpassed in virulence the language used by most Catholic controversialists during the Middle Ages. At the beginning of his career he expressed some friendly sentiments toward the persecuted Jews, and, in a special pamphlet published in 1523, he tried to remind the German public that *Jesus Christ Was a Born Jew;* but he was speedily disabused in his hope of converting the German Jews to his brand of Christianity and increasingly indulged in verbal assaults on Jews and Judaism. As he became more and more enmeshed in the power struggle of the age between the emperor and the princes, he found that anti-Judaism was quite popular among the German masses as well as among some of his protectors, such as the elector of Saxony. Ultimately, in two pamphlets written in 1543 and in his final testament composed shortly before his death three years later, he abandoned almost all self-control. To quote from just one of his vitriolic polemics, we cite the following outburst:

Oh, how they [the Jews] love the Book of Esther; it is so well in line with their bloodthirsty, vengeful, and murderous sentiments and hopes. There is no people under the sun more avid of revenge, more bloodthirsty, believing itself to be God's people, in order to murder and strangle the heathens.

Know my dear Christian, and do not doubt that next to the devil you have no enemy more cruel, more venomous and virulent, than a true Jew.[11]

It was indeed with Luther's approval, if not on his initiative, that in 1536 the elector of Saxony banished the Jews from his country. This was fully in line with the reformer's exclamation: "Who prevents the Jews from returning to Judaea? Nobody. We shall provide them with all the supplies of the journey, only in order to get rid of that disgusting vermin." True, much of this violent language may be discounted as typical of the age and the man. His attacks on the peasants who participated in the famous Peasant Rebellion of 1525, for example, were no less unbridled, although he himself was born to a rural family who had for many generations endured the hardships of medieval peasant life. During that uprising he published a pamphlet with a telling title: *Against the Robbing and Murdering Hordes of Peasants.* In general, Luther was such an ardent advocate of the unbalanced status quo that he tried to rationalize it in theological terms by saying:

God's kingdom is a kingdom of grace and mercy, not of wrath and punishment. . . . But the kingdom of the world is a kingdom of wrath and severity. In it there is only punishment, repression, judgment, and condemnation, for the suppressing of the wicked and the protection of the good.[12]

Far less violent, but intrinsically as sharply opposed to the Jewish people, was the other outstanding Christian reformer of the age, John Calvin. Having spent most of his life in France and later in Geneva, from both of which Jews had long before been eliminated by decrees of expulsion, Calvin generally evinced less concern about the presence of Jews. At times he tried to emphasize that the New Testament itself preached the preservation of Jews as a religious postulate, especially in his commentary on Romans 9–11:

Nevertheless, when Paul cast them [the Jews] down from vain confidence in their kindred, he still saw, on the other hand, that the covenant which God had made once for all with the descendants of Abraham could in no way be made void. . . . Therefore, that they might not be defrauded of their privilege, the gospel had to be announced to them first. For they are, so to speak, like the first-born in God's household. . . . Yet, despite the great obstinacy with which they continue to wage war against the gospel, we must not despise them while we consider that, for the sake of the promise, God's blessing still rests among them.

Even during his brief enforced absence from Geneva in 1539–1541, when he had the opportunity to meet Jews in Strasbourg and Frankfurt, Calvin did not change his basic position. In a pamphlet recording a disputation with a Jew, probably Josel of Rosheim, he tried to state his opponent's argument rather fairly, albeit with extreme brevity. He also spoke in a moderate tone in the replies restating his own views. However, in many other passages in both his major theological work and his commentaries on the Bible he betrayed his uncritical acceptance of many judgments of the medieval scholastics concerning Jews and Judaism in their time.[13] Only a few representatives of the more radical reformation, especially in Holland and Poland, sought a closer rapprochement with contemporary Jews.

Nevertheless, in the long run the new cultural and socioeconomic developments of Western Europe forced a reorientation to the Jewish question. Thus Hugo Grotius's memorandum of 1616 on Jewish status in Amsterdam and the decision of 1697 to allot to Jews 12 of the 124 seats on the London Stock Exchange, soon to become the world's leading bourse, were straws in the wind.[14] Both events were harbingers of Jewish emancipation, and it is no accident that both occurred in countries which had controlling Protestant majorities in their population.

Manifestations of the new spirit became more and more pronounced with the development of modern capitalism. We need not share Werner Sombart's exaggerations concerning the Jewish share in the evolution of the new capitalist system to admit that Jews played a more significant economic role than was warranted by their ratios in the population, especially in the most advanced capitalistic countries—Holland, England, France, Brandenburg-Prussia, and ultimately North America. The nineteenth century, especially, saw the rise of numerous Jewish banking houses, led by the House of Rothschild, whose influence on the economies of the capitalist world made itself strongly felt. Other aspects of the same trend were the liberalization of international trade, greater freedom of movement, and the entry of Jews into many new occupations, particularly in the liberal professions, the arts and sciences, and governmental service. All of these factors greatly contributed to the legal and political emancipation of Jews as well. Aided by the forces of enlightenment and the general democratization of Western countries, the breakdown of medieval ghettos and the establishment of civil and political equality for Jews became necessities, even more urgent for the modern state than they were for Jewry.

Many traditionalist forces among Central and Eastern European Jews viewed political emancipation with a jaundiced eye because it meant giving up most of their communal autonomy and would inevitably work profound changes in the accustomed ways of life. But civil emancipation did become a matter of historic necessity for European Jews as their rapidly increasing numbers forced them to look for new outlets for their economic enterprises and new opportunities for their workmen. On the part of the state, on the other hand, Jewish political emancipation was an even greater historic necessity: a democratic state simply could not tolerate the continued presence of a large and influential minority living on the basis of its medieval system of special rights and special duties. Equality of rights was in many ways the only alternative to complete elimination of Jews from such countries.[15]

The radical transformation of the Jewish position in society could not take place without much opposition from vested interests and otherwise prejudiced groups. The new anti-Semitic violence which developed in the modern epoch was expressed verbally as well as in deeds; it began stressing secular, cultural, economic, and political factors much more than the religious antagonisms which had dominated the medieval controversies. At the height of the period of capitalist growth Jews were accused not only of being the traditional exploiters and usurers, as in earlier periods, but also of being a people permeated with a drive for world domination through the instrumentality of finance. In this respect reactionaries went hand in hand with the newly rising social revolutionary groups in attacking Jews. The feudal lords whose control over society was being undermined by the new social forces were prone to blame the Jews for their downfall. Perhaps the most eloquent denouncer of such alleged Jewish desires for domination was Count Zygmunt Krasinski, one of the triad of immortal Polish poets of the first half of the nineteenth century. In his most celebrated dramatic poem, *The Undivine Comedy* (1835), he presented a banker (an obvious representation of a Rothschild) as the chief demonic force undermining society. Similar sentiments were expressed also by poets and thinkers in other lands; even in increasingly democratic England and among fighters for the liberation of oppressed nationalities, such as the Greeks. Lord Byron, then at the height of his European fame, put into the mouth of one of his heroes the peroration:

> Who hold the balance of the world? Who reign
> O'er Congress whether royalist or liberal? . . .
> Jew Rothschild and his fellow Christian Baring.
> Those and the truly liberal Lafitte
> Are the true Lords of Europe. Every loan
> Is not a merely speculative hit
> But seats a nation or upsets a throne.

Curiously, some extreme socialists of the school of Fourier and others joined this chorus of accusers. In 1845 one of the Fourierists, Antoine de Toussenel, published a book bearing the characteristic title, *Les Juifs rois de l'époque: Histoire de la fe'odalité financière.* This theme was taken up by Edouard Drumont at the end of the century and repeated with even greater vehemence by other anti-Semites, especially in Germany and czarist Russia.[16]

These slogans reached their climax in the nefarious concoction circulated under the name of *Protocols of the Elders of Zion.* Based upon a tract first prepared by the Russian monk Sergei Nilus, this desultory expose of a fanciful conspiracy captivated the imaginations of untold millions, including that of such a politically naive, even if economically powerful, personality as Henry Ford. The myth of the *Protocols* stimulated numerous remarkable suggestions for counteraction of the alleged Jewish plot. One such was the proposal by the czarist foreign minister, Count Vladmir Nikolaevich Lamsdorff, in reaction to the allegedly Jewish inspiration of the Revolution of 1905. In a secret memorandum the minister seriously advocated a confidential exchange of views between St. Petersburg, Berlin, and the Vatican, with a view toward organizing vigilant, international supervision over the activities of the Jewish revolutionaries and ultimately joining hands to combat the Jew as the common foe of Christian and monarchical order. The *Protocols* and the fantasy that it spread had antecedents deep in the Middle Ages, survived to play a considerable role in Nazi propaganda, and still has not lost its appeal among anti-Jewish spokesmen in the Soviet Union and the Arab world today. Despite repeated demonstrations of the pamphlet's spurious origin and clear proof of the falsehood of the entire underlying assumption of the alleged "Zionist" drive for world domination, the myth has remained a source of anti-Jewish hatred and recurrent violence in many parts of the world.[17]

Needless to say, those who circulated such libels did not trouble to seek corroborative evidence. Opposing statements by leading Jews from the ancient prophets to modern thinkers were unheeded. We need but mention a representative statement by Maimonides, who, at the end of his *Code of Laws,* thus summarized the objectives of the Jewish messianic expectation:

The sages and prophets have not yearned for the days of the Messiah in order that the Jews should rule the world, exercise dominion over the heathens, or receive homage from the nations, nor that they should eat and drink and enjoy life. Only in order that they may be free to dedicate themselves to learning and wisdom, without the interference of an oppressor or a disturber, so that they might secure life in the world to come. . . . And at that time there shall be no hunger, nor war, nor envy and rivalry for there will be an abundance of all good things.

Similarly, Moses Hess, one of the spiritual founders of the modern Zionist movement, felt confident in 1862 that his generation was "on the eve of the Sabbath of history and should prepare for our mission." It was for that purpose that he believed that the restoration of the Jewish people to Zion would redound to the benefit not only of the Jews but also of the whole world. "When I labor for the regeneration of our nation, I do not thereby renounce my humanistic aspiration," he insisted. For modern nationalism was, in his opinion, essentially but a reaction "against the leveling tendencies of modern industry, a civilization which threatens to deaden every original organic life force by introducing a uniform inorganic mechanism." It is in this context that he believed that a return to Israel would make it possible for the Jewish people to "develop anew from thence the eternal principles which unite humanity with the Universe and the Universe with its Creator."[18]

If such statements came at all to the attention of the disseminators of anti-Jewish hatred, they readily dismissed them as utterances of biased apologists. No similarly facile dismissals could be made in the case of another myth, which even more frequently embittered Judeo-Christian, and on occasion also Judeo-Muslim, relations: the blood accusation. The libel apparently went back to the days of the Maccabean revolt and the story spread by the Seleucid propaganda that Antiochus IV, upon his entry into the Temple of Jerusalem, had found a Gentile kept there and fattened by the priests for ultimate sacrifice on the altar. This myth first adversely affected the Christian population of the Roman empire, but from the twelfth century on it assumed ever more threatening anti-Jewish forms in medieval and modern Europe. In one of its earliest manifestations (in Norwich, 1144) a Cambridge monk named Theobald, a Jewish convert to Christianity, combined this myth of the Jews' need for Christian blood, especially before Easter, with the myth of a Jewish world conspiracy.[19]

In vain was this growing delusion among the masses combatted by the Christian world. In 1236, after a disturbance by a blood libel in Fulda, Emperor Frederick II, equally eminent as a scholar and a ruler, asked a number of Western kings to send him experts in the field of Jewish belief and observance to discuss the merits of this accusation. This congress came to the conclusion that there was no shred of evidence for Jewish ritual need of human sacrifices since even the consumption of animal blood had been strictly forbidden to Israel from biblical times. Eleven years later, in 1247, the papacy condemned the blood accusation: Pope Innocent IV issued a bull forbidding the dissemination of that libel, a condemnation that was to be echoed by many of his successors at the See of St. Peter. For example, in 1540 Pope Paul III addressed a special bull, *Licet Judaei,* to the bishops of Poland, Bohemia, and Hungary declaring:

We have heard with displeasure from the complaints of Jews of those countries how, for some years past, certain magistrates and other officials, their bitter and mortal enemies, blinded by hate and envy, or as is more probable by cupidity, pretend, in order to despoil them of their goods, that the Jews kill little children and drink their blood.

Nevertheless, rumor-mongering on this score never ceased. Even in the more critical and "enlightened" nineteenth century, the "Damascus accusation" of 1840 became an international cause célèbre. It was of little assistance to truth seekers that a canon of the Cathedral of St. Stephen's in Vienna, a convert from Judaism, took a solemn oath before the altar that, as a former Jew familiar with Jewish institutions, he knew that the blood libel was without any foundation. As late as 1899, thirty baptized Jews living in Jerusalem issued a most persuasive declaration reading:

As born Jews, who are intimate with all the ritual prescriptions, uses and traditions of the Jews, and all Jewish sects, and as Christians who believe in Him who is the truth and the light, we hereby testify solemnly before the All-knowing Triune God, by the salvation of our souls and by our honour and conscience, that the accusation against the Jews in general or any Jewish sect whatever, that they are either compelled to use or have used at any time Christian blood or human blood for ritual purposes, is an absolutely mistaken, false calumny.[20]

Yet even after such compelling testimonies, many groups in the population of most Christian lands have been prepared to listen to demagogues preaching hatred against Jews on the basis of the blood accusation. Not even the United States completely escaped this superstitious belief. A well-known incident in Massena, New York, in 1927 showed how prone the populace, including as responsible an official as the mayor, was to lend a willing ear to the long discredited calumny. The masses were also ready to believe, with even less opposition from Christian leaders, the equally pernicious libels of Jews desecrating the host, poisoning wells, and committing other atrocities motivated by perennial hatred of all Christian neighbors.

All these accusations were but a few of the numerous manifestations of popular hostility toward Jews nurtured by the general "dislike of the unlike." No matter how long Jews lived in a country, until the Emancipation era they were considered aliens by the majority of their fellow citizens, a conception which they did not negate for they considered themselves to be living in *galut* (exile). The general feeling that the Jew was an alien was intensified by the gradual rise of medieval nationalism. Though not quite so rampant as the nationalism of the modern period, this incipient movement nevertheless made itself felt ever more strongly with the passage of time. Halvdan Koht was undoubtedly right when he stated that "from the beginning of the twelfth century European nationalism has a continuous history."[21]

About half a century ago I publicly defended a theory, first orally and then in writing, that much of medieval and early modern Jewish history can be explained by the various reactions of the nationalist forces to the presence of Jews. I observed then, and with further study have become even more convinced, that once a state became what might conveniently be called a national state—that is, one in which the political and ethnic boundaries roughly coincided—a popular anti-Jewish reaction was to be expected, either in the form of massacres or in the ultimate expulsion of Jews from the country. Countries of multiple nationality, on the other hand, for the most part treated the Jews fairly. In fact, some multinational states saw in the Jewish presence a means of promoting governmental authority over an ethnically heterogeneous population, for the dispersed Jewish minority had little interest in the local ethnic conflicts and appeared as a relatively neutral, unifying force. This Jewish function was the more effective—as under the medieval system of "serfdom," which had a different meaning in different countries and periods—when Jews lived under the tutelage of the central power and thus had a natural interest in preserving its rule against centrifugal forces.

As ethnic homogeneity increased in the course of a lengthy symbiosis of the various groups within a country, the Jews, originally attracted by the policy of a prince, found themselves ultimately the only remaining minority and, as such, increasingly unwelcome both to rulers and subjects. Such a situation often degenerated into public disturbances and in the end led to formal decrees of banishment. To mention only some of the signal instances, this happened in England in 1290, in France in 1309–1394, in Spain in 1492, in Portugal in the shape of forced conversion in 1496–1497. In all cases, whether through sanguinary massacres or through a formal decree of expulsion, the violence accompanying such acts belonged to the most vividly memorable features of medieval Jewish life.[22]

In modern times, to be sure, the situation seemed to change. The position of Jews in national states, such as France, Italy, and to a lesser extent England, was superior to that in such countries of multiple nationality as czarist Russia or Poland—whether one speaks of Poland before the partition or of resurrected Poland. One must not forget, however, that the Western European nations had now become colonial powers. The homelands may have retained their national homogeneity, but the fact of their domination over a multitude of racial and ethnic groups elsewhere did not quite allow these countries to act as pure national states. At the same time, the modern developments of individualism and of institutions based in principle upon democratic equality also modified whatever national hostilities toward Jews might otherwise have remained active in these lands. Above all, there was the great fact of the secularization of Western societies, which fostered the assumption that Jews could be fully integrated into any Western nation without undergoing conversion to Christianity—a notion unthinkable in previous generations. Emancipation, at least in its early stages, presumed that, upon achieving equality of rights and thus seeing the gates to all public and private functions open to them, Jews would readily assimilate to the surrounding culture. They might still retain their religious diversity, but in progressively secularized societies, religion usually divested itself of its predominantly ethnic manifestations and could become a "private affair of the individual."

The validity of these assumptions began to be tested during the French Revolution. One need but peruse the deliberations at the French National Assembly to note how fully the spokesmen of the various points of view anticipated the debates which were to rage in the following two centuries. On the one hand, the conservative group led by Abbé (later Cardinal) Maury contended that the Jews were unassimilable and that, despite admission to all rights of French citizenship, they would remain forever a nation within the nation. At the same time a radical wing, represented by the Alsatian deputy Jean François Rewbell, insisted that economically Jews would remain exploiters who would utilize their newly won freedoms only the better to oppress the masses of peasantry and urban workers. The protagonists of Jewish equality, for their part, claimed that Jewish "separatism" was merely the effect of age-old oppression and would ultimately disappear under conditions of fraternity and equality. Yet even they expected from the Jews total assimilation except in the purely spiritual sphere. Characteristic of this point of view was the well-known exclamation of the Girondist, Count Clermont-Tonnère: "We ought to refuse all rights to Jews as a nationality, but to give them all to Jews as individuals." Most characteristically, he added in a passage rarely quoted: "If they do not wish to become citizens [under this condition], let them say so and be banished." In other words, even this progressive deputy envisaged only the medieval solution of either total integration (although now without conversion) or expulsion. Not surprisingly, later on in the French Revolution it was left to the Jacobins of Champagne on the extreme left to petition the Paris authorities for the outright banishment of all the Jews from France.[23]

In the protracted struggle for emancipation in Central Europe during the nineteenth century, the nexus between emancipation and assimilation loomed very large. Liberals on both the Christian and Jewish sides habitually thought in terms of this sort of solution to the Jewish question. The masses of Jews, on the other hand, particularly when the emancipation movement reached Eastern Europe, insisted upon preserving their ethnic identity, especially in such ethnically mixed areas as Czechoslovakia, the Baltic region, Rumania, and others. In many of the provinces of the Austro-Hungarian and czarist empires the Jews were often confronted with the unwelcome choice of either assimilating to the dominant minority of Germans, Magyars, or Russians or integrating into the masses of the native populations, some of which were still emerging as young, culturally growing nationalities. Out of the resultant turmoil arose the new demands for national minority rights for Jews and other nationalities combined with equality of rights for all.

In the more homogeneous national states like Germany, the fact that even the German Jews, however obviously patriotic and imbued with German culture they were, had not become sufficiently assimilated evoked the resentment of many extreme German nationalists. The latter claimed that the Jews had not kept their part of the bargain, had broken an unspoken contract between the state and the Jews by not becoming fully assimilated once equality had been granted. Germany, they argued, was therefore entitled to revoke emancipation. While the "contract myth" had no foundation in the historical records, it sounded plausible enough to nurture great resentment among the German masses, whose antipathy was not lessened by their envy of the speedy rise of Jewish affluence in the rapidly advancing economy of the Hohenzollern empire.[24]

German anti-Semitism was further nurtured by this very growth, of which an intrinsic part was the rise of German imperialism and militarism. Anti-Semitism was given an air of scientific respectability by the newly emerging racialist doctrines of Count Gobineau and his German followers, such as Eugen Dühring and Houston Stewart Chamberlain. And anti-Semitism was given a new theological dimension by the dissemination of the idea that Christianity was itself a Jewish plot. In their march toward imperial hegemony, many Germans resented the shackles imposed upon their policies by international law and the underlying ideology of Judeo-Christian ethics. Drawing upon the thoughts of such anti-Christian philosophers as Friedrich Nietzsche, many political leaders and agitators now combined the dreams of return to the pre-Christian Teuton morality with feelings of racial supremacy and the cultivation of a martial spirit among German youth. In 1909, long before Hitler's rise to power, one heard such warnings as those sounded by Ernst Wachler in the racialist *Der Hammer:* "Woe unto the people which will behave in a Christian fashion in an era when the struggle has begun for the possession of the earth." German publicist Heinrich Pudor declared:

From a heroic and master race the Teutons have become a people of dreamers, worshippers, and penitents. Wherefore? On account of their Christianity. . . . Get rid of Judaism and Christianity and go back to the sources of Teutonism. . . . Christianity is a Jewish invention. . . . All Christianity is Judeo-Christianity and as such the most stupendous fraud ever committed on races and peoples in world history.[25]

This sort of agitation, combined with the ultimate defeat of the German armies in World War I, prepared the ground for the rise of the postwar Nazi movement and the final seizure of power by Hitler and his cohorts. Many Germans listened with rapture to the preachings of the leading Nazi ideologist Alfred Rosenberg, who claimed that "reverence for the soldier fighting for the honor of his people is the new, recently developed living sentiment of our time. In the name of the new religion of national honor we may expect the awakening of Nordic-European consciousness." The result of these incantations and the willingness of the German people to give ear to the theme was the catastrophe of World War II, so familiar to us all and, for the Jewish people, the greatest holocaust in a blood-stained history.

Needless to say, not all forms of fascism went to the German extreme. Even when Mussolini adopted, under Hitler's pressure, some of the racialist concepts of National Socialism and, in 1938, promulgated racial laws for Italy paralleling those of Germany, he never forgot what he had declared in 1934—that "from Diocletian to Bismarck [history] teaches us that whenever there is a conflict between state and religion it is always the state that loses the battle. A battle against religion is a battle against the imponderable." Yet, in the course of his alliance with Nazi Germany he was infected by its racialist spirit. According to his son-in-law Count Ciano, he once exclaimed in 1941 that he resented Christmas as a holiday because it "reminds us only of the birth of a Jew who gave the world a debilitating and devitalizing theory and who especially contrived to trick Italy through the disintegrating power of the popes." Nevertheless, the Italian people in its majority did not follow the dictator's line; and even during World War II, when Italy was to all intents and purposes occupied by the German

Army, many Italians underwent great personal danger to save their Jewish neighbors from German extermination squads.[26]

The impact of the great catastrophe of World War II upon the Jewish people has assumed unprecedented dimensions. The endeavor to fathom its meaning for Judaism is still unfolding. Theologically, one of the great questions of the age, related to the ancient Jewish theodicy, has been why Eastern European Jewry, which had a far greater percentage of pious and observant Jews than most Western countries, was destined to suffer more severely than any other segment of the people. One speaker who articulated this Jobian dilemma was Rabbi Kalonymus Kalmish Shapiro, who soon after uttering these words fell victim to the Nazi onslaught. Shapiro referred to an ancient midrash which he understood to convey a promise by God, after the death of the "Ten Martyrs" of the Hadrianic age, that if such a tragedy were to occur again the world would be destroyed and the universe would return to its primordial chaos. Viewing the enormities of the Nazi death squads, the rabbi asked:

How can the Universe remain standing and not turn into primordial chaos? . . . Innocent children, pure as angels, as well as great and holy men in Israel, are being killed and slaughtered only because they are Jews . . . and the world's space is filled with their heart-rending shouts: "Save us, save us!" They, too, cry: "Is this the reward for devotion to Torah?" Yet the Universe is not destroyed but remains intact, as if nothing happened!

These questions are as yet unanswered. Now, after the passage of more than a generation since this outcry was voiced, new periods of violence have swept over the world, and the threat of universal destruction through a new atomic holocaust remains real.[27]

It is time indeed for the Jewish people and mankind at large to ponder deeply over the problems of violence and what can be done to defend man in an era of untrammeled violence.

NOTES

1. See my "The Emancipation Movement and American Jewry," in the revised English translation of a Hebrew essay published in *Eretz Israel,* IV (1956, Isaac Ben Zvi Jubilee Volume), 205–14; also in my *Steeled by Adversity: Essays and Addresses on American Jewish Life,* ed. by Jeannette Meisel Baron (Philadelphia, 1971), pp. 80–105.

2. Babylonian Talmud, Ta'anit 28a.

3. See Sebastian Miczynski, *Zwierciadlo Korony Polskiej* ("The Mirror of the Polish Crown") (Cracow, 1618), esp. chap. 6, entirely devoted to the alleged widespread spying by Jews who "communicate matters relating to the Crown to the neighboring enemies, the Turks."

4. See the large literature listed in the respective chapters of *SRH,* to which add the recently published document in my "Solomon Ibn Ya'ish and Sultan Suleiman the Magnificent" in the *Joshua Finkel Festschrift,* ed. by Sidney B. Hoenig and Leon D. Stitskin (New York, 1974), pp. 29–36.

5. See Moses Ibn Ezra's complaints in his *Shire ha-Hol* ("Secular Poems"), ed. by Heinrich (Hayyim) Brody (Berlin, 1935), I, esp. no. 176, v. 7.

6. *Seder Eliyahu Rabbah,* XX, ed. by Meir Friedmann (Vienna, 1901), p. 113 ff; Midrash Genesis Rabbah 42,4; 75,9, ed. by Julius Theodor and Hanokh Albeck, pp. 409, 881. On the conflicting dates attributed to the *Seder Eliyahu Rabbah* and *Zuttah,* see Viktor Aptowitzer, "Seder Elia," *Jewish Studies in Memory of George A. Kohut,* ed. by Salo W. Baron and Alexander Marx (New York, 1935), pp. 5–39 (arguing for its date in the ninth century); and Mordecai Margoliot, "On the Problem of the Antiquity of *Seder Eliyahu*" (Hebrew), in *Sefer Assaf,* ed. by Mordecai David (Umberto) Cassuto et al. (Jerusalem, 1952), pp. 370–90 (insisting on the third century date).

7. Azariah Rossi, *Sefer Me'or Enayim* ("Light of the Eyes: Historical-Chronological Studies), ed. by David Cassel (Vilna, 1864–1866), p. 446.

8. The reaction in Jewish circles to the new situation created by the sectarian divisions and wars of religion in sixteenth-century Europe is analyzed, on the basis of contemporary rabbinic writings, by Hayyim

Hillel Ben-Sasson in "The Reformation in Contemporary Jewish Eyes," *Proceedings of the Israel Academy of Sciences,* IV,2 (Jerusalem, 1972).

9. The thrice-told story of the Inquisition and its aftermath in modern Jewish history has produced an enormous literature, including some writings by new Spanish apologists for that institution. Suffice it to refer here to my analysis and the numerous bibliographical data presented in *SRH,* X, chap. 45; XIII, chap. 55 and 56; and XV, *passim.*

10. "Medieval Heritage and Modern Realities in Protestant-Jewish Relations," *Diogenes,* no. 61 (1968), 32–51; reproduced in my *Ancient and Medieval Jewish History: Essays,* ed. by Leon Feldman (New Brunswick, 1972), pp. 323–37, 544–48.

11. Martin Luther, *Werke,* Weimar edition, esp. LIII, pp. 412 ff., 433, 462, 522 ff., 572 ff.

12. Ibid., IV, pp. 242 ff.

13. See John Calvin, *Institutes of the Christian Religion,* iv, 16, 14 in the English translation by Ford Lewis Battle, ed. by John T. McNeill, The Library of Christian Classics, XX–XXI, (Philadelphia, 1960), II, pp. 1336 ff.; "Ad questiones et obiecta Judaei cuiusdam Responsio" in his *Opera quae supersunt omnia,* ed. by Wilhelm Baum et al. (Brunswick, 1863; Berlin, 1900), Corpus reformatorum, XXIX–LXXXVI, IX, 653–74; and other data assembled in my "John Calvin and the Jews," *Harry Austryn Wolfson Jubilee Volume,* ed. by Saul Lieberman et al. (Jerusalem, 1965), pp. 141–63, reproduced with some revisions in my essays in *Ancient and Medieval History,* pp. 338–52, 548–54.

14. See Hugo Grotius (de Groot), *Remonstrantie* (Memorandum Concerning the Order to be Established for the Jews in the Lands of Holland and West Friesland), reed. by Jacob Meijer (Amsterdam, 1949), with Meijer's comments thereon in his "Hugo Grotius's *Remonstrantie,"* *Jewish Social Studies,* XVII (1955), 91–104; and Arthur K. Kuhn's somewhat overstated view in "Hugo Grotius and the Emancipation of the Jews in Holland," Publications of the American Jewish Historical Society, XXXI (1928), pp. 173–80; Lucien Wolf, "The First Stage of Anglo-Jewish Emancipation," reproduced in his *Essays in Jewish History, with a Memoir,* ed. by Cecil Roth (London, 1934), pp. 115–36.

15. See my "New Approaches to Jewish Emancipation," *Diogenes,* no. 29 (1960), 56–81 (also in its French and Spanish editions).

16. Zygmunt (Sigismund) Krasinski, *Nieboska Komedya,* with an introduction and notes (Warsaw, 1912); in the English translation by M.W. Cook, entitled, *The Undivine Comedy and Other Poems* (Philadelphia, 1873); Lord George G.N. Byron, Don Juan XII, 5–6, in his *Poems and Plays,* ed. by E. Rhys (New York, 1915–1918), vol. III; Antoine de

Toussenel, *Les Juifs rois de l'époque, Histoire de la fe'odalité financière* (Paris, 1845). See also the various analytical studies by Robert F. Byrnes and Edmund Silberner listed under their names in the *Cumulative Index of Jewish Social Studies,* vols. I–XXV, compiled by Max M. Rothschild (New York, 1967); and particularly Silberner's comprehensive study in his *Ha-Sotsializm ha-ma'aravi u-she'elat ha-Yehudim* ("Western Socialism and the Jewish Question") (Jerusalem, 1955).

17. See esp. John S. Curtiss, *An Appraisal of the Protocols of Zion* (New York, 1942); Lucien Wolf, *Notes on the Diplomatic History of the Jewish Question* (London, 1919), pp. 57 ff.; and, in a broader context my "Changing Patterns of Antisemitism: a Survey," *Jewish Social Studies,* XXXVIII (1976), 5–38.

18. Maimonides (Moses ben Maimon), *Mishneh Torah (Code of Laws),* Hilkhot Melakhim, XII, 4–5; Moses Hess, *Rome and Jerusalem: A Study in Jewish Nationalism,* English translation with notes by Meyer Waxman (New York, 1943), pp. 48, 54 ff., 122 ff., 135; idem, review of Gustave d'Eichtal's *Les trois grands peuples méditerranéens et le Christianisme* in *Archives Israélites,* XXVI (1865), 484 ff.

19. Josephus, *Against Apion,* II, 8, in Thackeray's translation, p. 95; Elias Bickerman, "Ritualmord and Eselskult," *Monatsschrift fur die Wissenschaft des Judentums,* LXXI (1927), 171–87, 235–64; W. Schultze, "Der Vorwurf des Ritualmordes gegen die Christen im Altertum," *Zeitschrift fur Kirchengeschichte,* LXV (1953–1954), 304–06; and my remarks in *SRH,* I, pp. 192 ff., 382 n. 33.

20. See the numerous sources discussed in ibid., IV, pp. 132 ff., 306 ff.; XI, pp. 146 ff., 358 ff., *et seq.*

21. Halvdan Koht, "The Dawn of Nationalism in Europe," *American Historical Review,* LII (1947), 265–80, esp. p. 279; and other data reviewed in *SRH,* XI, pp. 193 ff., 379 ff.

22. See my "Nationalism and Intolerance," *Menorah Journal,* XVI (1929), 405–15; XVII (1929), pp. 148–58 (also reprint); "Medieval Nationalism and Jewish Serfdom" in *Studies and Essays in Honor of Abraham A. Neuman* (Philadelphia, 1962), pp. 17–48, reproduced in my *Ancient and Medieval History,* pp. 308–22, 533–44; and *SRH,* XI, chap. 50.

23. See the excerpt reproduced in the *Revue des Grandes Journées Parlementaires,* ed. by Gaston Lebre and G. Labouchère, I (Paris, n.d.), pp. 10 ff.; Robert Anchel, *Napoléon et les Juifs* (Paris, 1928), pp. 17 ff.

24. See Harry Scher's brief analysis of *Jewish Emancipation–the Contract Myth* (London, 1917) and the related considerations in my aforementioned essay (n.15) in *Diogenes,* no. 29, pp. 36 ff.

25. Wachler and Puder, cited by Ismar Freund in *Der Judenhass* (Ber-

lin, 1922), pp. 36 ff. Years earlier Paul de Lagarde, a leading orientalist and Christian hebraist and a major contributor to the rise of the Nazi spirit, had enunciated his credo: "Catholicism, Protestantism, Judaism, naturalism must give way to a new conception of life so that they be remembered no more than are the lamps used at night after the sun shines over the mountains." His impact on Alfred Rosenberg and others is discussed in my *Modern Nationalism and Religion* (New York, 1947), pp. 76 ff., 290 ff.

26. Mussolini's statements, cited by Nathaniel Micklem in his *National Socialism and the Roman Catholic Church* (London, 1939), p. 104; and by Count Galeazzo Ciano in his *Diaries,* 1939–1943, ed. by Hugh Gibson (New York, 1946), p. 423. See also, more generally, my *Modern Nationalism,* pp. 68 ff., 288 ff.

27. Shapiro's moving questioning and other data are cited in my testimony at the Eichmann trial of 1961. See the memorandum prepared for that testimony, published in my *From a Historian's Notebook: European Jewry Before and After Hitler* (New York, 1962), esp. pp. 46 ff. (reprinted from the *American Jewish Year Book,* vol. 63). See also my more recent "Queries in Retrospect," an address delivered at a colloquium on the Holocaust, presented by Dropsie University with Villanova University, April 11, 1973 (Philadelphia, 1973), pp. 11–18.

SHIMON SHAMIR

9 Muslim-Arab Attitudes Toward Jews: The Ottoman and Modern Periods

Analogy is a precarious method: when it finds differences it tends to polarize; when it finds similarities it tends to assimilate. A case in point is the nature of attitudes toward the Jew in Middle Eastern society, which is usually viewed through a juxtaposition with the similar problem in the experience of the West. In some cases this leads to an idealization of the position of Jews as a perfect contrast to their position in Christian Europe and in other cases to an obliteration of the positive features of the Middle Eastern situation by blending it into a Western stereotyped conception of the Jewish predicament in the gentile world.

The aim of this paper is to examine briefly these polarities as they apply to two stages in the history of the region in recent centuries, namely to the attitude of Muslim society toward the Jews in the Ottoman period, particularly in the Arabic-speaking provinces, and to the attitudes of Arabs toward Jews after the emergence of nationalism in this century.

A Tolerated Minority

It is commonly held by most Arab and many Western writers that in traditional society under Ottoman domination Jews lived in peace and harmony with their Muslim neighbors and suffered no persecutions. Ottoman society is depicted as a conglomeration of communities defined by various critera—such as religion, kinship, or locality—and held together by the Ottoman government, which defined the rights and duties of each. As long as the introduction of the nationalist criterion did not disrupt the social order, it is argued, Jews enjoyed a life of security and dignity in this "pluralistic" society and could prosper economically and flourish culturally.[1]

These notions are usually based on an idealized conception of the status of *ahl al-kitab* (the "people of Scripture" or "people of the Book") in Islam, an exaggerated interpretation of Arab-Jewish collaboration against the Christian powers, and a romanticized view of Jewish-Muslim cultural symbiosis, particularly in medieval Spain. Sometimes it is also inspired by the image of the Ottoman golden age, in which sultans granted shelter to Jewish refugees from Spain and other European lands and allowed some of them —notably Don Joseph Nasi—to occupy prominent positions in the empire's ruling elite. Rather than being viewed as a singular chapter in Ottoman-Jewish history, that experience serves as a basis for generalization on the status of the Jewish communities throughout the Ottoman period.

In the case of some Muslim writers, idealization of Jewish-Muslim relations in the Ottoman period can be attributed to a deliberate political posture or to a genuine unawareness of the plight of minorities, typical of the callous attitude of dominant majorities. With local Jews, Musa Alami tells us in his reminiscences on life in Jerusalem in the late Ottoman period, Muslims "associated on terms of virtual equality." Not only that, but "a family of Jews . . . were amongst the closest friends of his parents."[2]

Above all, the idyllic picture of Jewish life in Ottoman society, depicted by this school of thought, is the product of a comparison to Christian Europe. It is a fact that under Ottoman rule, as under most previous Muslim dynasties, Jews were not forced to convert to Islam, were not prevented from practicing their religion, and were not denied a legal basis for their existence within the state. The situation in many Western countries contrasted with the state of affairs in this region to such an extent that the temptation to eulogize the latter is perhaps understandable.

However, this view overlooks the fact that tolerance is not necessarily identical with lack of discrimination, legal recognition as such does not bestow security and dignity, and religious rights do not always amount to social acceptance. Jews in the Ottoman Empire were subjected to the whole system of restrictions imposed in Islam on the *dhimmis,* the tolerated infidels. These restrictions applied to such questions as payment of taxes *(jizya),* ownership of land, or choice of occupation. In spite of some well-known exceptions, non-Muslims were barred from that mixture of military, political, and administrative vocations which constituted the offices of the Ottoman ruling elite even when it was recruited from the local population (a fact which, incidentally, made it so difficult for Muslims of our time to accept the reality of Jewish statehood and Israeli military power).

A good many of these restrictions had been patently designed to demonstrate the inferior status of *dhimmis.* Thus, for example, *dhimmis* were not allowed to marry Muslim women (while Muslims were allowed to marry *dhimmi* women); their evidence against Muslims was not admissible in *sharia* courts; they were obliged to wear distinctive clothes and forbidden to carry arms or ride horses.[3] The degradation of non-Muslims was also expressed in ways that were not decreed by law but practiced in daily life. These included the obligation to make way for a Muslim in a narrow alley or the employment of distinctive modes of address to Muslims and non-Muslims.

A category of sources which authentically reflect social realities

—and have not yet been systematically exploited in studying the position of Jews—is that of the numerous contemporary descriptions of daily life on the popular level, in various localities, recorded in such forms as chronicles, occasional poems, or biographies.

Thus, for example, in the chronicle of Ahmad al-Budayri—a Damascene barber who had recorded, in the colloquial dialect, the events which took place in his town in the mid-eighteenth century —we find several passing references to Jews. On one occasion when several Janissaries arrested a Muslim of the *ashraf* class (descendants of the prophet's family), Budayri comments that he was treated roughly, "as though he was one of the Jews or the people of Ad and Thamud."[4] In this case, if one wishes, it may be claimed that the writer referred to the Koranic concept of Israelites rather than to the social position of his Jewish contemporaries, but there is no room for different interpretations in his other reference to Jews: Budayri there describes a seven-day feast, given by one of the Damascene dignitaries, to which a different group was invited each day, according to its social status, in descending order. The Christians and the Jews, he reports, were invited on the fifth day, thus ranking above only the peasants and the prostitutes.[5]

Another illustration may be found in an occasional poem written by an Egyptian sheikh, Hasan al-Hijazi, at the end of the seventeenth century and examined in a study by Gabriel Baer. The poem tells the story of a Jew called Yasif who, like many other Jews in the Ottoman state, rose to a high position in the fiscal system, the principal field open to Jews, and who, like many other Jews treading the same path, became immensely hated. When Yasif tried to implement some new fiscal regulations, he was killed by Egyptian troops, and the Cairo mob burned his body to ashes. Typically, the poem indicates that Yasif's appearance in Cairo "riding on his horse" was in itself revolting.[6]

These references to the inferior status of Jews are corroborated by many European observers. In his authoritative book *Manners and Customs of the Modern Egyptians,* Edward W. Lane wrote of the Jews of Egypt that at the time of his study (1833–1835) they "are under a less oppressive government in Egypt than in any other country of the Turkish Empire . . . ," but "they are held in the utmost contempt and abhorrence by the Muslims in general." Lane reports:

Not long ago, they used often to be jostled in the streets of Cairo, and sometimes beaten merely for passing on the right hand of a Muslim. At present, they are less oppressed; but still they scarcely ever dare to utter a word of abuse when reviled or beaten unjustly by the meanest Arab or Turk; for many a Jew has been put to death upon a false and malicious accusation of uttering disrespectful words against the Kur-an or the Prophet. It is common to hear an Arab abuse his jaded ass, and, after applying to him various opprobrious epithets, end by calling the beast a Jew.[7]

Thus the evidence on the position of Jews in the Ottoman Empire, to be found in the various contemporary sources, points in one direction: under the Ottomans, and, especially in the periods subsequent to the height of their power, Jews were often maltreated and subjected to excessive impositions.

The realization that Jews in this part of the world were oppressed as well creates the temptation to shift to the other extreme and conclude that this case is no more than another variation on the persecution of the Jews in Europe.[8] This impression is reinforced by the fact that in the nineteenth century blood libel—the most demonic type of anti-Jewish persecution contrived by Christian Europe and the manifestation of the darkest undercurrents of its anti-Jewish bias—made its appearance in this region. Blood libels were reported in Aleppo (1810, 1853), Beirut (1824), Antioch (1826), Hamma (1829), Tripoli (1834), Damascus (1840, 1848, 1890), Dayr al-Qamar (1847), Cairo (1844, 1901–1902), Alexandria (1870, 1881), Damanhur (1877), and in several other places. The most famous of these libels was the Damascus affair of 1840, in which several Jews were tortured to death.[9]

Nevertheless, the similarities should not be allowed to blur the fundamental differences between the two cases. The sharp dichotomy of Christian and Jew, so prevalent in Europe, was not paralleled in Muslim-Jewish relationships in the lands of Islam, and certainly not in the heterogeneous Ottoman Empire. Jews were indeed "second-class" subjects in the sultan's domains, but their position was not unique. They constituted a part of the millet system (*dhimmi* communities) of the Ottoman state, and essentially their status was similar to that of the millets of the Armenians, the Greek-Orthodox, and the other denominations. The singularity of the Jewish condition in Europe and the loaded tension of Christian-Jewish bipolarity were absent in the Muslim-Jewish relationship.

That is not to say that the positions of Jews and Christians in Muslim society were identical. Jews do appear in the Koran as persecutors of prophets and enemies of the believers, but they were never accused of theocide and their religion was never categorically denounced, as in Christianity. The Jewish millet was indeed in a disadvantageous position compared to other millets, but there were also cases where the opposite was true. In the *tanzimat* period, for example, when Christian millets were increasingly associated in the popular mind with the encroachments by Western powers, Jews were in certain cases spared from violence directed specifically at Christians.

Therefore, it is one thing to point out that Jews in Islam were obligated to wear distinctive clothes and quite another to state that the yellow badge of shame was invented by the Muslims. The distinctive clothes that the Jews wore did not single them out from other groups which had their own distinctive clothes, and they did not reflect the deep condemnation which was characteristic of the Christian attitude. Similarly, it should be noted that blood libels were introduced into the area by Christians, not by Muslims, and in a sense were a reflection of the measure of westernization accomplished in the nineteenth century. On a more concrete level, they reflected the fierce competition which evolved between local Christians and Jews in business and occupational opportunities opened up by the process of westernization—a competition in which Muslims were often mere bystanders.

The pitfall of equalizing the disparities is particularly threatening to historians who rely primarily on Jewish sources. Characteristically, the descriptions of the condition of Jews in the region provided by these sources are dominated by a terminology and a conceptual framework which stress the universalistic nature of the Jewish predicament. Contemporary letters, petitions, and memoranda, many of them dispatched to Jewish communities in Europe,[10] depict the difficulties encountered by Jews in the East as *gezerot, hamat ha-mezik, pera'ot, tzarot hatzorer*—expressions used to describe the systematic persecution of Jews in Europe, or for that matter anywhere, throughout Jewish history. The references to Muslim rule in these dispatches imprinted on the minds of their readers (sometimes perhaps deliberately) an image of an oppressive force motivated by the same inherent animosity to the Jewish people which motivated Gentiles everywhere.

When these sources report on the brutal looting of Jews in a certain town by marauders or nomads, it is hardly possible to learn from them that, in fact, this reflected the deterioration of security from which non-Jews in that region also suffered. When they describe extortions ruthlessly imposed on a Jewish community in a provincial capital they do not show that within the decaying and hard-pressed provincial administration a governor often attempted to milk dry millets, merchant guilds, village communities, or any other groups which possessed some wealth and were within his reach. It is true that Jewish communities were often more vulnerable and defenseless than other groups, but this does not change the fact that their misery reflected the general decline of the empire rather than a deliberate anti-Jewish policy. Only comparison to local non-Jewish sources, particularly Turkish and Arabic, would set the facts in their proper perspective and provide an evaluation which tends toward neither excessive idealization nor undue darkening of Jewish realities in the Ottoman period.

Arab Nationalism Versus "Zionism"

With the emergence of Arab nationalism and its conflict with the Jewish nationalist movement, the dilemma assumed a new form. Protagonists of the Arab cause took up the argument that Arab nationalism has no conflict with Jews as such; that only Zionism, which is an alien and disruptive force, is the enemy of Arabism; and that Arabs can live and have lived in perfect harmony with the Jews in their midst and with Judaism in general. It is claimed that Arabs pointedly distinguish between Jews, who are a religious denomination perfectly acceptable to the Arabs, and Zionists, who purport to represent an actually non-existent Jewish nation, which would never be accepted by the Arabs.[11]

The proposition that modern Arabism has no antagonism toward the Jews is even less tenable than the allegation of Jewish-Islamic symbiosis in traditional society. Interestingly enough, the Arabs themselves, who vehemently reject the premises of Zionism, often expound, explicitly or implicitly, the notion that Zionism is an innate phenomenon in Jewish history and emanates from the intrinsic logic of its particular cause. Negib Azoury, the precursor of political Arab nationalism, defines Zionism as *"l'effort latent des Juifs pour reconstituer sur une très large échelle l'ancienne monarchie d'Israel."*[12] Political and intellectual leaders, particularly of conservative Islamic trends, have often called upon Muslims to draw inspiration from the fact that even the Jews, "the most despised religion," managed to accomplish a revival in the modern world and set out to reestablish their past glory as a political power.[13] All such pronouncements take for granted that Judaism, like Islam, is originally and potentially a political community and that the Zionist endeavor represents a collective effort of world Jewry.

When Arabs have resorted to violence, as a response to Zionism, they have vented their wrath on Jews, not discriminating between Zionist and non-Zionist. In fact, the victims of Arab riots in Palestine, after the establishment of the Mandate, were the centuries-old Jewish communities of the old city of Jerusalem (1920, 1929), Hebron (1929), and Safed (1929). The Jews massacred in these places were of the "old Yishuv," which was hardly involved in the Zionist movement and often came out openly against it. The same is true with regard to anti-Jewish violence in the Arab countries. The Palestine conflict, especially after 1936, intensified the antagonism toward the local Jewish communities. With the gradual withdrawal of British and French control, assaults on local Jewish communities in several Arab states became more murderous. In Syria attacks on the Jewish quarter of Damascus were particularly frequent in 1938, when several Jews were stabbed to death. Another wave of assaults took place in 1944–1945. In Egypt the first large-scale anti-Jewish riots took place in Cairo in 1945, when a synagogue, a hospital, and several other Jewish institutions were destroyed. Anti-Jewish violence reached its peak in Iraq, the first major Arab state to be granted independence. Several Jews were assassinated in Iraqi towns in 1936 and 1937. The worst, however, was to come in 1941, under the rule of Rashid Ali, in the so-called *farhud* of Baghdad. The *farhud* carried all the attributes of a European pogrom: looting, burning, raping, and killing. Some 170 to 180 Jews were killed and hundreds were wounded. In all of these cases the targets were the Jewish communities as such, the declarations of their leaders disavowing any affiliation with Zionism being disregarded.[14]

With the establishment of the State of Israel, anti-Jewish violence took the form of systematic persecutions. With the exception of several countries, such as Lebanon and Morocco, where the authorities took steps to protect their Jewish subjects, most Arab governments introduced harsh anti-Jewish measures, confining Jews to ghettos, placing them under surveillance, conducting frequent arrests and show trials, confiscating property, and molesting Jews in many other ways. The local Jewish communities practically became hostages in the Arab countries, and mobs took out on them their hostility towards Israel and their frustrations from recurring defeats in their encounters with the Israeli army. In 1948 more than a hundred Jews were killed in Syria and Egypt alone. In 1956 and 1967 Jews were fiercely attacked in several places.

The present-day sufferings of Jews who have remained in the ghettos of Arab countries, notably Syria, are too well known to need any elaboration here. What may be interesting to note, however, is the fact that even the Palestinian *fedayeen* organizations— which, more than any Arab government, stress in their propaganda the distinction between Zionist and Jew—have also chosen regular Jewish institutions as their targets, notably in a series of terrorist operations in Europe between October 1972 and February 1973.

Arabic publications, unlike the propaganda literature published by Arabs for external consumption, refer to Zionism and world Jewry synonymously and denounce both in the same venomous language. The volume of anti-Jewish publications issued in the Arab states has reached staggering proportions. The *Protocols of the Elders of Zion* have been issued in several editions, including one published by the Egyptian government. Other propaganda treatises have been written on such outlandish subjects as "Human Sacrifices in the Talmud."[15]

Muslim leaders have produced books and pamphlets, and issued several resolutions and *fatwas* that are vehemently anti-Jewish. Thus, for example, the Islamic Congress held in Amman in September 1967 laid down in its resolutions that "all Muslim peoples, together and individually, must boycott the Jews and treat them as sworn enemies." The *ulama* of al-Azhar were particularly active in issuing anti-Jewish rulings.

The communications media, controlled in most Arab countries by the government, have also from time to time expounded the same concepts. Anis Mansur, one of the leading Egyptian journalists, had this to say on the subject:

The Jews are real wild beasts, interested only in taking revenge on the oppressor and oppressed, i.e., all of mankind. They are the enemies of mankind and what they do in the occupied land Hitler did not manage to do. They use kinds of torture and terror unknown in History. Therefore people all over the world have begun to think kindly of the genius who did not burn the remaining Jews. . . . Treason is in the nature of the Jews. They have no respect for the religion of others and are devoted to no people but themselves. They are racialist, respect whites only and expel even black and yellow Jews. Jews lie when they speak of dual loyalty, to their fatherland and to Israel. They are loyal to Israel alone. Every Jew is an Israeli. They migrate to Israel from East and West. Thus they are traitors to every country and spy on it. With the same loyalty and sincerity the Jews have sold Hitler and Germany to Russia and America. People all over the world have found out that Hitler was right. The Jews respect neither right nor religion nor moral values. They are bloodsuckers, interested in destroying the world so that Israel will survive. They are interested in the destruction of the world which has expelled and rejected them, heaped scorn on them for hundreds of years, burnt them in Hitler's crematoria . . .one million . . .two . . .six million of them.[16]

Thus, the allegation that Arabs harbor no animosity toward the Jews is not too difficult to disprove. But, once again, the refutation of one allegation induces some observers to shift to the other extreme. It is now argued that the Arabs took over where the Nazis left off and, carrying the banner of the struggle against the "Jewish conspiracy," have become the most ardent anti-Semites of our time.

This view should not be dismissed too lightly. As seen above, Arabs today do disseminate the anti-Semitic doctrine, and they do it with great intensity. Coupled with Arab threats to annihilate Israel, this strain in the Arab posture cannot but be seen as a serious menace. However, it should be borne in mind that there are some significant differences between the Arab stance and European anti-Semitism. Most of the Arab anti-Semitic literature is not indigenous but an importation from the outside. It is mostly produced and distributed, directly or indirectly, through government agencies and does not emanate from the grass roots. As shown in the first part of this paper, Islam does not nurture anti-Jewish prejudices to the same extent as Christianity, and the European myth of the Jews as a satanic force associated with the Antichrist and as a metaphysical symbol of eternal condemnation does not exist in Arab tradition. Jews, as such, cannot be seen as aliens in this part of the world and their position has never been marked by uniqueness. The whole racist element of European anti-Semitism is irrelevant for Arab society. Finally, anti-Jewish prejudice in Arab-speaking society does not have the historical associations, as in Europe, with recurring attempts to wipe out the Jewish people. In this sense anti-Semitism is a deliberate transplant.

Nevertheless, this does not necessarily have to remain so. The cumulative effect of continued dissemination of anti-Jewish themes through the media and indoctrination of the young generation with anti-Jewish convictions through the school system may eventually naturalize anti-Semitism in Arab society. At that point the method applied in this paper, to avoid both Scylla and Charybdis, would no longer apply.

NOTES

1. For illustrations of this allegation see Y. Harkabi, *Arab Attitudes to Israel* (Jerusalem, 1970), chap. 5.

2. Geoffrey Furlonge, *Palestine Is My Country, The Story of Musa Alami* (London, 1969), pp. 27–28.

3. See S.D. Goitein, *Jews and Arabs* (New York, 1955), pp. 67 ff.

4. Ahmad al-Budayri al-Hallaq, *Hawadith Dimashq al-yawmiyya,* ed. by Ahmad Izzat Abd al-Karim (Damascus, 1959), p.112.

5. Ibid., p. 39.

6. Gabriel Baer, "Anti-Jewish Poetry in Ottoman Egypt," paper read at the International Conference of Jewish Communities in Muslim Lands, Hebrew University, Jerusalem, 1974.

7. Original edition, pp. 512–13.

8. Notably Cecil Roth in *New Palestine,* 1946, and *Jewish Forum,* 1946.

9. Habib Faris, *Al-dhaba'ih al-bashariyya al-talmudiyya* (The Talmudic Human Sacrifices) (Cairo, 1890); J.M. Landau, *Jews in Nineteenth-Century Egypt* (New York, 1969)

10. See, e.g., the documents published by A. Ya'ari in his *Igrot Erez Yisrael* (Tel Aviv, 1933); and *Masot Erez-Yisrael* (Tel Aviv, 1936).

11. Harkabi, *loc. cit.*

12. N. Azoury, *Le Reveil de la Nation Arabe* (Paris, 1905), p.v.

13. D. F. Green, ed., *Arab Theologians on Jews and Israel* (Geneva, 1974).

14. Hayim Cohen, *The Jews of the Middle East, 1860–1972* (Jerusalem, 1973), chap.1. Shortly after the conclusion of the Seminar on Violence and Defense, Albert Memmi published his *Juifs et Arabes* (Paris, 1974), a response to Muammar Qaddafi's "invitation" to the Jews to return to the Arab lands "where they had always lived in peace." Memmi's book is a powerful refutation, drawing upon personal experience, of the myth of the idyllic life of the Jews under Arab and Muslim rule.

15. This theme appears, for example, in many Arabic works of Muhammad al-Ghazzali, a former ideologue of the Muslim Brotherhood in Egypt.

16. *Al-Akhbar,* Cairo, 19 Aug. 1973.

URIEL TAL

10   Violence and the Jew in Nazi Ideology

There can be no discussion of violence in Central and Western Europe in the modern era without reference to the Holocaust. While this paper does not discuss the violence of the Holocaust per se, its focus is the conceptual framework that was created by Nazism and consequently helped to prepare the ground for the Holocaust.[1]

The semantic and ideational meaning of the concept of "violence" has been defined by some of the leading ideologists of Nazism,[2] such as Carl Schmitt, Ernst Forsthoff, Ernst Rudolf Huber, Ernst Krieck, and Ernst Jünger. According to Jünger, "violence" *(Gewalt)* is "the transformation of strength into that political power *(Macht)* that motivates history. . . ."[3] By "strength" Nazi ideologists meant the internal power to resist external impact, influence, stress, pressure, or force. Strength was understood in terms of a personal inner power often articulated in terms derived from pietistic language. We see this in Krieck—". . . innere Kraft die sich in dem innersten unserer Seele regt [inner strength that stirs us at the core of our soul]"—or even more so in Ernst Jünger —". . .ein Machtwort erginge in meinem Innwendigen an mich [a mighty message befell me in my inwardness] . . . und meine Seele entflammte [and my soul took fire] . . . in Kämpfes Ungestüm [in the violence of struggle]. . . ."[4] Strength was understood as a form of one's individual solidity, a kind of power stemming or emerging from one's individual faith, conviction, or integrity; it was a certain kind of firmness, a form of moral or intellectual courage. Violence, or might, on the other hand, was considered the result of the transmission of strength from the individual to society, from man to the citizen, from society to the state, from the nation to the race, from the state to the Reich, and from the Reich through the party to its embodiment, to its highest, purest realization, its incarnation in the Führer.[5]

Therefore, violence did not necessarily or exclusively mean simply the use of brute force. Of course, it goes without saying that this kind of explicit, overt force, mainly in terms of "political might," was one of the main manifestations of Nazi violence from its very beginnings. Carl J. Friedrich made this clear by enumerating some of the main characteristic features of totalitarian regimes: the predominance of an official ideology covering all vital aspects of man's existence; the rule of a single political party passionately and unquestioningly dedicated to the ruling ideology; a technologically conditioned almost total monopoly of the control of all means of power, including mass communication or education; and a system of terroristic police control often methodically exploiting scientific psychology or sociology.[6]

However, violence as an integral part of the Nazi ideology and regime as a whole was meant to be applied rather indirectly. From its very beginnings, among the Free Corps and the Schutz und Trutz Bund during the first years of the Weimar Republic,[7] as well as among its first student organizations,[8] and more so later with the establishment of the Third Reich,[9] Nazism intended to develop, groom, educate, and mold a new type of man, a man who did not need the power of the police or any other kind of *Anwendung von Zwang* ("application of coercion") to make him conform to the norms of the state or of society. The type of person Nazism tried to create was one who would demand of himself to act, think, feel, and believe according to what the regime expected of him, or according to what he expected the regime might expect from him. The entire complex of ideological and normative expectations applying to a member of the Aryan race was to be internalized and acted upon by the individual as a matter of course, lest he lose his peace of mind. In the long run, instead of exercising violent power by means of police coercion, Nazism intended to indoctrinate its youth so that no external violence would be needed in order to ensure the faithfulness of the German, or, more precisely, his total identification with the state, the race, the Reich, and their culmination and essence: the Führer.[10]

This complete identification with the totality of the Reich indicates the deeper meaning of violence in the Nazi era. Ernst Krieck emphasized that instead of the use of police power, the political philosophy of Adam Müller was to be "... imprinted on the mind of our youth, for according to Müller the state means: ' . . .die Totalität der menschlichen Angelegenheiten, ihre Verbindung zu einem lebendigen Ganzen [the totality of human affairs, their binding into one living whole]. . . . ' "[11] Similarly, Ernst Forsthoff's definition of the *Totalität des Politischen* was accepted by many Nazi youth leaders as ". . . the essence of the inner strength . . . typical of the new Germanic man. . . ."[12]

Freedom Through Totalitarianism

Against this background let us now concentrate on analyzing a number of Ernst Krieck's lectures, some of which are as yet unpublished.[13] While in the final years of the Third Reich the authorities and party were critical of Krieck,[14] in the 1920s and when the Third Reich was established he was a recognized guide for young intellectuals, mainly products of the Nazi student unions of the Weimar Republic, and also for teachers, educators, and S.S. leaders. In one of his most important lectures, apparently delivered in 1932 at a meeting organized by S.S. Obersturmführer Johann von Leers, who was once "Schulungsleiter in der NSDSt.B. Reichsleitung,"[15] Krieck explained that the concept of violence–might signified "freedom." In style and content this resembles the first part of his book *Völkisch-politische Anthropologie,* Part I "Die Wirklichkeit" ("The Reality"), especially the section entitled "Das völkisch-politische Bild vom Menschen" ("The Folk-political Image of Man") (Leipzig, 1936, pp. 42–119).

Thus, according to this philosophy, the totalitarian regime that a dictatorship controls does not lead to a negation of human freedom but to its realization. Political totalitarianism is the guarantee of freedom, for in a system in which politics encompasses all of life the individual man is free of society from various points of view:

a) According to the Carl Schmitt school, said Krieck, social life is composed of dichotomies and antitheses—friend–foe, war–peace, resolution–argument, healthy naturalism–degenerate religion, strength–weakness, bravery–cowardice[16]—but the power of a dictatorship protects man from stumbling into such bipolarities and protects him from the fear and dread with which constant confrontation of choices burdens him; in particular dictatorship releases man from the negative extreme of the antitheses, from foe, weakness, cowardice, isolation, individuality, and degeneracy. Political totalitarianism is therefore a redeeming force, saving man from the constant fear of forces that are his opposite, that are foreign to him or endanger his existence.

b) Society is composed of masses and consequently of violent forces which dominate and oppress the individual; in a political regime based on dictatorial power, however, the individual attains his freedom on the one hand by being released from the mass and on the other by identifying with the political elite headed by the Führer. In a democratic order man is subject to ". . .Die Macht der Öffentlichkeit [the power of the public] . . . im totalen Staat befreit der Führer den Menschen von den Massen, von der bedrückenden Öffentlichkeit, von der degenerierenden Intellektualisierung des wahren Lebens, vom Parlamentarismus [in the total state the Führer frees man from the masses, from the repressive public, from the degenerating intellectualization of true life, from parliamentarism]. . . ."[17]

c) Society confronts the state and enslaves the individual in this struggle against the state, as exemplified by liberal society, which binds the individual to a parliament–party struggle and thus deprives him of responsibility for himself; responsibility is given to the parties and the parliament, which are no more than a sort of conglomeration of egotistical amorphous forces, narrow-minded and lacking public responsibility—a sort of sum total of the mass, which is faceless, characterless, unrealistic, and aimless. The power of a dictatorship, however, protects the individual from the Leviathan nature of this society, primarily by creating an identity between society and state by means of a process known as *totale politisierung aller Sozialprozesse* ("total politicization of all social life").

d) Society places man in a situation of "orphanhood" from any authority, while the power of a dictatorship provides man with authority, bestows authority upon him, spreads the wings of authority over him, and thus releases him from orphanhood, from isolation, and, to a great extent, from license as well.

e) In Western democratic society man is abandoned to economic forces which for him as an individual are arbitrary since as an individual he has no control over them. The power of a dictatorial regime, however, controls the economy as well, and thus man's very identification with that power and his surrender to its authority makes him a party also to the economic factors operating in the state. On this point Krieck no longer sang paeans of praise to the Gottfried Feder school, as expressed mainly in Feder's *Der deutsche Staat auf nationaler und sozialer Grundlage* ("The German State on National and Social Foundation") (Munich, 1931, 5th ed.), as he had done earlier. Now that the Feder school was no longer acceptable to the regime, Krieck praised the economic laws aimed at strengthening the position of capitalists and heavy industry, among them the "Gesetz über Betriebsvertretungen und über wirtschäftliche Vereinigungen" ("law concerning business representation and economic associations"), passed early in 1933,[18] and the "Gesetz über die Einziehung volks und staats-feindlichen Vermögens" ("law concerning the confiscation of property which is hostile to the state"), passed at the end of that year.[19] Here too Krieck stressed that the essence of these laws, dealing with labor relations and production, was the liberation of the working man from the particularist interests of what he called "miserly social pressure groups," bestowing upon him real freedom by the identification of his particularistic interests with universal interests of the state, the race, the party, the Reich, and the Führer: "Freedom means the liberation of man from himself through total identification with the general will, which is embodied in the Führer. . . ."[20]

This ideology, the main point of which is the attainment of individual liberty through identification with the general will personified by the Führer, still had several diverse trends in the late 1920s and early 1930s. Ernst Jünger represented the individualistic, or perhaps rather aristocratic, position in that he stressed that the citizen should refrain from completely annulling his individual will before the general will embodied in the Führer. If he does so, Jünger said, he will be incapable of blending with the general will through his own decision and desire. Just as there is some modicum of willing devotion or conscious self-sacrifice epitomized in the battlefield, in war, or, as Kurt Ziesel said, "in creative war" *(vom schöpferischen Kriege),* it is desirable to have room for it in the political regime of a totalitarian state. The ideal totalitarian regime is one which allows the individual his individuality so that it can combine with the general will. This is true, claimed Jünger, in regard to the concept of the omnipotence of the state, for if the state chokes off all individual will, it will also choke off the individual's will to surrender himself to that *Omnipotenz.* On the other hand, Ernst Forsthoff as well as E.R. Huber contended that "die totale Inpflichtnahme jedes Einzelnen verpflichtet zu der Aufhebung des privaten Charakter der Einzelexistenz [the total dutifulness of each individual requires the abrogation of the private nature of individual existence]. . . ."[21]

The central part of Professor Ernst Krieck's address on "Die Intellektuellen und das Dritte Reich," apparently delivered in 1938, is published here for the first time. Attached to this English translation of the original are detailed notes and source materials contributing to a deeper understanding of this important text. The manuscript, as it appears in the Goebbels Collection in the YIVO archives (New York),[22] is not annotated, and all the bibliographic and historiographic data cited below, attached to the body of the text, have been prepared and inserted for this translation.

One of the chief difficulties confronting a totalitarian state (*der totale Staat*), and by this I mean Carl Schmitt's political-ideological system of past years and not the one he favors today, is the absorption of intellectuals in the political regime.[23]

In 1933, after we overcame un-German literature (*undeutsches Schrifttum*),[24] and again in 1934 with the publication of the loyalty declarations *(Bekenntnisse)* of scientists and scholars, such as the members of the Teachers Union (*N.S. Lehrerbund*),[25] we were still convinced that intellectuals would be guides and mentors for the nation and lead to an ideological renaissance *(weltanschauliche Erneuerung)*, to the reawakening of the Germanic spirit and thereby to the revival of the racial culture. The ideological foundations of this culture were laid by Eugen Dühring, who was Friedrich Engels' rival, by H.S. Chamberlain, who was the Comte de Gobineau's successor and rival, by Möller van den Bruck, who minted and revived the term "Third Reich" but remained imprisoned in the dreams of a conservative revolutionary, and by Dietrich Eckart, the Führer's close friend. In practice, however, this culture was constructed by the Führer himself and by Alfred Rosenberg, who is in charge of all aspects of National-Socialist ideology, and also by Walter Darré, one of the fathers of the movement for German colonization and expansion in Eastern Europe.[26]

We believed that the intellectuals would take a lesson from the Führer's ideological teachings, from his profound understanding of spiritual creativity and even of profound reading, as he clearly indicated in *Mein Kampf* and carried out together with Hermann Esser, his friend from the days of the revolutionary struggle.[27]

For real spiritual life does not exist in a vacuum, nor in a professor's study, nor through ignoring natural reality, but precisely through what Thomas Mann in his destructive work called the *Politisierung des Geistes.* . . .[28] Only the conquest of the spirit by the force of the regime, of policy, and also by physical force will set the spirit in its real place, which is in civilizations and not in spiritual abstract culture. The purpose of the spirit is to serve the race, the state, and, as Alfred Bäumler said, the spirit is to be encompassed in the totality of racialism *(Arteigenheit, Artgleich-heit)*[29]

Unfortunately only part of the intellegentsia chose that path, and many are having difficulties in finding their place in the *totale Führerstaat.* Since the great day of 1 August 1934[30] when the positions of party leader, head of state, and commander-in-chief were combined in the Führer, the traditionally liberal intellegentsia has begun to feel alien to our national homogeneity.

One of the illuminating examples of the dilemma which intellectuals, ideologists, and even fathers of the National-Socialist revolution find themselves in is that of Gottfried Benn. In his book *The New State and Intellectuals*[31] he still discerned very well that our national revolution *(Die Revolution vom Nationalen her)* was from the outset opposed to the individualistic approach characteristic of the intelligentsia. A few of these educated men were charmed by historical materialism, which is nothing but a "devilish Jewish invention," and the rest remained bound by the shackles of rationalism and by the Kantian tradition of the critique of pure reason, a tradition in which man is inveigled into sterile speculation and into criticism of the a priori conditions of knowledge to the point that the a posteriori confrontation with the object of knowledge and experience is completely denied to him, and this too is a typically talmudic Jewish invention. The intellectuals in the Weimar generation who are prepared to entrust their egos to a political-racial totality, or to the Führer, are few. The general will, as Ernst Forsthoff showed,[32] is realized in the Führer, and it is thus that the Aryan leadership realizes the essence of the German, and there is no room for other essential qualities like those of the Enlightenment, rationalism, liberalism, communism, or Judaism.

However, Gottfried Benn himself was a victim of the narcissistic urge of liberal intellectuals, and after the revolution was completely realized, he remained a revolutionary, a romantic, a dreamer, a prophet and a seer, and he was therefore correctly forbidden any literary-public activity.

Gottfried Benn erred as regards racism as well. Formerly he enthusiastically supported the idea of biological cultivation *(biologischen Züchtungsgedanken),* and was strict with himself when he had to examine his own racial purity, this examination having an element of moral self-criticism or even expiation and inner purification of a man who knows he is standing before the seat of judgment of nation, race, and blood. And despite all this, to this day he has not been able to understand what Friedrich Georg Jünger stated as early as 1926,[33] that the time for humanism and liberalism has passed and that nowadays blood and race are the place upon which man attains a consciousness of himself and thus freedom. Race and blood are unavoidable primeval forces with primeval power *(Urzwang)*, and in accepting the yoke of these forces man is liberated from enslavement to reason, logic, and other sterile forms of the human spirit.

Many of the intellectuals who did not grow up in the National-Socialist revolution have not learned how to free themselves from a position on the sidelines, from the contemplative, reflective approach, nor how to invest their whole might and strength in what Jünger called the intoxicating thing *(das Berauschende)* contained in racial nationalism. Diametrically opposed as it is to Marxism, which seeks to justify itself with the help of science, and to theology, which seeks to justify itself with the help of metaphysics,[34] National-Socialism requires no justification *(Rechtfertigung)* from any ideological system at all. Might *(Macht)* and honor *(Würde)*, race and blood, these are total facts; that is a kind of reality whose authority derives from itself. Jünger further stated that a "community of blood" *(Blutgemeinschaft)* does not need to justify itself, for it is an existential fact whose authority derives from itself, it is here *(sie ist da)*, and thus any moral grounding is superfluous.

Jünger, however, like revolutionary, visionary philosophers endowed with romantic yearning—and let us not forget Edgar J. Jung[35]—followed the path of Gottfried Benn and likewise failed to discern that with the establishment of the Third Reich the period of revolution came to an end and that of realization began, a period during which Germanic man is called upon to entrust his will to the Führer so that his private will is identified with the Führer's.

What then should we demand of the intelligentsia in the Third Reich?

a) Our first demand is that the members of that social group should free themselves from the heritage of cultural pessimism[36] which originated in the second half of the nineteenth century. This despair of culture, of the purpose of mankind's existence, of the future of the human spirit which was sown in the German soul by Schopenhauer, Gobineau, Nietzsche, and in our day also by Spengler, penetrated the consciousness of contemporary intellectuals, actually because of the supposed kinship, I stress "supposed," of this pessimism to the National-Socialist outlook.

It is true that from the historical, developmental point of view, we owe much to cultural pessimism. This view brought home to us the fact that rationalism cuts man from living, nonderivative contact with cosmic reality, with nature, in other words with the womb from which Germanic man emerged and in which his great vitality was formed—in other words his essence *(sein Wesen)*. This detachment made Germanic man so decadent that most of the pessimists prophesied physical annihilation *(Ausmerzung)*[37] for us and thus also the spiritual decline of our cultural heritage.

However, the idea of detachment is only another form of the principle of Marxist self-alienation *(Selbstentfremdung),*[38] which itself is only a continuation of the Judeo-Christian tenet according to which man is destined to be an alien, a stranger, an exile, a pilgrim in this world, until he is redeemed through the force of divine charisma.

About those who believe in this destructive pessimism which deprives Germanic man of consciousness of his strength and of the hereditary natural power with which he was blessed, thanks to his Nordic ancestors,[39] the Führer said not long ago that if we did not need intellectuals, who knows, it would perhaps be possible to destroy them *(". . . so könnte man sie ja, ich weiss nicht, ausrotten oder so was . . .)."*[40] We must therefore demand of our intellectuals that they change from melancholy pessimists to optimists who have faith in the Führer and, by virtue of that faith, in themselves as well.

b) Another demand is liberation from the bonds of individualism and adherence to the concept of race. Many intellectuals continue to laud the value of the individual as if individual life, and not the victory of the Aryan race, were the most important thing. Hence the historian Walter Frank questioned whether in our age, when great rulers and powers enter and exit from the stage of history, when nations are fighting for existence and nonexistence, for power and honor, the people who concentrate on themselves, on their own individuality, deserve to live *(des Lebens würdig)*. Similarly Hanns Johst, one of the leaders of National-Socialist culture, stated that the whole and not the individual, the race and not the man, are the important essentials.

The individual does not have immanent value; he is only one cell in the organic tissue called race; he lives thanks to it and for its sake. The scientific system of Eugen Fischer,[41] according to which hereditary characteristics should be considered the motive force of history, is the key to understanding the value of the individual. And there are scientists in the world rising to disagree with the possibility of proving the existence of race scientifically. However, we have learned from Chamberlain's and especially from the Führer's teachings that the verification of the existence of race, and perhaps of existence in general, does not require artificial scientific tools.

The fact of the existence of race is not doubtful, because man carries it in his heart, his spirit, his soul, or because man wants race to become a fact. And precisely this attitude, which moves the source of objectivity to the subject, is accepted even by outstanding scientists such as Otmar Freiherr von Verschuer. The best of our writers as well, in their important controversy against the decadence of Romain Rolland,[42] testified that the source of scientific truth is in feeling—not in critical reason, as stipulated by Kant,[43] and not in empirical findings, as stipulated by the English empiricists.

History is the arena for the struggle between the lofty, noble, pure racial type and what E. Jaensch described as the "antitype" *(Gegentyp),*[44] that is between good and bad, between Aryans and Jews (*Germanentum* and *Judentum*) between blood and metaphysics, between light and darkness, between primeval forces *(Urgewalten)* and the weak-mindedness of the rationalists.[45]

We must therefore demand of the intellectuals that they accept without compromise or hesitation the Führer's statement that the days of "personality principle" *(Persönlichkeitsprinzip)* are indeed over."[46]

Postscript

Salo Baron, in the first chapter of his monumental work *A Social and Religious History of the Jews,* analyzed the Jewish people's historic approach to power and concluded that in the course of history the Jews developed ". . . the refusal to recognize the powers of the day. Power itself often became the cause of suspicion and resentment rather than of admiration and acquiescence. . . . The religious and ethnic power of perseverance, rather than the political power of expansion and conquest, became the cornerstone of Jewish belief and practice. Such 'power' was naturally defensive and passive and mutual non-aggression was one of its major safeguards. . . ." This concept has its source as far back as the very beginning of the history of Israel, when we find " . . . early recognizing [of] the ultimate futility of even the greatest human power. . . ."

And since the very existence of Israel symbolized the negation of power and the priority of the spirit, Baron sums up as follows: "It was scarcely surprising that Nazism's concentrated fury hit the people whose entire career had longer and more persistently than any other embodied . . . historic fundamentals . . ." such as ". . . messianic humanitarianism and internationalism. . . . There have been many German thinkers who, glorifying power as do the spokesmen of no other nation. . . . reiterated that humanitarianism is a ruse of the weak, invented by the weak (especially the Jews). . . . The Jewish people . . . felt . . . that it possessed powers other than political, which were their full equivalent. . . ."

Primary and archival sources cited above bear witness to the fact that Baron's system is applicable to the Nazi period as well. From the beginning of modern anti-Semitism and racism in the last third of the nineteenth century, up to and including the Holocaust,[47] Judaism served as a symbol of nonsurrender to policies seeking to suppress individuality, intellectual freedom, and spiritual autonomy, substituting for the individual's inner strength violence in its complex sense—that is, total conformism, the extinction of individual will by the will of the Reich and the Führer.

NOTES

1. Cf. my review of Josef Ackermann's *Himmler als Ideologe* (Zurich-Frankfurt, 1970) in *Freiburger Rundbrief* (Freiburg i/Br., 1975–1976), pp. 14–22; see also the stimulating essay by Yehuda Bauer on "Implications of the Study of the Holocaust on our Historical Consciousness," The Institute of Contemporary Jewry, The Hebrew University, Study Circle on Diaspora Jewry in the Home of the President of Israel, Fifth Series, no. 5 (Jerusalem, 1972).

2. Some of the Nazi ideologists, such as Möller van den Bruck, Oswald Spengler, Carl Schmitt, Ernst Krieck, Ernst Jünger (and their teachings)

became controversial during the Third Reich, in particular at the beginning of World War II, but this does not necessarily diminish their historical impact. Moreover, in many cases the ideologists were apparently criticized precisely because of their far-reaching influence. It seems that Krieck's case is especially symptomatic; cf. the extensive material in the files of the "Beauftragter des Führers für die Uberwachung der gesamten geistigen und weltanschaulichen Schulung der NSDAP," Institut für Zeitgeschichte Archiv, Munich (henceforth cited IZGA), microfilms MA-611, pp. 59055–59201, especially "Gutachten Baumler on Krieck's Lebensphilosophie"; also ibid., pp. 59286–543, 59583–641, 59650–693. Anton Hoch, Chief Archivist, and his staff were exceedingly kind in allowing me to utilize the archival materials of the IZGA and in giving me the benefit of their professional advice.

The relationship of Carl Schmitt to Nazi ideology, policy, and anti-Semitism has been thoroughly investigated by George Schwab against the background of Schmitt's entire political thought on German statehood. Accordingly, Schmitt continued to oppose Nazism until 1933, arguing "that only those parties not intent on subverting the state be granted the right to compete for parliamentary and governmental power." Referring to Schmitt's *Legalität und Legitimität* (Munich, 1932; Berlin, 1968), Schwab correctly concludes that "this obviously meant driving the extremists on both sides of the political spectrum from the open arena"; cf. *The Concept of the Political by Carl Schmitt,* translation, introduction, and notes by George Schwab with comments by Leo Strauss (New Brunswick, N. J., 1976), p. 14. Schwab has shed new light on the rather controversial part Schmitt played both in the Weimar Republic and the Third Reich and was right in pointing out that Carl Schmitt was not simply one of those who directly "paved the way for the Führerstaat." See also G. Schwab, *The Challenge of the Exception: An Introduction to the Political Ideas of Carl Schmitt between 1921 and 1936* (Berlin, 1970), chaps. 3, 5–9, and conclusion. Additional archival source material on Nazi criticism of Carl Schmitt after 1936 is to be found among the "classified" propaganda booklets published by the governmental department of Alfred Rosenberg: *Mitteilungen zur Weltanschaulichen Lage,* III, no. 1 (8 Jan. 1937), 1–15, Bundesarchiv, Koblenz, N.S.D. 16/38. I am indebted to Heinz Boberach, Chief Archivist at the Federal Archives, Koblenz, Germany, for his advice and permission to quote these sources.

3. Ernst Krieck, "Die Intellektuellen und das Dritte Reich" (1938?). This paper, called "Vortragsmanuskript," parts of which are published herein for the first time, was found among various additional typewritten and as yet unpublished manuscripts in the Goebbels Collection of Clip-

pings and Offprints, parcel no. 4, YIVO Institute for Jewish Research, New York. The paper was generously put at my disposal by Ezekiel Lipschutz, Archivist at YIVO.

The contribution of the historian Jacob L. Talmon to the study of violence is well known. In addition to his Hebrew work *In the Era of Violence* (Tel Aviv, 2nd. ed. 1975), the following definition is extremely significant for our study: "Everyone talks of rights but everywhere violence triumphs. Rights are won by force alone, and every act of violence is committed in the name of rights . . . the right to employ violence has been given the dignity of a dogma . . ." (Talmon, *The Unique and the Universal: Some Historical Reflections* [New York, 1965], p. 165; see also pp. 119–64 on the universal significance of modern anti-Semitism).

4. Krieck, p. 2. On the historical form and impact of pietistic language, cf. August Langen, *Der Wortschatz des deutschen Pietismus* (Tubingen, 1968), pp. 390 ff. Also cf. Peter von Polenz, "Sprach purismus und Nationalsozialismus," in Eberhard Lämmert et al., *Germanistik eine deutsche Wissenschaft,* (Frankfurt a/M., 1967), pp. 111 ff. See also Koppel S. Pinson, *Pietism as a Factor in the Rise of German Nationalism* (New York, 1968 [1934]), pp. 153–79.

5. Krieck, pp. 2–4. On the political, legal, and ideological background, cf. one of the essential sources, Ernst Rudolf Huber, *Verfassungsrecht des Grossdeutschen Reiches* (Hamburg, 1937–1939), p. 213. Cf. also the excellent chapter "Der totale Führerstaat," in Eleonore Sterling, *Der Unvollkommene Staat-Studien über Diktatur und Demokratie* (Frankfurt a/M, 1965), pp. 281 ff.

6. Carl J. Friedrich, "The Unique Character of Totalitarian Society," in *Totalitarianism,* ed. by Carl J. Friedrich (New York, 1954, 1964), pp. 52–53.

7. Robert G.L. Waite, *Vanguard of Nazism: The Free Corps Movement in Postwar Germany (1918–1923)* (Cambridge, Mass., 1970 [1952]), chap. 8, pp. 183 ff; Uwe Lohalm, *Völkischer Radikalismus: die Geschichte des Deutschvolkischen Schutz und Trutz Bundes, 1919–1923* (Hamburg, 1970), VI, parts 2 and 4.

8. Anselm Faust, *Der Nationalsozialistische Deutsche Studentenbund— Studenten und Nationalsozialismus in der Weimarer Republik* (Dusseldorf, 1973), I, pp. 128–40.

9. One of the important primary sources is Rudolf Benze, Gesamtleiter des Deutschen Zentralinstituts für Erziehung und Unterricht, *Erziehung im Grossdeutschen Reich* (Frankfurt a/M, 1943), 3d. ed., Auflage, p. 14 ff.

10. Baldur Schirach, *Die Hitler-Jugend, Idee und Gestalt* (Berlin, 1934);

cf. "Rede des Reichsjugendführer Baldur von Schirach auf dem Empfangsabend des Aussenpolitischen Amtes der NSDAP an 12. Mai 1935 über 'Wesen und Aufbau der Hitler-Jugend,' " in *Dokumente der deutschen Politik,* vol. 3 (Berlin, 3rd. ed. 1938), 262–73, reprinted in Hans Jochen Gamm, *Führung und Verführung Pädagogik des Nationalsozialismus* (Munich, 1964), Dokument 58, pp. 315 ff.

11. Krieck, p. 8. At this point the far-reaching impact of Othmar Spann's *Der wahre Staat* (Leipzig, 1921) on Krieck's ideology seems obvious; cf. Krieck's *Volkisch-politische Anthropologie* (Leipzig, 1936) (henceforth *Anthropologie*), pp. 97 ff. Spann is another example of a prominent early proponent of Nazism whose teachings became highly controversial after Nazism was transformed from an ideology into a political regime. On his influence on E. G. Jung's messianic interpretation of the Reich, see Hans-Joachim Schwierskott, *Arthur Möller wan den Bruck und der revolutionäre Nationalismus in der Weimarer Republik* (Berlin, Frankfurt, 1962), p. 110.

12. Krieck, p. 8.

13. See above, n. 3.

14. *IZGA,* MA-611, pp. 59163–424.

15. Krieck, pp. 42 ff.

16. Cf. Kurt Lenk, "Schmitt's Dezisionismus," in *Volk und Staat strukturwandel politischer Ideologien in 19. und 20. Jahrhundert* (Stuttgart-Berlin-Cologne-Mainz, 1971), pp. 120–31.

17. Krieck, p. 40.

18. *Reichstagsblatt,* I, no. 31 (5 April 1933), 161.

19. Ibid., no. 55 (27 May 1933), 293; no. 81 (15 July 1933), 479.

20. Krieck, p. 38. Cf. Kurt Sontheimer, *Antidemokratisches Denken in der Weimarer Republik* (Munich, 1968) p. 171; cf. the rather biased essay by Martin Greiffenhagen, "Der Totalitarismusbegriff in der Regimenlehre," in M. Greiffenhagen et al., *Totalitarismus Zur Problematik eines politischen Begriffs* (Munich, 1972), p. 23 ff. As to the socioeconomic background of David Schoenbaum, see "The Third Reich and Business," in *Hitler's Social Revolution: Class and Status in Nazi Germany, 1933–1939* (New York, 1967), pp. 113–51.

21. Cited by Krieck, p. 35. This dilemma between the individual and society has historical roots in German pietism; cf. K. S. Pinson's book on pietism (*op. cit.,* n. 4), chap. 2, "Individuality and Individualism," pp. 63–75, and chap. 3, "The One and the Many," pp. 76–101.

22. Ibid., n. 3.

23. Heinrich Muth, "Carl Schmitt in der deutschen Innenpolitik des Sommers 1932," in *Historische Zeitschrift* (Munich, 1971), pp. 75–147. Cf.

Sterling, *op. cit.,* pp. 283 ff. See also George L. Mosse, *The Crisis of German Ideology: Intellectual Origins of the Third Reich* (New York, 1971 [1964]), pp. 237 ff.

24. Richard Drews and Alfred Kantorowicz, *Verboten und Verbrannt: Deutsche Literatur 12 Jahre unterdruckt* (Berlin, 1947); Joseph Wulf, *Literatur und Dichtung im Dritten Reich: eine Dokumentation* (Gutersloh, 1963) (henceforth *Deutsche Literatur*), pp. 41, 44–67. This collection of sources, like some others by Joseph Wulf, shows evidence of prejudiced editing and does not present a sufficiently balanced or objective picture. At the same time, a considerable number of the documents included in these collections are definitely of scientific value, and we utilize them in this paper when the material stands the test of objective historiography. See also "Die 'Unbildung' der Schriftstellerorganisationen," and "Die Bücherverbrennung," in Dietrich Strothmann, *Nationalsozialistische Literaturpolitik: ein Beitrag zur Publizistik im Dritten Reich,* Abhandlungen zur Kunst, Musik, un Literaturwissenschaft, no. 13 (Bonn, 3rd. ed. 1968), pp. 67–80.

25. "Bekenntnisse der Professoren und Studenten," in Léon Poliakov and Joseph Wulf, *Das Dritte Reich und seine Denker-Dokumente* (Berlin-Grunewald, 1959) (henceforth *Denker*), pp. 104–16. On the attitudes of Martin Heidegger, cf. the somewhat biased essay by Paul Hühnerfield, "Wissensdienst für Hitler," in *In Sachen Heidegger: Versuch über ein deutsches Genie* (Munich, 1961), pp. 96 ff.

26. This opinion of Krieck's on the principle forerunners of the racist Nazi ideology has been confirmed by contemporary historiography: see Fritz Stern, *The Politics of Cultural Despair: A Study in the Rise of the Germanic Ideology* (Berkeley and Los Angeles, 1961), part III, pp. 183 ff.; Uriel Tal, *Christians and Jews in the Second Reich, 1870–1914* (Jerusalem, 1969) (Hebrew), pp. 175–234; Werner Jochmann, "Die Ausbreitung des Antisemitismus," in Mosse E. Werner, ed., *Deutsches Judentum in Krieg und Revolution, 1916–1923* (Tubingen, 1971), pp. 409–510; Karl Schwedhelm, ed., *Propheten des Nationalismus* (Munich, 1969), pp. 36–55, 105–23, 139–58, 159–75. See also Reinhard Bollmus, *Das Amt Rosenberg und seine Gegner—zum Machtkampf im nationalsozialistischen Herrschaftssystem,* Studien zur Zeitgeschichte, hrsg. vom *IZG* (Stuttgart, 1970), pp. 27–60, 153–250.

27. Werner Maser, *Adolf Hitler's Mein Kampf: eine kritische Analyse* (Munich, 1969), pp. 60–61; cf. A. Hitler, *Mein Kampf,* 496–73 Auflage, Volksausgabe 1939, pp. 36 ff.

28. Thomas Mann, *Betrachtungen eines Unpolitischen* (Berlin, 1920, 15th–18th ed.), pp. xxiii–xxxix.

29. A. Bäumler, *Nachschrift von U. Coede: "Vorlesungen über Geschichtsphilosophie, 1939."* YIVO Archives, Hauptamt Wissenschaft, 236, MK-3. On Alfred Bäumler's approach to the secularization of theological patterns of thought and articulation, see Uriel Tal, "Forms of Pseudo-Religion in the German Kulturbereich Prior to the Holocaust," in *Immanuel: A Semi-Annual Bulletin of Religious Thought and Research in Israel*, no. 3 (Jerusalem, 1973–1974), pp. 68–73.

30. Krieck is referring to the regulation of 1/8/1934 which merged the top state function *(Staatsoberhaupt)* with the top government function *(Reichskanzler)* in the person of the dictator, or, as the source has it, the Führer (*R.G.B.I.* 1934, part I, p. 747); cf. Ernst Rudolf Huber, *Verfassungsrecht des Grossdeutschen Reiches* (Hamburg 1937–1939), p. 213; cf. Peter Diehl Thiele, *Partei und Staat im Dritten Reich: Untersuchungen zum Verhältnis von MSDAP und allgemeiner innerer Staatsverwaltung* (Munich, 2nd. ed. 1971), pp. 1–32.

31. Gottfried Benn, *Der neue Staat und die Intellektuellen* (Stuttgart-Berlin, 1933), p. 9: ". . . Der neue Staat is gegen die Intellektuellen entstanden." Cf. Eykman Christoph, "Spiel, Peristaltik und Mutation: Gottfried Benns Verhältnis zur Geschichte," in *Geschichtspessimismus in der deutschen Literatur des zwanzigsten Jahrhunderts* (Bern-Munich, 1970), pp. 95–111. Also see Gottfried Benn's description of the forms of thought, emotion, and articulation in Stefan George's influential work "Das neue Reich" (1919): ". . . Es ist das Formgefühl, dass die grosse Transzendenz der neuen Epoche sein wird, die Fuge des zweiten Zeitalters, das erste schuf Gott nach seinem Bilde, das zweite der Mensch nach seinen Formen, das Zweischenreich des Nihilismus ist zu Ende . . . ," quoted in Ernst Loewy, *Literatur unterm Hakenkreuz, Das Dritte Reich und seine Dichtung, eine Dokumentation* (Frankfurt a/M, 1969 [1966]), pp. 85–86. See also the extensive documentation on the "Stefan George Kreis" and on George's ideological and aesthetic influence, *Hauptamt Wissenschaft* 236 MK-5, YIVO Archives. See also George L. Mosse, "Caesarism, Circuses and Monuments," *Journal of Contemporary History*, VI, no. 2 (1971), 179–82.

32. Ernst Forsthoff, *Der totale Staat* (Hamburg, 1933), pp. 29–43.

33. Friedrich Georg Jünger, *Aufmarsch des Nationalismus* (Berlin, 1926), p. 65 ff.; also quoted in Loewy, pp. 81–82.

34. Ernst Krieck, *Völkische-politische Anthropologie*, part I (Leipzig, 1936), pp. 57–69.

35. Cf. Bernhard Jenschke, *Zur Kritik der konservativ-revolutionären Ideologie in der Weimarer Republik: Weltanschauung und Politik bei Edgar Julius Jung* (Munich, 1971), chaps. 3, 4, and 6.

36. See studies by Fritz Stern and Uriel Tal, cited above, n. 26. See also n. 31 in Christoph Eykman's *Geschichtspessimismus und Geschichtsphilosophie*, pp. 7–41.

37. On the origin of this symptomatic term, cf. Cornelia Berning, *Vom "Abstammungsnachweis" zum "Zuchtwart"—Vokabular des Nationalsocialismus* (Berlin, 1964), pp. 31–32.

38. Cf. Hubert Kiesewetter, "Der Rechtshegelianismus und das Dritte Reich," in *Von Hegel zu Hitler: eine Analyse der Hegelschen Machtstaatsideologie und der politischen Wirkungsgeschichte des Rechtshegelianismus* (Hamburg, 1974), pp. 233 ff.

39. Cf. Hans Jürgen Lutzhöft, *Der Nordische Gedanke in Deutschland, 1920–1940,* Kieler Historische Studien, vol. 14 (Stuttgart, 1971), pp. 111–84.

40. Vierteljahrshefte für Zeitgeschichte (Munich, 1958), Heft no. 2, p. 195 ff.; cf. the outstanding analysis of Hitler's rhetoric in Detlev Grieswelle, *Propaganda der Friedlosigkeit: eine Studie zu Hitlers Rhetorik, 1920–1933* (Stuttgart, 1972), pp. 148 ff.

41. Otmar Freiherr von Verscheur, "Die Aufgaben des Instituts für Erbbiologie und Rassenforschung"; cf. "Erblinien machen die Geschichte" in *Der Völkische Staat biologisch gesehen* (Berlin, 1933), pp. 17–19, quoted in *Denker,* pp. 416–17.

42. R. G. Binding, etc., "Sechs Bekenntnisse zum neuen Deutschland," in *Deutsche Literatur,* pp. 88 ff; cf. Loewy, pp. 75–76.

43. Cf. Kurt Sontheimer, *Antidemokratisches Denken in der Weimarer Republik: die politischen Ideen des deutschen Nationalismus zwischen 1918 and 1933* (Munich, 1968), p. 109: ". . . Die Idee des Krieges als einer Fügung des Schicksals, der man sich zu stellen habe, war in Deutschland trotz Kant viel vertrauter als die Idee des Ewigen Friendens, die man gern verachtlich als Humanitätsduselei abtat. . . ."

44. Erich Jaensch, *Der Gegentypus: psychologisch-anthropologische Grundlagen deutscher Kulturphilosophie* (Leipzig, 1938).

45. Cf. Ernst Krieck, *Das nationalsozialistische Deutschland und die Wissenschaft* (Hamburg, 1936), 35 pp.

46. A. Hitler, *Mein Kampf,* 469–73 Auflage Volksausgabe 1939, pp. 500 ff.

47. Cf. the penetrating study by Saul Friedlander, "Some Aspects of the Historical Significance of the Holocaust," in the *Jerusalem Quarterly* I, no. 1 (1976), 36–59. The essay is a major contribution to both Jewish and universal aspects in the study of mass movements and genocide. The text is an expansion of the Second Philip M. Klutznick International Lecture

on Contemporary Jewish Life and Institutions, delivered at the International Scholars' Conference on "The Holocaust—A Generation After," held in New York City, March 3–6, 1975, under the auspices of the Hebrew University Institute of Contemporary Jewry's International Committee.

MICHAEL CONFINO

11   Soviet Policy Versus the Jewish State

The intent of this paper is to address two main sets of issues and subjects: first, to present some basic features of the historical development of Russia's foreign policy in general; and, second, to analyze the problems created by the Soviet penetration in the Middle East and by Soviet involvement in Middle Eastern affairs.

Expansionist Strategy

Let us turn to the first of these subjects and outline the main features in the historical development of Russian and Soviet foreign policy. The first and most conspicuous feature during the last 250 years, from the beginning of the eighteenth century to the middle of the twentieth century, was the relative simplicity of Russian foreign policy—that is, a simplicity from the point of view of the relative stability of its aims and objectives and from the point of view of the relative uniformity of its methods. With respect to these aims and methods, the continuity is so striking that it seems at times that the course and orientation of Russian foreign policy remains almost unaffected by such factors and developments within the country as the personality of the leaders, the form of government, and the social and political regime.

This important feature—the relative simplicity—should be related here to what may be seen as its corollary with regard to foreign-policy making *toward* Russia and the Soviet Union. As stressed by Richard Pipes: "Overly sophisticated signals bewilder Russian leaders and can mislead them. . . . In principle, it does not pay to be too clever with Russian politicians: they are inclined to interpret ambiguity as equivocation, equivocation as weakness, and weakness as a signal to act."[1] In other words, waging a too sophisticated policy toward the Soviet Union creates many risks of misunderstandings, and the greater the sophistication the greater the risks. I need not elaborate on what a "misunderstanding" in foreign policy between superpowers may mean in our time.

To define very briefly the nature of the aims and methods mentioned above, one could say that until the 1950s these aims and methods, which appear so strikingly simple, were basically those of a continental power, a power with an enormous continental mass. This enormous hinterland is the basis of its foreign policy— not only the territorial basis but also a basic factor in shaping the political attitudes and mental structures of the people who formulate this policy. In other words, both the country's territorial vastness and its historical experience contributed to creating a certain pattern of thinking in matters of foreign policy. This historical experience includes, for example, the Northern War at the beginning of the eighteenth century between Russia and Sweden, in which the great military leader Charles XII finally lost to Peter the Great, who skillfully used Russia's hinterland. A similar pattern occurred a century later during the Napoleonic War, and again in World War II, with the Nazi invasion of Soviet Russia. Thus the Russian rulers should have felt a relatively high degree of security, thanks to this territorial depth of their defenses—an important fact not only in waging war but also in conducting foreign policy. Actually, and curiously enough, the Russians almost never seemed to feel secure enough in their huge empire and usually behaved as if they needed more space.

This brings us to the second feature of Russian foreign policy. While Russian foreign policy was that of a continental power, the drive and ethos of this policy was also one of continuous expansion. For this there is no need of proof other than the maps of Russia from the fifteenth century on, for they reflect the slow expansion from the small duchy of Moscow to the enormous empire of the U.S.S.R. today, engulfing many nationalities. An important feature of this territorial expansion was the fact that all the territory gained was contiguous to the mainland, to the territorial mass of the state. (The sole exception was Alaska, sold to the United States in 1867). These territories were in many respects ruled as colonies in the traditional sense of the word. The fact remains, however, that in the past Russian expansion proceeded according to the principle of territorial contiguity; Russia did not seek to have overseas dominions, and, accordingly, the traditional role of her navy remained negligible.

A further remark may be relevant here regarding the influence of the "continental factor" on the making of Russian foreign policy. A substantive change occurred in this respect in the late 1950s and early 1960s. Around that time Soviet political thinking and strategy began to show clear signs of a reorientation stemming from several factors, among them a reassessment of sea power and the role of ballistic weapons. This change also included a readiness and increased activism regarding the establishment of Soviet zones of influence in noncontiguous areas. In this respect the Middle East appears as one of the first such areas in which the Russians have tried to gain a permanent foothold.

The third feature regarding the position of Russia or of the Soviet Union in international relations was and still is the rule not to have enemies on two fronts and, of course, not to wage war on more than one simultaneously. With regard to the eighteenth and nineteenth centuries, this rule may also be formulated as follows: not to wage war without an ally in the West. In the eighteenth century Russia's western ally was Britain, during most of the nineteenth century her allies were Prussia and Austria; and later on, from the 1890s to 1914, it was France. This rule was a basic tenet of Russia's foreign policy. It was due to the fact that in spite of the enormous manpower, the country's territorial depth, etc., Russia's rulers were usually quite aware of her many weaknesses and her likely incapacity to overcome the strains of waging war on two fronts. This feature is a legacy of the past but also one which has perhaps the greatest relevance in our times because of the present state of relations between the Soviet Union and China. One of the reasons for the USSR's Western policy and détente is obviously the wish to avoid simultaneous conflict with China and in Western Europe.

The fourth and last feature of this foreign policy is its capability and skill in supporting and justifying Russian or Soviet selfish nationalist and imperialist policies by using altruistic arguments or broad humanitarian ideologies. Thus, for instance, in the past Russia very often used the argument of liberating the Slavs or the Orthodox Christians from the yoke of the Tartars, then of Turkey, as a respectable pretext for her own expansion. Moreover, this argument was used with regard to such peoples and religious communities in nineteenth-century Turkey, notwithstanding the fact that many other Slavs—Poles, Ukrainians, Byelorussians—were under Russian rule. According to this double standard, Slavs et al. were to be liberated from others but certainly not from Russian domination. Nevertheless, in this particular case, it served quite well the main aim of Russia's foreign policy—the control of the Turkish Straits.

During the Soviet period the continuity in using this technique is very clear, although a change of content occurred in the argumentation: the Communist ideology came to play the role that the Slavic race and the Orthodox faith had under the czars (besides the temporary use during World War II and briefly thereafter of the "Slav solidarity" slogan in order to mobilize support from the Slavic peoples). Under the Soviets, instead of being, as in the past, "the big sister of all the Slavic peoples," Russia became "the fatherland of the international proletariat." The practical result of this postulate was the pretension and claim that everything that serves Soviet Russia also serves—automatically—the international proletariat, the masses, and progress in general. Therefore, the interests of the proletariat—of the masses, of progress—are the same as the interests of Russia.

Actually, this argumentation amounts to a mixture between the foreign policy of Soviet nationalism and a terminology of progressive internationalism. On the one hand, there is the theory that Russia is the fatherland of the world proletariat, that it has a universal mission to liberate all humankind from exploitation, that its final goal is the reign of Communism all over the world, and that this goal justifies all means. On the other hand, all this ideological construction is mobilized to the service of a nationalist policy which takes into account only the interests of the USSR as a great power, the strengthening of its global position militarily, politically, economically, and so forth.

Soviet foreign policy, then, is a dynamic one, and its essence is a fundamental nonrecognition of a status quo. In this light, any situation, treaty, or agreement is viewed, by definition, as temporary, as subject to change. They last as long as the USSR finds them advantageous, or as long as there are other parties determined and strong enough to enforce them. Otherwise, they have to be changed at the first favorable opportunity.

Another point is the Soviet Union's readiness to exploit in its favor circumstances arising from such situations, or international developments that the Soviet Union itself cannot create or bring about. (Pertinent examples of this feature are the Soviets' stand toward the Arab oil embargo during the Yom Kippur War and their maneuvering in the Cyprus crisis.)

Finally, in spite of the numerous examples showing a manipulative attitude toward ideology, it would be a mistake to believe that Communist ideology (of the Soviet brand) has no influence on the Soviet leadership, its decisions and orientations in domestic matters as well as in foreign affairs. In spite of their pragmatic approach, ideology plays an important role in the Soviets' thinking their ways of perception of realities and actions. Ideological statements are not lip service irrelevant to current affairs and political actions; they should be taken seriously.

The Conflict with "Zionism"

Looking at the historical roots of the Soviet attitude toward the Middle East, my impression is that the traditional description of a continuous Russian interest in the Middle East for 250 years or so is rather exaggerated and needs qualification. Historically the real interest of Russia in the eighteenth and nineteenth centuries and of the Soviet Union in the 1920s and 1930s was mainly directed toward the two southern neighbors of Russia (which are part of the "Near East" or the "Middle East" in the old meaning of the term), namely Turkey and Iran. Historically speaking, those were the areas of interest of Russia as a great power.

Secondly, the specific target which mostly interested the Russians when they were dealing with the so-called "eastern question" in the late eighteenth and the nineteenth centuries was the Turkish Straits, specifically the Bosporus and the Dardanelles. This was, historically speaking, the area of direct interest to Russia and the Soviets. The Middle East as such, that is the Arab Middle East and Israel, were in the past a secondary and even marginal area of interest for Russia. And, of course, there is no need to elaborate at length on the fact that the Crimean War (1854–1856) did not take place because of a quarrel between Orthodox and Catholic monks in Bethlehem, whose respective patrons were Czar Nicholas I and Napoleon III.

The active policy of the Soviet Union in the Middle East began in 1954, 1955, and 1956, specifically with the arms deal between Czechoslovakia and Egypt in 1955. This deal was not, as is often believed, a consequence of the raid by the Israel Defense Forces against Egyptian military installations in the Gaza strip (February 28–March 1, 1955). Actually, besides Uri Ra'anan's convincing studies,[2] recent evidence indicates that close contacts between the parties of the deal were already underway in early February 1955. Those were the first steps; Soviet involvement in the Middle East has been growing ever since.

Ideologically it is not superfluous to mention here the traditional hostility of Bolshevism to Zionism and to Jewish immigration to the land of Israel. This traditional hostility begins with the early Russian Social Democrats, like Plekhanov, continues with the writings of Lenin and Stalin against Zionism, and is practically applied by the Bolshevik Party and the Soviet regime.

Politically speaking, in the 1920s and 1930s Arab nationalism appeared in the USSR's assessment as the only anti-imperialist force in Palestine. The Arab riots of 1929 and 1936, led by the Mufti, were hailed by the USSR as "basically progressive." On the other hand, Zionism and the Jewish Yishuv (settlement) appeared as "objectively" reactionary and as allied with British imperialism.

Thus, in the light of this political line, the Soviet Union's attitude in 1947–1948 stands apart as a brief departure from its traditional hostility to Zionism. The support that the Soviets gave to the plan of partition of Palestine into two states, one of them a Jewish state, was an unexpected turn in Soviet policy. It was prompted by their basic goal, namely the quickest possible expulsion of the British, whom they considered as the main imperialist power and the leaders of the international anti-Soviet camp. In other words, one of the main motives behind this stand was the Soviet interest in the confrontation with the West. This departure from the traditional policy did not last very long. Relations with Israel began to deteriorate around 1953, leading also to a temporary disruption of diplomatic relations. In 1954 the first Soviet veto against Israel (to be followed by many others) was cast in the United Nations Security Council following a Syrian complaint on an alleged Israeli violation of the truce agreements. Since 1955 Soviet foreign policy has been consistently pro-Arab, leading eventually to a continuous penetration and growing involvement in the area.

This policy of greater regional involvement in the Middle East will be better understood within the broader context of the reorientation of Soviet foreign policy following the decisions of the Twentieth Congress of the Soviet Communist Party held in February 1956. This reorientation was of momentous importance regarding the Soviet attitude toward the neutralist (or Third World) countries. The old "two camps" slogan and undifferentiated "imperialist lackey" model no longer suited Soviet purposes. They were abandoned and replaced by the view that these neutralist countries may objectively have a progressive international role and, because of their often touchy nationalist regimes and "anti-imperialist" orientation, they can be potential Soviet allies, or at least passive supporters. In other words, this change of international orientation was mainly conceived as part and parcel of Soviet strategy in the confrontation with the West, that is, the United States and Western Europe (and later the rivalry and strained relations with China).

For that main reason—namely the confrontation with the West —the USSR had a policy of greater involvement in the Middle East as well. But this involvement also meant, of course, facing Middle Eastern realities and working out a regional policy (or policies) within the global one. Thus, as succinctly analyzed by A.S. Becker and A.L. Horelick,[3] this policy of greater involvement has been driven by the complex interplay of two sets of factors. The first are the larger global impulses and objectives that prompted the Soviet Union to establish and then extend a bridgehead in the Arab Middle East (and in this context the weightiest factor is relations between the United States, and the USSR). The second set of factors includes those bearing on the Soviet relationship to the states in the area proper and to the explosive intraregional conflicts in the Middle East: the inter-Arab conflict and the Arab-Israel conflict. Within this context, and in order to increase its own influence in the Arab world, the USSR cultivated patron-client relationships with several radical, nationalist Arab states, especially Egypt, Syria, and Iraq. The Soviets nurtured this relationship not only by providing their clients with arms and economic assistance but also by aligning themselves more and more (and ever more openly) on the side of their clients in the two polarizing intraregional conflicts. Paradoxically, in so doing the Soviet Union found itself at times closely tied to the achievement of goals in the Middle East that were intrinsically marginal to Soviet interests.

However, these marginal goals were obviously outweighed in Soviet long-term strategic planning by the view that a strong position in the Middle East not only is important per se but also opens opportunities in other directions: radicalization of politics in adjacent areas; possibilities of turning NATO's southern flank and disrupting its East Mediterranean end (Greece and Turkey); and the establishment of a base for operations in East Africa and for a strategic link with India (as exemplified during the India-Pakistan War). Finally, and of great significance in their calculation, the Soviets aim at restricting American influence in the Arab world up to the point, if possible, of complete elimination of the United States. In this respect, recent events in Egypt might be seen as a major setback for the Soviets and a success for U.S. foreign policy. This might indeed be so provided that the present orientation of Egyptian policy is a lasting and sincere one; provided also that the United States will be capable of paying the high price the Egyptians require; and, finally, provided that Israel will be willing to pay an exorbitant price in order to secure the success of this U.S.-Egyptian relationship, which may turn out to be basically detrimental to Israel's interests.

Within this complex set of goals and objectives, what are presently the important trends in Soviet tactics and maneuvering more directly concerning Israel? I shall try to answer this question by addressing myself to and commenting on several propositions widely shared by scholars and analysts regarding the present trend of Soviet foreign policy in the Middle East.

First, let me put aside a set of opinions voiced in the aftermath of the Yom Kippur War and during these last months: (a) that the

Soviets will play the role of a stabilizing factor in the Middle East conflict; (b) that they will try to achieve some formal recognition (a "formalization") of their position and achievements in the area and will be satisfied with that; (c) that, whether detente applies or not to the Middle East, they will act in either case in coordination with the United States, aiming at a sort of condominium in the region; (d) that they will not support the Palestine Liberation Organization (PLO) because this would damage the international image of the USSR as a "constructive and responsible power"; that their attitude will be, as in similar cases in the past, to avoid the risks of giving official backing to uncontrollable and politically unpredictable guerrilla groups (as, for instance, in South America) and to deal only with states and governments.

Unfortunately, these opinions seem to be wishful thinking in view of the very slim circumstantial evidence on which they are based and in the light of past experience and present signals. The weaknesses of these opinions are apparent when one considers two other interesting (yet quite different) propositions: (a) that the Soviets are not interested in a settlement of the Arab-Israeli conflict because they need the tension it maintains in order to open opportunities for further Soviet penetration and, therefore, (b) that the USSR cannot be interested in the destruction of the independence of the State of Israel since Israel obviously is an indispensable ingredient in the conflict. Both these propositions are inaccurate and dangerously misleading.

Exact formulations are important for rendering thoughts and statements clearer and more precise. Obviously, the Soviet Union may be interested in a settlement of the Arab-Israeli conflict, but the relevant question is what kind of settlement. The Soviets will certainly be interested in: (a) a settlement on their own terms; (b) any settlement agreed upon by the main Arab states *and* the PLO; (c) any such settlement (as stated in "b") in which the USSR and the United States will have the status and role of guarantor. These are a few examples taken at random from among various types of settlements that would be acceptable to the Soviets.

If so, what is or may be the Soviet Union's attitude toward Israel? It seems that the Soviet attitude is and will remain empirical and instrumental; that is, if Israel's existence as an independent state helps or does not seriously hinder Soviet interests, the USSR will, directly and/or indirectly, support its existence. If, on the contrary, the Soviets arrive at the conclusion that the existence of Israel as an independent state is an obstacle to the achievement of high priority Soviet interests, they may support or propose (directly or indirectly) settlements of the conflict in which Israel's independence is not contemplated. These various orientations depend to a great degree upon the "correlation of forces" in which —needless to say—the policies of the United States and of Israel have an enormous weight, if properly conducted; the Soviet Union, which usually does not wage an adventurist foreign policy, understands intentions and determinations if they are clearly formulated.

On one issue, however, it seems to me that there are no more limitations to Soviet action, and in this topic I do not share the prevailing view among scholars and analysts: I think that the Soviets will give substantial official political support to the PLO, leading eventually to a declaration that the organization is entitled to create a state and to head it. Whether the Soviets also agree to the political program of the PLO, which contemplates the extinction of Israel, will for some time remain a matter of speculation that will go on long after Soviet political support and material aid to the PLO have already become weighty facts in the Middle Eastern realities.

In the light of recent developments it seems that in the present and next stage of the conflict the Soviets will above all try to avoid another setback such as the one suffered in Egypt (whatever its scope and real depth). It seems also that their basic position toward the "step-by-step" approach initiated by Henry Kissinger is that sooner or later this policy will arrive at a deadlock. Until then the USSR will probably support the radical and extremist Arab states (Syria, Iraq, Algeria) and increasingly the PLO; it will try to manipulate them (particularly Syria and the PLO) against Israel and the United States and align itself with the harder Arab positions and demands.

The rationale of this stand—as the Soviets probably see it—is that at least it makes the task of American diplomacy more difficult and that, under the circumstances, following a harder line is a more advantageous bargaining position for achieving a more favorable compromise for the Soviet Union and the Arabs.

Whether and when such a compromise (or any compromise at all) may be reached is, of course, an open question. It also is an open question what exactly the Soviets mean when they speak of the "1967 borders" (as in the formula: "Israeli withdrawal to the lines of June 4, 1967, and implementation of the legitimate national rights of the Palestinian people"). As a matter of fact, the Soviets have never officially recognized Israel's 1967 frontiers as international boundaries, and one should not be surprised if some day they also draw out of the dust of the UN archives the stillborn boundaries of the 1947 partition plan.

Fortunately, between possible Soviet goals and their implementation there is still a very great distance. And there is also the great role of a lucid United States policy and of Israel's determination and strength.

NOTES

1. Richard Pipes, "Some Operational Principles of Soviet Foreign Policy," in *The USSR and the Middle East,* ed. by Michael Confino and Shimon Shamir (Jerusalem, 1973), p. 23.

2. Uri Ra'anan, *The USSR Arms the Third World: Case Studies in Soviet Foreign Policy* (Cambridge, Mass., and London, 1969), *passim.*

3. Abraham S. Becker and Arnold S. Horelick, *Soviet Policy in the Middle East.* Santa Monica, Calif., 1970, *passim.*

SELECTED BIBLIOGRAPHY

Becker, Abraham S., and Horelick, Arnold L. *Soviet Policy in the Middle East.* The Rand Corporation, 1970.

Confino, Michael, and Shamir, Shimon, eds., *The USSR and the Middle East.* Jerusalem, 1973. Published for the Russian and East European Research Center and the Shiloah Center for Middle Eastern and African Studies, Tel Aviv University.

Hoffmann, Erik P., and Fleron, Frederic J., Jr., eds. *The Conduct of Soviet Foreign Policy.* London, 1971.

Lederer, Ivo J., ed., *Russian Foreign Policy: Essays in Historical Perspective.* New Haven and London, 1962.

Pipes, Richard. "Some Operational Principles of Soviet Foreign Policy," in *The USSR and the Middle East,* edited by Michael Confino and Shimon Shamir, Jerusalem, 1973.

Ra'anan, Uri. *The USSR Arms the Third World: Case Studies in Soviet Foreign Policy.* Cambridge, Mass., and London, 1969.

Rubinstein, Alvin Z., ed. *The Foreign Policy of the Soviet Union.* New York, 1960. *Soviet Objectives in the Middle East,* A Report of the Institute for the Study of Conflict. London, 1974.

DAVID SCHERS

12   Anti-Semitism in Latin America

This chapter deals with the particular characteristics of violence
and defense in Jewish life in Latin American countries. The research carried out in this field is very limited. As a result, the paper
will be based on material dealing with Latin American societies in
general and their Jewish communities in particular, on data provided by recent research on Latin American Jewry, on general
information about violence in Latin America, and on information
provided by some interviews and other sources. We shall review
the main features and trends in the development of Jewish communities in Latin America, pointing out exogenic and endogenic
factors which influence Jewish institutional and individual attitudes and behavior. Against this background we shall try to analyze violence and anti-Semitism in Latin America, in relation to
specific features of the political culture and behavior. Reactions to
anti-Semitism and violence in general, with special reference to
specific cases, will be dealt with as well in an attempt to achieve
a better understanding of the real Jewish problem—not anti-
Semitic physical violence, but pressures for assimilation.

Jewish Communities in Latin America: The Main Features

Jewish communities in Latin America may be classified by the size of their population: (a) large communities with a population of over 100,000 (Brazil, Argentina[1]); (b) medium-sized communities with a population of between 25,000 and 50,000 (Chile, Mexico, and Uruguay); (c) small communities with a population of between 10,000 and 15,000 Jews (Colombia, Venezuela); (d) very small communities in the remaining Latin American countries, where the number of Jews is less than 5,000.

Our observations are based mainly on data obtained in four South American countries: Argentina, Brazil, Chile, and Uruguay, in which the great majority of Jews of Latin America are concentrated. The development of contemporary Jewish communities in these countries started at the end of the nineteenth century and the beginning of the present century. There is no historical continuity between these communities and previous Jewish settlements of the colonial era. The immigrants who established the modern Jewish communities came mainly from Eastern and Central Europe, and this fact was of considerable importance in the development of their institutional, cultural, and political character. The immigrants brought with them the social and cultural patterns of Jewish life in Europe and tried to implement similar institutional structures in their new countries without realizing their lack of suitability to local prevailing conditions. These structures, although useful for the generation of the migrants, did not suit the needs of new generations, and, as a result, traditional institutions lost members, prestige, and influence.

External pressures on Jews were and still are factors which act on these communities in direct and subtle ways. National unity and integration are stressed in these countries. Consequently, less place is left for legitimate and accepted expressions of ethnic specificities. The situation was therefore different from the one prevailing in the United States and Canada, where cultural minorities and cultural pluralism were accepted and encouraged.[2]

In Argentina and in other Latin American countries there is religious freedom, but the political culture stresses nationalism and total integration as central national aims. Permissiveness for relations of immigrants and their offspring to their "mother country" characterizes the large concentrations of Spanish and Italian immigrants and in a certain measure legitimizes Jewish ties to Israel.[3] However, the rapid process by which the children of these immigrants lose their distinct characteristics and become full Argentinians is a factor which distinguishes them from the Jewish second and third generations, who continue to be different in religious, ethnic, and other aspects of identity.

Most Latin American Jews thus have been exposed to a conflict between a liberal-democratic immigration policy, which encourages the welcome of the immigrant, and an integrationist-homogenizing-nationalist tendency, which makes the offspring of the immigrant indistinguishable from the general population. However, it must be remembered that these and other generalizations are based mainly on the situation in Argentina and that there are differences in this as in other aspects between the various Latin American countries.

The ideological backgrounds of the waves of immigrants found expression in the institutional development of the communities. *Landsmanshaften,* synagogues, mutual aid organizations were formed by religious, "progressive," and Zionist groups who came from Europe and brought their own political and ideological views with them. The Zionist movement became influential and succeeded in winning over most of the Jewish communities. The Holocaust and the creation of the State of Israel were factors which had a strong influence in fostering Jewish activities and Jewish identification. They neutralized the negative influence on Jewish life of the almost total stoppage of Jewish immigration during World War II.

The Jewish identity of the generations born in these countries is at a lower level from the point of view of such indicators as language, religious behavior, and traditions. They also differ from the previous generation from an occupational, economic, and educational point of view.

The new generations are influenced by integrative processes that the older generation did not face or faced to a lesser degree. They feel that their rights and duties as native-born citizens make it harder for them to identify as Jews. The first generation usually tries to compromise between its acceptance of the principle of integration and its will to keep its Jewish identity. However, to an increasing degree Jews abandon the institutional frameworks of Jewish organizations, and even the informal foundations of Jewish life are weakened. The rising standard of living and the weakening of ties with Jewish life have brought many Jews into conflict with their Jewish identity. The dichotomy between Jewish life and loyalty to the general society leads some of the youth to adopt leftist-extremist attitudes; others—but only a few—turn to Zionism, which leads some of them to Israel; the majority, under cross pressure, do not deal openly with the problem and become alienated.

We are dealing with Jewish communities whose individuals are attracted into assimilation by economic and social conditions and pressured by cultural and political factors in the same direction. What are the endogenous processes that these communities are going through? From a demographic point of view, these are Jewish communities with a diminishing population due to a very low rate of fertility, some net emigration, and mixed marriages. The institutional framework developed by these communities was instrumental in meeting the needs of the first, immigrant generation but faced problems of adaptation of the new generations, which were more exposed to the influence of the general society. As a result, many older institutions lost members and influence while others, those based mainly on sport and social activities, gained relative importance in membership and number of activities. The minimum common denominator which keeps these members together is the satisfaction—conscious or unconscious—of being among Jews. It may be assumed that from the point of view of identification with Judaism and Jewish identity the influence of "gregariousness" is not enough. Jewish schools, day schools, and half-day complementary schools, enroll approximately one-third of the Jewish children. This influence seems to be important, but only future basic research will prove this point. It seems that the determining variables in shaping Jewish identity are the family and the community and that school is only a reinforcing variable.

Endogenous factors supporting the maintenance of Jewish identity are weaker than exogenic factors leading to assimilation. As stated above, the influence of the Holocaust and the creation of the State of Israel tended to counteract assimilating tendencies. However, at present it seems that neither the family nor educational and other institutions are ideologically and organizationally equipped to face the increasing exogenous influences.

The Jewish population in Latin America belongs to the middle and upper-middle urban classes. The position of these classes is different in countries like Argentina and Uruguay than in countries such as Brazil, according to the socioeconomic structure in each country.[4] Nevertheless, the class situation of these communities is a factor which helps to explain their interest in political stability and their sensitivity to changes which may harm their economic positions, as in the case of Cuba or Chile during Allende's time. The increasing number of Jewish professionals does not change the situation, basically because only a part of them—although an increasing number—are salaried employees, most of them belonging to the independent middle classes. The political situation leads many Jews to accept regimes which provide security and stability even if these regimes are not politically democratic or socially progressive. Departures from liberal and progressive attitudes create tensions and conflict with the sectors of the Jewish youth who tend toward leftist social and political ideologies. Despite the generational and other differences between Jews from specific sectors and countries, the general trends are, as stated above, a diminishing population, an institutional weakening, and an increasing assimilation.

Violence in Latin America

A good summary of different tentative explanations of violence in Latin America is presented in *Conflict and Violence in Latin American Politics,* a book of readings edited by Francisco José Moreno and Barbara Mitrani.[5] The psychocultural explanations are based mainly on the Mexican situation, which presents the "machismo" syndrome, feelings of inferiority, and childrearing norms as explanations for violence. The political approaches argue that the political system which does not fit the needs of the socio-economic structure creates a situation in which politics is replaced by violence as a means of solving a conflict. Another factor is that when politics becomes almost the only way open for upward mobility, competition among ambitious contenders becomes intense and violent.

Socioeconomic approaches point to the stress created by urbanization, by poverty, and by the demonstration effect. The revolution of rising expectations breeds frustration and frustration leads to violence. This is not only a matter of higher expectations of the poor, for the middle and upper classes also fear losing their privileges. It seems that the combination of all or some of these factors created a tendency to violence in Latin America. All of the articles in the volume cited above seem to take for granted the general belief that this tendency is very strong. However, there is little convincing evidence supporting the popular belief that Latin America is more violent than other areas of the world. Vietnam, Cyprus, the Middle East, Ireland, and Biafra provide examples of political violence which is neither less widespread nor creates fewer victims than recent Latin American events.

It is true that the Mexican Revolution (1910–1920), with about one million victims, or the Colombian Violencia (1946–1965), are examples of outbursts of widespread persisting violence. However, in trying to find some figures about recent periods, the results are anything but clearcut,[6] and the methodological problems concerning such comparisons are so serious that there is no other alternative but to rely on qualitative and even impressionistic observations.

The popular linking of violence with the Latin American continent stems in part from the frequent coups d'état and the political instability that characterize most countries of the area. However, one has to remember that these changes of government by military intervention often did not involve bloodshed. A common practice in several countries has been for defeated politicians and military personnel to be given diplomatic posts or be sent abroad in exile. Nevertheless, the introduction of clearcut ideological cleavages and international factors in the political struggles have brought a new kind of repression and violence which make the present a time of widespread political violence. Uruguay is an example of urban guerrilla attempts to engage in conflict and violent warfare instead of directly seeking the electoral support of the masses, which has been lacking. On the other hand, Chile is an example of the violent repression of leftist sectors which claimed many victims.

The success of the revolutionary rural guerrilla in Cuba created a wave of sympathy for the revolution and many attempts to imitate its strategy. However, rural guerrilla fighting failed and reached its lowest ebb with the death of Che Guevara in Bolivia. The centers (*focos*) of guerrilla power were isolated and unsupported, and counterinsurgency warfare was effective. A revision of rural guerrilla strategy brought several revolutionary groups to the conclusion that Latin American conditions require a different approach. Carlos Marighella, in his *Mini-Manual of the Urban Guerrilla*, points to the fact that the supply of arms, food, medical supplies, and information is easier in the city. Students-turned-guerrillas melt easily into the urban environment and may become an effective fighting force,[7] but they cannot realize their plans because of their failure to mobilize popular support. For example, popular support for the Tupamaros was limited to their romantic "Robin Hood" image, and the population was not ready to support them in their efforts to become rulers of society.

Urban guerrillas have brought violence into the cities, where the Jewish population is concentrated. They have kidnapped and attacked individual Jews, while some of the Jewish urban guerrillas have been executed or imprisoned. Nevertheless, the violence and counterviolence were not anti-Jewish, nor did they have Jewish overtones.

It seems that a combination of all or part of the factors mentioned above have created a tendency to violence in Latin America. However, in order to be anti-Semitic, violence needs other ingredients which may convert a general propensity to use violence into a particular tendency to use it against Jews.

Animosities in Latin America

As in the case of violence, there is a popular image of Latin American countries, particularly Argentina, as countries where anti-Semitism is widespread and influential. This image does not seem to be based on comparative research, but certain data and news about anti-Semitic events provide some supporting evidence.[8] Why is Argentina a focus of anti-Semitism? Firstly, because Nazi-fascist movements and tendencies have been relatively successful and because of the influence of Nazis who escaped from Germany.[9] Secondly, government attitudes against anti-Semitic manifestations have not been firm enough because of anti-Semitic circles within the government, the army, and the police. Thirdly, there has been a visible target—a big Jewish community in a completely "white" city. Buenos Aires is one of the largest cities in the world and one of the few with no serious racial problems; it has a homogeneous population of European origin and Catholic faith. Jews are different by religion, culture, identity, and family names.

Violent anti-Semitic activities peaked in the early 1960s when the Tacuara and other rightist groups launched attacks against Jewish institutions and individuals. As in many other cases, attacks on individuals were presented as reactions against antipatriotic Communists. The infamous Sirota case, in which a kidnapped Jewish girl was found with a swastika engraved on her breast, was one of a wave of anti-Semitic actions at that time.

What are the factors which may help to explain the appearance of this wave? Basic socioeconomic and political conditions at that time had created feelings of frustration. (a) The economic situation, the alienation of the Peronist masses, and the disenchantment with the Frondizi government, which did not fulfill its promises, created enough frustration to foster the necessary preconditions for violent conflict. (b) There was also the cultural-historical influence of religious anti-Semitic beliefs of Catholic origin. Alienated groups of youngsters and teenagers, led by fascist adults, were the carriers of anti-Semitic feelings and used them to discharge their frustration. (c) A strong government stand could have stopped these actions and, in fact, did so after local and international pressures were brought to bear. But, meanwhile, influential circles in the police and the army were quite lenient in dealing with the aggressors and gave them encouragement. (d) The reactions to the Eichmann affair, which was considered a violation of Argentinean sovereignty, also played a part. Thus we may conclude that the wave of violent anti-Semitism was the result of a combination of the characteristics of the political culture, socioeconomic factors, and historical circumstances.

The character of anti-Semitic activities in Argentina is less violent than other types of urban violence and terrorism. Posters, leaflets, tar bombs, swastikas, articles in the press—these are the main expressions of anti-Semitic feeling. When more violent means are used, such as bombs or gunfire, they are generally directed against property. Although these may be very traumatic experiences for Jews, they are nevertheless not the murderous attacks characteristic of Russian pogroms or of the Nazi massacres.

New trends in anti-Semitism appear under the cover of anti-Zionism. Hussein Triki, the able representative of the Arab League, used this approach in the 1960s, but he faced strong opposition in Argentinean circles and was finally expelled. The international situation created by the oil crisis, the renewed efforts of Arab propaganda, backed by tremendous economic means, can help to make this renewed kind of anti-Semitic propaganda more effective. It is not very probable that this will have direct violent expressions, but pressures on the Jewish population to reconsider their deep feelings and ties with Israel may have unpleasant psychological and political results.

Gina Germani points to the widespread existence of traditional anti-Semitism and the acceptance of some inveterate prejudices against Jews in rural areas and among lower strata of the population. Ideological anti-Semitism, by contrast, is based on elaborate principles linked to the characteristics of the "authoritarian personality," and it is common among the upper classes.[10] With the reappearance of the justification of every possible means, mainly terror, for the implementation of revolution, there seems to be a new tendency in certain leftist circles to use anti-Semitic popular prejudices as a political tool. The use of anti-Semitism by the extreme right is frequent and is liable to intensify in case of crisis.[11] The campaign against the Jewish minister Gelbard in Argentina was organized by the Right but also had some leftist overtones. This sort of concatenation and manipulation of ideological and popular anti-Semitic tendencies should not be excluded as a source of renewed outbursts of anti-Semitism.

A common reaction to modern anti-Semitic pressures and accusations is a tendency of the Jews to try to show profound patriotism and loyalty. This tendency, together with the sensitivity of Jewish youth to social causes, has brought many of them to the belief—common among idealist Jewish revolutionaries in various other countries and periods—that their redemption lies in the redemption of society, leading them to join local movements of national and social liberation. Repression of and disenchantment with these movements may bring some of these youngsters back to Jewish activities, but it seems that most of them will find sanctuary in political apathy and individual advancement. What seems problematic and difficult are the internalized anti-Jewish prejudices which characterize many of the Latin American Jews and create conditions for ideological and/or passive assimilation, the latter being dominant.[12]

Reactions to Anti-Semitism

We can place reactions to anti-Semitism within the general framework of Jewish attitudes toward life in the Diaspora. When the walls of the Jewish ghetto disappeared from the European scene, the Jews had to find answers to their central problem of how to adapt to the new conditions of modern societies and how to neutralize anti-Semitism.

Several solutions were suggested. One was to turn the Jews into "productive members of society." The Jewish agricultural colonization in Argentina and ORT technical institutions were expressions of this very popular approach. Other solutions included reform of religious rites in order to adapt them to modern life. Anti-defamation propaganda was also suggested. All of these solutions were tried in Latin American communities with different degrees of success or failure. Although colonization succeeded at first, there are now very few Jewish farmers and there are fewer and fewer Jewish workers. In the secular anticlerical atmosphere the success of religious reform is very limited.

Political action and propaganda are still among the most popular means aimed at neutralizing the negative influences of anti-Semitism. This method seems to require less time and effort for its implementation than other more basic solutions, and, perhaps because reactive in character, it is generally employed when anti-Semitism strikes.

A typical organization of Jewish political representation and defense in Latin America is the DAIA, Delegacion de Asociaciones Israelitas Argentinas. Founded in 1933 to counteract Nazi anti-Semitic policies in Germany, the DAIA has a long tradition of struggle against anti-Semitic phenomena in Argentina.[13] Similar representative organs exist in every Latin American Jewish community. In some of the smaller communities they fulfill the functions of a community organization, but this is not the case in the largest communities of South America (Argentina, Brazil, Uruguay, and Chile).

The reactions of the DAIA to the 1961–1962 attacks on Jewish individuals and institutions may provide an example of the means commonly used by the Jewish communities in reacting to the threat of anti-Semitism. On this occasion there were some other reactions, not organized by DAIA, which may help us to understand new trends in the attitudes of Jews to anti-Semitic violence. In addition to the usual appeal to government officials, the reactions of the DAIA included: strongly worded public declarations denouncing the anti-Semitic activities; telegrams sent to Jewish communities and institutions in Europe and the United States; and public demonstrations, of which the Jewish trade strike of June 28, 1962, was the most outstanding. The idea of such action met with opposition from those within the Jewish community who believed in quiet action as expressed in the Jewish press. The traditional attitude of *shtadlanut,* asking the government for protection, did not fit the activist position of the leadership of the DAIA. It seems that the position of this particular leadership was instrumental in creating an active militant stance and demanding response.[14]

Besides the question of general strategy, the community was divided around the question of how to react to the fact that some of the attacked victims were Communists. The DAIA, it was argued, should not defend Communists. The institution's attitude was that the DAIA, as always, did not adopt political positions but was defending a Jewish person whose rights had been violated. It seems that general support for the strike in particular and a more activist response in general had its origins in a grass-roots reaction against the traditional Eastern European attitude of "playing down" anti-Semitic events in order to keep a low profile—a basically defensive and passive attitude. The spirit of the Warsaw Ghetto and the influence of Israel seem to have been instrumental in fostering this attitude.

Jewish collective self-defense had its beginnings in spontaneously organized groups of young people who decided to train themselves in judo, boxing, and other techniques in order to meet the provocations of anti-Semitic hooligans. Groups of this type decided to act in the 1960s, including in their programs the idea of retaliation when necessary. Their attitude seems to have been instrumental in effecting a decrease in acts of anti-Semitism. It created serious difficulties for the attacking groups, and the danger of an escalation of incidents with victims from both sides acted as a deterrent and helped the government to take a firmer attitude. Jewish self-defense found it difficult to act because anti-Semitic groups had allies within the Argentinean police and army. Nevertheless, they became a factor which anyone trying to attack Jews had to consider. In this sense, the willing readiness of the Jews to use force if needed helped to limit and reduce violent expressions of anti-Semitism.

The Jewish communities in Latin America are undergoing processes similar to those of other communities in the world. However, some special features of the general society make the existing pressures for assimilation stronger and the possibilities of integration without losing the specific Jewish identity more remote. Despite the prevalence of violence and terror, their use against Jews is diminishing. Even rightist governments and political groups do not tend to employ anti-Semitic means as tools of political struggle.

The international situation and the growing influence of Arab factors have created favorable conditions for the appearance of a new wave of anti-Zionism, which could be harmful in the struggle for survival being fought by these Jewish communities.[15] Strong ties with Israel are one of the effective means which offer to many Jews in these nonreligious communities a positive way of identification with Judaism. But new and renewed pressures offer Jewish youth a total identification with local nationalism even as they promote the internalization of anti-Jewish prejudices. The acceptance of the Jew as a human being by the general society only on condition that he abandon his Jewish identity is essentially a sophisticated expression of anti-Semitism, even though no physical violence is employed. Defense against such sophisticated pressures is very difficult, especially when they are accompanied by attractive conditions conducive to personal economic and social advancement. Dramatic episodes of anti-Semitic violence are much easier to identify and may call forth reactions of pride and commitment among the attacked group. The silent erosion of Jewish identity is less apparent and thus harder to combat. It seems that in the near future the struggle against assimilation and new forms of sophisticated anti-Semitism in Latin America will be less dramatic but no less difficult than in the past, including in their programs the idea of retaliation when necessary.

NOTES

1. Recent research by the David Horowitz Institute for the Research of Developing Countries, Tel Aviv University, shows that figures for the Jewish population of Argentina were overestimated. See, for example, Comité Judió Americano, *Comunidades Judías de Latinoamerica* (1971–1972) (Buenos Aires, 1974); Jewish World Congress, *The Jewish Communities of the World* (Hebrew) (Tel Aviv, 1973). In this paper we rely on preliminary findings of the David Horowitz Institute's research and its forthcoming reports.

2. Moshe Davis, "Centers of Jewry in the Western Hemisphere: Comparative Approach," *Jewish Journal of Sociology* (June 1963), 4–21.

3. Ibid.

4. U.N. Economic Commission for Latin America, *Social Change and Social Development Policy in Latin America* (New York, 1970).

5. Francisco José Moreno and Barbara Mitrani, eds., *Conflict and Violence in Latin American Politics* (New York, 1971).

6. Charles Lewis Taylor and Michael C. Hudson, eds., *World Handbook of Political and Social Indicators,* 2nd ed. (New Haven and London, 1972).

7. Robert Moss, *Urban Guerrilla Warfare,* Adelphi Papers 79, The International Institute for Strategic Studies (London, 1971); Charles A. Russell, James A. Miller, and Robert E. Hiddner, "The Urban Guerrilla in Latin America: A Select Bibliography," *Latin American Research Review,* IX, no. 1 (Spring 1974), 37–79.

8. Gino Germani, "Antisemitismo ideologico y antisemitismo tradicional," in *Comentario* (Buenos Aires) no. 34 (1966), 55–63; Joaquin Fischerman, "El Antisemitismo en el Gran Buenos Aires," in *Comentario,* no. 72 (1970), 29, summarizing research conducted for the DAIA; unpublished reports on anti-Semitic events.

9. Nathan Lerner, "Antisemitism and the Nationalist Ideology in Argentina," in *Diaspora and Unity,* 17–18 (1973), 131–38; Yehuda Adin, "Nationalism and Neo-Nazism in Argentina" (Hebrew), *Bitfutzot Hagola,* no. 33 (Summer 1965), 1–20.

10. Germani, *op. cit.*

11. Federico Branco, "La AAA revela su personalidad," interview with an AAA leader, *Vision* (Mexico), 44, no. 3, (15 Jan. 1975), 22–23.

12. Additional support for this phenomenon was found by Edy Rogovsky and Chaia Sverdlik in research under the auspices of the David Horowitz Institute, report forthcoming.

13. Nathan Lerner, *Jewish Organization in Latin America,* Research Report No. 4, the David Horowitz Institute for the Research of Developing Countries, Tel Aviv University, December 1974.

14. Interviews, August 1974; personal observations, Buenos Aires, 1960–1963; Yehuda Adin, *op. cit.*

15. The idea of "survival" as the main problem of Jewish communities in Latin America is suggested by Irving Louis Horowitz, "Jewish Ethnicism and Latin American Nationalism," *Midstream* (Nov. 1972), 22–28.

BEN HALPERN

13   Self-Denial and Self-Preservation: Responses to Anti-Semitism Among American Jews

The topic of violence and Jewish self-defense necessarily involves a number of controversial conceptions, such as anti-Semitism, which require definition. The conception of violence itself deserves some attention even though its meaning may seem quite obvious.

Hannah Arendt has made some useful distinctions between violence and power which are important for our discussion:

> One of the most obvious distinctions between power and violence is that power always stands in need of numbers, whereas violence up to a point can manage without them because it relies on implements. . . . The extreme form of power is All against One, the extreme form of violence is One against All. And this latter is never possible without instruments.[1]

> Violence is by nature instrumental; like all means, it always stands in need of guidance and justification through the end it pursues. . . . Power needs no justification, being inherent in the very existence of political communities; what it does need is legitimacy.[2]

Briefly one might say that power rests on the ability to control human actions by means of symbolic systems, and violence is the use of physical means to control human actions without recourse to symbolic systems. Violence often occurs, therefore, at the outer boundary of symbolic authority. To justify itself, it either establishes such authority where there was none or restores it where it is threatened. Thus, in order to maintain the bounds of authority parents and policemen resort to violence, one should hope in a restrained manner, by spanking children, or subduing lawbreakers. War and revolution are attempts to establish such boundaries in relation to people who do not share the same symbolic system or respect the same authority.

These two forms of violence in social relations, whether or not truly justifiable—that is, functional—are certainly common. One type might even be said to be traditional or conventional; its main function is that of sustaining an existing system and reinforcing its authority over those who share the same symbolic system. The other, the use of violence in establishing boundaries between different symbolic systems—in other words defending one's turf—could be dispensed with only if a single order of legitimacy, backed by a single authoritative power, were recognized worldwide by everybody involved in all possible social relationships. Barring the messianic eventuality of an anarchistic utopia, one sort of violence, the violence involved in social control, is necessary for the maintenance of any kind of social system; and quite a different type of violence is probably inevitable whenever opposed symbolic systems and their adherents meet, in the same or contiguous territories, in order to establish the bounds of each one's authority.

The definition of anti-Semitism is more problematic, particularly in relation to anti-Jewish violence. To be quite historical, the term anti-Semitism should be used only with reference to those who call themselves "anti-Semites." Such people are not found in historical documents until the late nineteenth century. But it would be pedantic, to say the least, to adhere to such a strict nonanachronistic use. There is no fundamental difference between what calls itself anti-Semitism after 1870 and similar phenomena which existed under different names for centuries before. My own view, in fact, is that anti-Semitism is inherently and universally related to the very existence of Jews. That obviously implies that I mean something more general than the specific expression of anti-Semitism among certain groups who apply that name to themselves. To single out what is specific to such groups, I shall use the expression "political anti-Semitism."

What, then, is the general meaning that I attach to the term "anti-Semitism"? Very roughly and schematically, I suggest that anti-Semitism is the hostility provoked by virtue of the fact that the Jews are a group constituted by an ideology.[3] More concretely, I suggest that Jews are subject to the same kind of hostility as Communists in capitalist lands or Huguenots in Catholic France—or as East Asians in North Africa in recent years. Jews belong to a broad category of people who are defined as outsiders by virtue of their cultural difference: that is, because they have a symbolic system at odds with that of those among whom they live.

The Roots of Anti-Semitism

In the Jewish case, the antagonism between their symbolic system and any other with which it comes in contact is implicit in the fact that Jews are defined as a group by monotheistic faith. Such a faith implies that its members have access to a universal truth, thus excluding the validity of any contrary belief.[4] Such a group necessarily places itself in a position of antagonism to others and arouses their hostility.

This is what I refer to as basic anti-Semitism. Since it is inseparable from Jewishness, it applies even to those Jews who no longer adhere to the founding beliefs of the Jewish community. I cannot develop here the historical and sociological explanation of this fact.[5] Let me simply refer to an empirical fact which can be verified out of one's own experience. The only way one can cease to be a Jew is by conversion. If a person has not converted but simply fails to believe any longer in the faith that defines him as a Jew, he still remains a Jew. He is subject, accordingly, to the same kind of social relationship, basically one of hostility or antagonism, that Jewishness necessarily provokes by nature of the kind of claim it makes for its own symbolic system.

If one is to speak about the roots of anti-Semitism in America, one must begin with the basic roots of anti-Semitism anywhere, namely that there are Jews living among non-Jews. It is important to note at once that the relationship does not necessarily imply violence. What it implies is antagonism, and antagonism, of course, tends under certain conditions to provoke violence. This danger is always latent wherever a symbolic system claims universality but fails to achieve it. A group committed to such a symbolic system has an inherent propensity to extend the domain of this system universally, and therefore it is constantly inviting boundary clashes with others who do not accept those claims. This much is true of Judaism, of Communism, of all the monotheistic faiths—of any ideological belief that has a universal claim.

A second, quite familiar, aspect of the Jewish position is that the Jews have been for centuries, or millennia, a defeated ideological group. Whatever propensity they have to extend their claims of universality has to be inhibited for their own self-protection. Indeed, it is so successfully inhibited that any commitment to convert Gentiles is practically denied by the normative tradition. It nevertheless exists and every now and again crops up in history, as in the case of Isaac Mayer Wise. He was anxious to convert all the Gentiles and believed Jews had a mission to continue apart, not simply in order to bear witness to the prophetic truth but to overcome the deficient monotheisms of the Gentiles and convert them to the real model. He was of course exceptional. Mostly, the normative tradition retains a propensity to establish Jewish universality only in the form of messianic beliefs. This means that the conversionist urge is, for all practical purposes, completely inhibited in day-to-day relations with Gentiles.

That does not alter the fact that there is such a claim, and everyone is aware of it, whether the Jews exercise it or not. By their very existence among others, the Jews represent an ideological denial of opposed values, including the claims to universality of other monotheistic faiths. This is one of the controversial issues in the historiography. Some, like James Parkes, have argued that there is no true anti-Semitism until Jews become a guest people among Christians; anti-Semitism is thus a specifically Christian phenomenon.[6] It is obvious from the way I define anti-Semitism that I would not agree with this assertion. I regard the hostility to Jews in Hellenistic civilization as being anti-Semitic, not merely, as Parkes claims, a normal kind of friction such as always occurs at the boundaries between rival ethnic groups.

The Jews, as noted earlier, are a defeated group, and consequently they have inhibited, in self-protection, any active pursuit of universal dominion for Judaism. The basis for their living among others has usually been a self-denying ordinance by which active Jewish proselytizing is renounced, both in principle and in practice. But Jewish survival has also been preserved by a self-denying ordinance on the part of Gentiles. Jews living among Gentiles are inherently a subversive threat, whether actual or potential. But over the centuries this threat has been widely tolerated because the alternative was to make martyrs of the Jews. Martyrdom was indeed visited upon the Jews on many occasions, but more generally it was avoided by the host society, for a policy of martyring a minority may well entail a threat to general law and order. Repressive policies may express the ultimate logic of the Jewish-Gentile ideological antagonism; but the conclusion is not one worth pursuing so long as Jews are only a logical, or at most a potential, threat, and the cost of making martyrs out of them may be to upset the general respect for law and order upon which the whole society rests.

Such a cost-benefit calculation was evidently widespread all through Jewish history, producing the large measure of tolerance that permitted Jewish survival over millennia. In the case of Jews living among Christians, tolerance was reinforced by a whole array of theological and mythic acknowledgements of a special Jewish status: Jews must survive until the second advent as witnesses to the proof-texts of Christian belief; they have a vital role in Christian sacred history not only as Christ-killers but as exemplars of the symbol of the wandering Jew, who must remain to be converted in the end of days. In any case, to be tolerated necessarily implies that one must be watched, kept under some kind of repressive regime, however minimal, because what is tolerated is really what one cannot get rid of—or at least not at a reasonable cost. Thus, tolerance implies the preference that what is tolerated should disappear and no longer have to be tolerated. Toleration also implies the need to take precautions against those qualities of what is tolerated which explain why one would like to get rid of it. Thus the Jews, or any tolerated minority with an ideologically subversive potential, exist under conventional restrictions, if not infraviolent methods of restraint. These precautionary measures range all the way from the ghetto to the kind of polite exclusion that prevails under the most favorable conditions when a host society has to tolerate an ideologically opposed minority.

If outright violence occurs in such a context, it implies that the conventions by which the minority's position are defined have broken down. Indeed, it usually means that the conventions of general law and order in a society have broken down, releasing against Jews a hostile potential which had been conventionally kept in check. In any kind of revolution or peasant upheaval, or in any case where religious enthusiasm is freed from the control of the authoritative establishment and the masses are inflamed, there will often be pogroms, massacres, and other violence against the Jews; sometimes, by way of mass pressure on the constituted authorities, there will be expulsions.

The characteristic picture of Jewish relations with Gentiles since the conclusive defeat of any possible Jewish universal mission is thus the following: they are tolerated by conventions which are maintained by authorities in the name of more general considerations, such as economic utility. This often is accomplished in the face of latent or overt resistance on the part of popular conscience.

Jews are not accepted by popular belief as really deserving this kind of toleration; and whenever lower-class resistance breaks the general restraints of conventional authority, one of the results may be the venting of hostility against the Jews in the form of violence. Such occasional violence, however, is quite different from the conventional low-grade hostility involved in their regular repression or toleration.

One must further note that Jews have a specific historical significance in the annals of the several peoples among whom they have lived, and it is far from being the same significance in every case. To understand the specific form of the Jewish-Gentile relationship, or any specific outbreak of violence against Jews, it is necessary to take into account not simply the general paradigm of Jewish-Gentile antagonism referred to above but also the specific nation's historical experience with the Jews. In the case of Germany, for example, there is a very intimate, continuous, and acute relationship of Jews to the national history, rooted in the fact that Jews were not effectively expelled from Germany before the Reformation. Thus, Germany's experience with Jews was different from that of a country like England, which expelled them in the thirteenth century, lived over three centuries without them, and then finally saw them return as newcomers. Germany, or various principalities in Germany, had a continuous relationship with Jews during a time when the popular conscience not only denied their legitimacy as residents but rebelled against it. Jews were tolerated there as an illegitimate group almost in the same way that we tolerate prostitutes or bootleggers. This may seem a drastic statement, but it is not too far off the mark, even though one would have to revise very carefully some of the traditional formulations of the above general description in the light of Guido Kisch's work on Jewry law.[7] It may well be that Jews were not treated legally under the general category of strangers, but sociologically—and certainly morally—it is clear that they were regarded as people who really did not belong. In late medieval Germany Jews lived among Germans who felt that they should have been expelled; but, owing simply to the incapacity of the Germans to get together to do this all at the same time, they stayed. Around them was woven that whole demonological complex of myths which reached such a high degree of cultivation in German culture.

Of course, the anti-Jewish myth flourished in areas other than Germany where there were no Jews at all. In Germany it was nourished by constant contact with those demonic creatures and became a festering hatred. In the nineteenth century and later, this endemic hostility was complicated by the symbolic involvement of the Jews in conflicts which split German society, as they did French society. Continental Europe in the nineteenth century was deeply split over legitimacy and revolution, authoritarianism and liberty. The Jews, whose emancipation symbolized for many clericals and counterrevolutionaries the forces of the French Revolution, became a salient issue in the politics of the country. The contrast with America is obvious. If one seeks in American national history a salient hostility attached to a particular group, or a deep political division in American society focused on the status of a particular group, we have to look to the blacks, but certainly not to the Jews. The status of Negroes is a political issue which has divided the United States since before the Civil War. The Jewish position in American history, and in English history as well, is that of an inconspicuous, nonsalient group.

The national histories of English-speaking peoples have been relatively indifferent to Jews. In American history there never was a Jewish status—at least in the federal structure—that had to be revised by emancipation.[8] According to Cecil Roth, Jewish history in England has been fairly smooth because at the time of the readmission in the days of Cromwell it was impossible to achieve a defined Jewish status.[9] Thus, Jews were admitted by way of exception, without any special status, and they continued to be a nonsalient element in English history. Because their status had never become an issue seriously dividing society, readmission of Jews to England proceeded with the support of Roundheads such as Cromwell, on the one hand, and adherents of the Restoration and the House of Orange, on the other. So, too, in the United States the status of the Jews has not been a party issue. Political anti-Semitism was imported from abroad, and it was an exceptional event for Jewishness to be made a political matter at all. This is in sharp contrast to the history of Europe. It is also in sharp contrast to the history of the blacks in America, not to speak of some other groups, such as the Catholics.

A further implication of the general assumptions I have laid down is that there is no natural transition from anti-Semitism to genocide. If genocide, or more generally violence, occurs there must be a specific historical reason for its occurrence, not contained within the basic syndrome of Jewish-Gentile relations. The basic relationship is a long-standing, if unstable, mixture of antagonism and toleration; and that of course implies a range of attitudes. At one extreme, one may have almost total toleration, but to go beyond that to assimilation or merger is a resolution not logically involved in the syndrome. If ever historically achieved, it requires some additional explanation. On the other hand, one may have a high degree of anti-Semitism—that is, a low degree of tolerance—and if history goes beyond that to genocide or to expulsion, then something has happened to the relationship not contained within its own logic but requiring special explanation. The usual cause may be traced to the breakdown of law and order generally.

To sum up, the potential for violence toward Jews in American history involves schematically some such set of possibilities as the following. On the one hand, there is a constant element of boundary-maintaining repression, which is a necessary part of toleration; that is, whenever Jews go beyond what is tolerated they are reminded of the limits of their toleration by certain repressive techniques which are quite automatic in the social system—they are snubbed, told they are pushy, and so on. Within the general American syndrome of toleration there also may be cases where the boundaries between a Jewish sphere and some particular gentile sphere are not clear. The best example would be the urban slums in the immigrant era. In that event boundaries are enforced and demonstrated by street warfare and gang fighting. Definitions of "turf" take place in this way for Jews as well as for other newcomers. In American history there is no profound and specific political involvement with Jews that could produce violent attacks upon them at the outermost hostile extreme of Jewish-Gentile relations; but there have been cases, in the breakdowns of conventional law and order that take place from time to time, in which Jews became symbolic targets for the venting of general hostility. If this account of the situation is correct, it follows that the most extreme expressions of anti-Semitism are imported into America from abroad.

The Beginnings of Anti-Jewish Violence

Attacks on Jews have occurred sporadically all through American history, and most of these probably have never been recorded. The first major hostile acts against Jews in American experience occurred during the Civil War,[10] and the most important incident was the expulsion of Jews from the area of Tennessee by General Ulysses S. Grant. There were other issues—for example, Jews had to fight to get representation in the chaplaincy during that war— but the main incident was the expulsion of Jews as a class from Paducah and other parts of what was then Tennessee. This was a classic anti-Semitic action. One of the perennial aspects of anti-Semitism is that it is always involved with lies and false accusations, collectively applied. The expulsion of the Jews from Tennessee was ordered on the explicit grounds that Jews as a class are speculators, disloyal, and so forth—familiar libels in the long tradition of hostile stereotypes about Jews.

Obviously this action took place in a situation in which martial attitudes ruled. In such a situation, conventional restraints, forms of authority and legitimacy, are suspended, and discretion is in the hands of the commander to act outside normal regulations. One of the characteristics of American history is the wide latitude for this kind of movement outside the accepted framework, even in normal times. The annals of vigilantism are familiar, of course, and Rap Brown correctly stated that violence is as American as cherry pie. American society, even in normal times and particularly in its early frontier years, has been not just open and loose but frequently lawless. In fact, one historian of religion in America speaks of the American church as one of the "younger Churches" and of American Christians as "new Christians." The American church, in other words, no less than the Christian church among the pagan Germanic tribes, had to convert the heathen—the heathen in this case being immigrants who had been Christian abroad. The assumption was that west of the Mississippi, or even on the Mississippi, wherever one meets the frontier, one had to deal with drifters and riverboat gamblers, people who had thrown off all moral and ethical restraints, a mob among whom the rule of the six-gun holds sway.[11]

In the eyes of churchmen, the authority of legitimate symbolic systems had to be regained from this outlaw society by conversion, by extensive home missions, and by revivalist campaigns. So, too, secular law and order had to be regained from the outlaws by vigilante groups, for they thought that only by violence could the boundaries of legitimacy be reestablished. The relations between component groups in American society also took on a similar character. One need not speak only of the treatment of Negroes: Irishmen were beaten up in their anti-draft demonstrations, convents were burned, Italians were taken out of jail and lynched. In Kentucky, Tennessee, and southern Illinois, Hungarian miners were expelled and their homes burned. On the other hand, the IWW rebelled with equal violence. If the whole history of America is not filled with such continuous violence, at least it is by no means a minor theme in our national symphony.[12]

In the light of that experience, the question one has to ask is why there was so little violence against Jews. Not only were salient cases few, but, compared to anti-Semitic outbreaks elsewhere, they were relatively minor. Most accounts of anti-Semitism in America fol-

low the Civil War incidents with an account of the exclusion of
Joseph Seligman from resort hotels in the 1870s; or they move to
the anti-immigrant agitation of the 1890s. But the next violent
episode to gain wide attention was the Leo Frank case in 1913.[13]

Frank, a Jewish factory manager in Atlanta, was accused of rape
and murder and tried in a courthouse virtually open to the out-
doors, with a mob outside yelling instructions at the jury throughout. He was accordingly convicted, and there followed a long
agitation, deeply involved with the politics of the area, for the
commutation of his sentence and for his pardon. Just before leaving
office in 1915, the outgoing governor did commute Frank's sentence to life imprisonment. Thereupon, amid threats of mob violence, Frank's throat was cut by a psychotic prisoner who said he
was attempting to prevent an attack on the prison which would
endanger the other prisoners. The wounded Frank was then
dragged out of jail and lynched, and the corpse of the hanged man
trampled before being delivered to the undertakers.

This case became historically salient because of public, especially
Jewish, agitation over a presumed miscarriage of justice comparable to that of the Dreyfus case. Also in connection with the Frank
case, Tom Watson, a Populist agitator, developed an intensive
anti-Semitic campaign and made it politically successful. Finally,
following the example of the Knights of Mary Phagan, a night-
rider group arising out of the Frank case,[14] a renewed Ku Klux
Klan was organized, bringing to fruition Watson's propaganda.

This episode raises a number of questions. It appears, for example, that Tom Watson more or less stumbled onto anti-Semitism
as a useful political instrument. He was certainly anti-Semitic in
the same basic way as others, and he was generally a hostile character, so that his expected position on anti-Semitism–tolerance is very
much on the low-tolerance, high-hostility side. Nevertheless, it
appears that he took up the Jews as a theme for his political
agitation owing to the chance occurrence of the Leo Frank trial.
He reacted only after the intervention of Northern and Jewish-
sponsored defenders of Frank who, he felt, were impugning Geor-

gian justice and interfering in Georgian life. He then found that the anti-Semitic theme was effective, and he played it for all its worth.

Among the Northerners who signed protest petitions against the execution sentence passed on Frank was none other then Henry Ford, the same Henry Ford who in the 1920s became the prime mover of the next massive anti-Semitic campaign. Ford had bought the *Dearborn Independent* and used it as a medium for purveying the *Protocols of the Elders of Zion* to the American public. In the very act of doing so, however, he claimed not to be an anti-Semite. Even while selling the *Protocols* as truth, he blandly announced that he had nothing against the Jews as such; indeed, he had first learned about the "Jewish conspiracy" to dominate the world from a Jew on Ford's World War I peace mission. Ford did not identify which of the two Jews on his "peace ship" had allegedly been his informant, but one of them, Herman Bernstein, sued him for libel.[15]

Throughout Ford's involvement in anti-Semitic agitation he contended that he was acting in the best interests of the Jews themselves. This, of course, is standard practice today, when no one declares himself anti-Semitic: at most one is an anti-Zionist. Such a posture was not invented in our times but was characteristic of such undoubted political anti-Semites as Watson and Ford in America or even Stoecker in Berlin. Where this was not the case —and the title anti-Semite was openly avowed by Americans—it usually appeared as an import from the outside in such bodies as the American Nazi Party, and among some adherents of fascism.

Apart from those cases where the anti-Jewish obsession is primary, other anti-Semitic incidents—even those of violent potential like the Frank case and the closely related emergence of the Ku Klux Klan, or the anti-Semitism among the Populists earlier— have arisen in America out of peripheral attachment of Jewish issues to some major violent form of American popular activism, primarily oriented to other issues. The Ku Klux Klan is a major example of this. Jews, however, were indeed woven into a whole complex of nativist antagonisms, such as anti-Negro and anti-Catholic hostility. After World War I Jews became increasingly identified with the Communist foe, while at the same time they continued to focus mass anti-capitalist hostilities as well. Henry Ford's agitation was a major element in compacting the symbolic identification of Jews with these other objects of hatred.

A complete account of anti-Jewish violence in America would have to include big-city friction in immigrant communities. Statistically speaking, this is probably the most common kind of violence to which Jews were exposed in America: hoodlums pulling the beards of old Jewish men, sporadic street fights, harassment of Jewish youngsters, particularly coming out of Hebrew school, and fights between neighborhood gangs. This was regularly dismissed as "kid stuff" when the police did not wish to intervene. Included in this category were such acts as smearing swastikas on gravestones, setting fire to Hebrew schools and synagogues, tearing up Torah scrolls, as well as molesting old people in the street. Indeed, such actions do occur regularly on the fringes of urban quarters between one ethnic group and another.

One of the constant accommodations to this, of course, has been the development of Jewish gangs. The rise of Jewish criminality—or, at any rate, the prominent notice of it by gentile politicians—had a crucial relationship to the rise of the kehillah movement in New York.[16] The response of the new community organization was to conduct surveillance and establish contact with Jewish criminal elements in order to maintain the good name of Jews. But Jewish gangsters, like those in the slums, also had their positive social functions. A man like Big Harry Zelig served as a kind of godfather to the whole ghetto. If anyone in the neighborhood had trouble with Irish, Polish, or Italian hoodlums, he could expect Big Harry Zelig or his cohorts to see to it that the matter was taken care of.

This is, of course, a standard ethnic situation in the immigrant ghetto. In this particular ethnic confrontation a specific additional element was that the police were Irish. They would occasionally break up Jewish strike demonstrations and beat up members of Jewish funeral processions. Such a syndrome of police brutality, characteristic of earlier years, revived in the 1940s and became politically significant in the days when an appreciable proportion of the New York police were Christian Fronters.

To sum up, the basis for violence against Jews in America cannot simply be said to be anti-Semitism. There is, of course, endemic anti-Semitism in America as there is wherever there are Jews. But the transition from anti-Semitism to violence is not continuous; some additional specific cause has to be supplied to explain it. There is no particular saliency of Jews in American history which causes their presence to be a violently handled issue. What does occur is the involvement of Jews, fortuitously but with increasing continuity, in other issues which are salient and violently handled. Issues that provoked American violence and involved Jews in the past included populism, anti-Communism, anti-radicalism, and so on. This line of development may still be on an upgrade in some respects, while in other respects it has run its course. There has also been an importation of foreign types of political anti-Semitism leading to violence, particularly in World War II. Finally, there is violence arising from the problem of establishing boundaries between various ethnic groups in urban quarters. This last category rounds out what I think is a fair description of the forms in which violence has been encountered by Jews in America.

How, then, did Jews respond both to anti-Semitism and to violence? As a general rule, it is fair to say that all through Jewish history there has been a high propensity to respond; Jews are very sensitive to attack and do not have to be pushed to the wall before they react. The form of Jewish response is necessarily related to the circumstances under which they must defend themselves.

In the Warsaw Ghetto, for example, Jews had to respond to violence under conditions comparable only to those faced by a trapped bear in a bear pit,[17] a position that was unique among the resistance movements. In World War II resistance generally occurred when resisters to occupation could anticipate their rescue from the outside. They coordinated their actions with the approach of forces coming to liberate them. They were in contact with these forces and received arms and equipment from them. They had outside support and were part of the war strategy of some major belligerent force. In the Warsaw Ghetto no one was approaching to rescue the resisters, no one was supplying them with arms, notwithstanding the trickle that came in through the Polish underground, and no one coordinated strategy with them or had a strategy that included them. In fact, what they did was to exercise their choice of the method by which they were going to be killed. That was the limit of their freedom. External situations in Jewish history have repeatedly presented a similar suicidal choice, owing to the isolation inherent in the Jewish position.

Even short of such extremes, Jewish responses to attack must contend with the element of isolation. Methods of resistance for those who are essentially without allies may include a variety of choices. The search for allies is the predominant response of emancipated Western Jewries, even at the cost of Jewish self-abnegation. But even among Jews in isolation there are methods other than suicidal resistance. Jews may assume a protective coloration of passivity. One of the most ironical episodes in recent Jewish history was Mahatma Gandhi's advice during the Hitler epoch that Jews should adopt a policy of passive resistance. If there ever was a gratuitous suggestion, it was this one. There has been no more consistent demonstration of passive resistance as a method of living than that exemplified in Jewish history. The mere existence of the Jews in exile is an act of continuous passive resistance.

The Impact of Liberalism

America is one of that array of nations which opened up to the Jews a possibility of emerging from their isolation, the prospect of finding alliances, of being part of a more general cause. The Emancipation and Enlightenment opened up this possibility to Jews throughout Western Europe—in fact, the whole definition of Jews as being Eastern or Western European really hinges on that one fact. Western Europe ends at that line in the east where emancipation more or less succeeded by the last quarter of the nineteenth century, and Eastern Europe begins where it did not succeed until 1917, if at all.

The Jewish community in the West, and certainly the immigrant Jewish community in America, adopted by consensus (which implies, of course, that some were opposed) the view that Jews can make alliances, that the Jewish interest is not an isolated interest but can be united with other more general interests. More specifically, Jewish interests were seen as identical with the interests of a liberal order of society, which in America becomes essentially the interests of the American way of life. One of the characteristics of America is that everyone accepts the American Revolution.[18] This trauma in American history was not one that divided the nation, and whoever did not accept the American Revolution could only become an expatriate. The limit of permissible opposition is to argue that America is not a democracy but a representative republic, but that, too, is an acceptance of the American Revolution. When the American Jewish community allies itself with the general cause of liberalism as the basis for the emancipation and enlightenment of the Jews, it feels that it is not allying itself with a partisan group within the society but with the American way of life, with the most basic principles of American consensus.

This has a certain significance in terms of the political assumptions of Jews regarding their life in America, which may be a bit different even from the corresponding assumptions of Jews in Western Europe.[19] For example, it is not absolutely essential to a liberal Jewish attitude that there should be no independent Jewish politics or that separatist political activism by Jews on behalf of Jewish interests should be ruled out. American Jews, however, accept as a rule that politics must be nonsectarian. They resist instinctively making a Jewish cause of Jewish causes. That certainly is one possible way of being liberal. One could well draw the conclusion from the emancipation of the Jews that thereafter there is nothing but a religious aspect to Judaism. Consequently, there should be no Jewish politics; if Jews engage in politics it should always be in some general framework. This is the view that became dominant among American Jewry: no Jewish vote, no Jewish parties, and no Jewish political organizations.

But this is not the only way in which Western liberalism can express itself in a Jewish context. In fact, one of the conclusions one can draw from a consistent, or even radical, liberalism is precisely that Jews, like everybody else, are entitled to organize politically in pursuit of their own interests. One precursor of this view was the German Gabriel Riesser, who certainly was not a parochial or illiberal Jew. Riesser had broad, general political interests and involvements and was an important figure at the 1848 Frankfurt Parliament of the Germans. But he published a journal that he defiantly called *Der Jude*—almost in the same way that the blacks now call themselves "black." The implication was the same as when Herzl published *Der Judenstaat,* even though one of the then-current anti-Semitic usages was to refer to a Jewish or liberal newspaper as a *Judenblatt*—a kike sheet. "Jew" in Riesser's day meant the same thing as "Yid" or "kike." Precisely in terms of his liberalism, Riesser insisted that there must be an open, public defense by Jews of Jewish interests because these are essentially liberal interests, and that this must not be veiled in a nonsectarian front organization or submerged in more general propositions which do not mention Jews but only happen to apply to Jews. In this attitude, of course, he was expressing a liberal radicalism somewhat at odds with that of the Jewish establishment. The same thing might be said, to a degree, about Adolphe Crémieux, who, simply as a liberal, insisted on a militant prosecution of Jewish interests, as in his fight against the special Jewish oath.

It is my impression that a radical liberalism which requires that Jews should openly defend their own interests in their own person, and not by veiling them in more general expressions or using nonsectarian organizations to present their claims, became characteristic of a second wave of Jewish liberals in continental Europe. The first wave would establish something like the French Consistory, which subordinated itself and limited itself to governmental terms of reference, or the Gemeindebund, the religious organization of the German Jews. The second wave would establish something like the Alliance Israélite Universelle, at least in its early period (or like the Centralverein Deutscher Bürger Jüdischen Glaubens).

These bodies, especially the latter,[20] were characterized by a rebellion against the idea that Jews should not conduct their own defense but should rely instead on nonsectarian organizations to carry on the fight against anti-Semitism, or that this struggle should be conducted, if possible, as a general fight for liberal principles and not one concerned with specifically Jewish grievances. Instead they argued—more as liberals and Germans than as Jews, to be sure—that it was their duty of honor as German citizens to set up a Jewish body to defend Jewish interests.

This, then, is an alternative conclusion that may be derived from Jewish liberalism, and, in the case of Germany, it even led to proposals to establish a German Jewish party like the Catholic party.[21] Such religious parties were characteristic of European history, and Jewish liberals at certain times thought that this would have been an appropriate thing to do. These, however, were expressions of Jewish liberalism which barely found any application in America—perhaps because of the consistent, relatively radical separation of church and state in America. The universal attitude of the American Jewish community was to pretend that there was no Jewish vote; that attempts by politicians to use Jewish names or Jewish issues in order to garner votes were an offense against the Jews of America and had to be fought; certainly that there can be no Jewish parties; and, above all, that the Jewish community is nonpartisan and does not align itself officially, whatever the political preferences of individual members of the community may be.

Another important characteristic of American Jewish life is that it is organized in terms of voluntary association. We have no corporate framework imposed by the general structure of society or by law. This again is quite different from Central Europe—

indeed, different from most countries in Europe. Even in England, where free association is the basic principle, there are certain traditional corporate relationships establishing a pattern to which the Jewish community conforms. In America the entire community is basically established by free association of members, and the legally binding statutes of any Jewish organization are those it can have enforced in court as the laws of a corporate entity. These regulations are, of course, freely adopted and apply only to the members who freely associate with such a corporate entity.

The Question of Organized Defense

As a consequence, Jews have never succeeded in establishing a communal roof organization except in relation to issues concerning Jews abroad. Anything relating to American Jewish domestic issues has always been handled by Jews in the most pluralistic fashion. Whoever wanted to get involved in a problem as a representative Jew had as much right to this title as anybody else. The resulting confusion sometimes inspired efforts to coordinate organizational attacks on issues of Jewish interest; but when the issues involved were domestic Jewish problems, efforts toward unity usually collapsed. When they were at all successful, very often for a provisional period, it was because of some overwhelming emergency facing Jews the world over which arose outside America.[22]

This aspect of Jewish organization in America had a clear impact on Jewish issues during the Civil War, notably the chaplaincy issue and the expulsion from Paducah and other places in Tennessee. Who defended the Jews in those cases? A national Jewish body, the Board of Delegates of American Israelites, had been set up to represent Jews. This body was organized in response to a foreign issue, the Mortara case. While the Board was involved to a degree in the chaplaincy issue, its authority was denied by other American Jews in this and other matters of domestic concern. So long as it was a question of protesting persecution of Italian Jews by the Pope, then it was possible for American Jews to unite for this purpose—especially, I might add, since such protests were strongly supported by Protestants. The wave of know-nothingism and the general anti-papal mood among Protestant Americans from 1840 to 1860 assured Jews of general sympathy in such cases as the Damascus ritual murder charge and the Mortara kidnapping. The Board of Delegates' competence in matters like these was not severely contested, but what was resisted was any attempt to use that organization to impose a communal discipline in matters of Jewish education and ritual and so on, including the chaplaincy issue.[23]

The fight against Grant's expulsion order illustrates a different aspect of Jewish self-defense. Like many other instances of Jewish self-assertion in the West (including, for example, the struggle for the right to serve in the British Parliament without taking an oath as a Christian) the fight was waged by concerned individuals, with little or no involvement of any communal structure. In the Paducah case it was one of the expelled men, Cesar Kaskel, who organized a wave of protest action, and he enlisted the support of public opinion, non-Jewish as well as Jewish. There was no Jewish organization, no Anti-Defamation League or other defense agency to which he could apply to really take this matter in hand. The Board of Delegates, whom Kaskel consulted briefly, was not an effective body for such a purpose.[24]

Early in the twentieth century the American Jewish Committee also was established, primarily to deal with Jewish problems abroad. Not until 1913 was the Anti-Defamation League established to defend Jews against domestic anti-Semitism. By that time, the New York Kehillah had been organized in response to charges of Jewish criminality made by the police commissioner, Theodore A. Bingham. Having established a Jewish community organization in specific response to defamatory attacks against New York Jews, what functions did the organizers assign to it? In order to answer defamatory charges, the Kehillah set up a statistical bureau and proved that Jews were not inordinately inclined to criminality; in fact, their share of criminal cases was less than proportionate. The Kehillah also proved later that health conditions in the Jewish slums were relatively better than elsewhere. Thus, one function of a defense agency is to investigate and, if possible to refute, charges made against Jews.

Another, more interesting function is that of self-discipline. In specific response to Bingham's charges, a Jewish detective bureau was established in the Kehillah to check on Jewish criminality. Investigation was used as a preventative technique, to keep Jews in order by internal discipline.[25]

This, of course, is not the only reason for the interest of people like Judah Magnes in the Kehillah. They were scandalized not simply by chaos in the administration of the Jewish dietary laws but by the whole idea of a disorganized Jewry. Magnes and others like him at the time were disciples of Ahad Ha-am and Simon Dubnow, and they believed in communal organization for its own sake. But what made organization possible was the attack from the outside. American Jewry does not begin with a kehillah, an organized community which, among other functions, responds to attack; at best, it creates such an organization in response to attack, with a good deal of defensive and apologetic emphasis on self-discipline and self-control. In other words, the basic feeling is one of hesitation to do anything which would stamp the Jews as an independent political or infrapolitical entity. This, of course, does not apply to Magnes or to many other people who were the real pillars of the kehillah movement, but it can be said to be the basic consensus, the ruling opinion, which established the framework within which such leaders as Magnes were forced to work.

In the same period the Leo Frank case broke into the news. There was no communal Jewish involvement in this, but there was a very active, immediate, and continuously spreading response to a charge of perversion and crime against a respectable Jew. This Jewish reaction took place at once, as soon as Frank was charged, and it operated spontaneously through the channels of his family and social ties. It got to be a general Jewish issue right away, mainly through tribal and family susceptibilities. Eventually it involved Louis Marshall and others in Frank's defense, but not as representatives of an organized community. Precisely this massive Jewish reaction, especially when general Northern white support was successfully enlisted, touched off the full-scale, newspaper-promoted anti-Semitic reaction that accompanied this trial. It is obvious that anti-Semitic animus would have characterized the trial in any case, but one of the main themes of the anti-Jewish agitation around Frank's trial, and one of the universal grievances of anti-Semites, is this spontaneous Jewish solidarity. Southern anti-Semites bitterly complained that no sooner do you touch a Jew than all the Jews in America rise up in arms, start hiring high-priced lawyers from the North, and organize petitions with clergy-men and industrialists and everybody under the sun over a simple matter of an individual crime.[26]

A similar, but somewhat more complicated picture is presented by the case of Aaron Sapiro. Sapiro was a lawyer who brought a libel suit against Henry Ford's *Dearborn Independent,* which had attacked him for his work in organizing rural cooperatives. By the 1920s there were organizations in existence, particularly the American Jewish Committee, which could assume the job of defense against such attacks. But they had decided that the best way to treat Ford was not to puff up his importance. This did not mean passivity. Among the things done owing to organized Jewish pressure was the denial of mailing privileges to the *Dearborn Independent* on occasion, just as Ford on his side insisted that all his automobile dealers had to buy a certain number of issues of the *Dearborn Independent.* In other words, every bit of power available to a man like Louis Marshall was freely used, so long as it was done quietly. Inhibitions about freedom of the press did not really prevent action, but it was felt that the American Jewish Committee should not appear in these matters, owing simply to tactical considerations. Only when Ford backed down in the end, because of Sapiro's persistence and other circumstances, did the American

Jewish Committee enter into the picture, at the invitation of Ford. (It was a mere accident, incidentally, that the Committee rather than the American Jewish Congress was used. Ford's first application was made to Stephen S. Wise, president of the Congress, but he did not happen to be available.[27])

The situation in regard to Jewish self-defense had changed considerably during World War I. In part internal developments were responsible. Those ideological factions inclined to favor comprehensive community organization, Jewish parties, and other active political measures on behalf of the whole Jewish community rose to dominance and ruled the American Jewish consensus in the period of World War I. Immediately following the war they established the American Jewish Congress in the face of the American Jewish Committee's resistance. Thereafter their influence waned, but they continued to have at least a loud voice in Jewish affairs. There were also significant external factors. Beginning in the 1920s a politically motivated anti-Semitism began appearing more prominently on the American scene. It was partly native in origin: that is to say, produced by the accidental peripheral involvement of Jews in other issues that generated nativist organizations. The Jewish organizations were ideologically targeted in nativist agitation, particularly against radicals. They were even more central in the agitation of types of political anti-Semitism imported from the outside by such movements as the Christian Front and especially the American Nazi Party. I might add parenthetically, with reference to Father Coughlin, that here again, as in the case of Tom Watson and Ford, it is almost fortuitous that anti-Semitism became so salient in his propaganda. He, like others before him, found that for the purposes of his agitation on other issues an anti-Semitic theme paid off; he therefore played it to the full.

For the Christian Front anti-Semitism was hardly a mere peripheral question but rather a fully elaborated ideological attack on Jews as being centrally involved in everything distasteful in the contemporary world. As for the American Nazi party, anti-Semitism is clearly its major obsession. In the face of that kind of threat

Jewish defense organizations quickly went beyond the standard hush-hush and pressure tactics that they had customarily used and developed an additional counterespionage capacity. They did for the anti-Semites what the kehillah had done for the Jewish community: they set up investigatory agencies, sometimes working together with government agencies, in a strategy intended to undermine the organization of anti-Semitic groups. This method might have been facilitated, if not suggested, because of the way in which the Ku Klux Klan came to grief. The Klan fell apart because of corruption among its leaders. They used their positions as a personal racket, and when this was exposed the movement split up. The same kind of possibility was explored with reference to the Christian Front; and, from this, Jewish defense agencies developed a policy of constant surveillance of anti-Semitic activities, of organizing public counterdemonstrations every time anti-Semites demonstrated in Jewish sections, and of attempting citizens' arrests. By the 1930s, then, Jewish defense agencies had adopted much more militant and direct methods of work.

During the 1930s the Jewish establishment was confronted by challenges from within. The anti-Nazi boycott movement was initiated without their consent. It was taken up afterwards by some established leaders, like Stephen Wise. In this and other cases, the growing militancy of established Jewish leaders was an attempt in part to maintain their leadership in a Jewish community which, aroused by the lash of Hitler, was pressing for more and more militancy. Moreover, during World War II there was a rising curve of anti-Semitism in American public opinion, continuing even after Pearl Harbor right up to the opening of the second front.[28] There was a polarization of opinion in America regarding the Jews. The so-called "apathetic middle" drifted more and more to opposite poles. Some became more strongly pro-Jewish and usually also favored the opening up of a second front. Some became more strongly anti-Jewish. These tended to be America Firsters and Liberty Leaguers, especially in the early war years. Before Pearl Harbor attacks on Jews following anti-Semitic street-corner meetings and anti-Jewish hoodlumism with a political orientation developed in Boston and New York. Under these pressures Jewish organizations became more active and demanded positive government action against anti-Semitic assaults.

The Jewish community councils and mayors' committee on unity were immediate consequences of this activity.[29] The problem both in Boston and New York was to establish some sort of control over Christian Front proclivities within the police. This could only be done if Mayor La Guardia in New York or Governor Saltonstall in Massachusetts intervened and took suitable measures. Jewish communities (often under pressure from the outside, by journals like *PM* and the *New York Post*, or by a certain Belsky who ran a Jewish newspaper in Boston which exposed anti-Semitic attacks hushed up by the Jewish community leaders and the Boston papers) organized community relations councils and sought government action against racist agitators. Jews were allied in this cause with Negroes. They joined black leaders in pressing for legislation against discrimination in employment, public accomodations, and so on.

This brings up a final, contemporary topic which can only be mentioned briefly, namely black anti-Semitism. This is one of several cases of conflict between Jews and other minorities otherwise allied with them. Jewish defense activity against Christian Fronters is another instance. In this case Jews had to contend with the hostility of the Irish or the Catholic Church—that is, of groups who were part of the New Deal coalition to which Jews belonged. During the 1930s Jewish defense organizations had increasingly adopted the view that the Jewish interest is not simply identified with those of the poor, of the minorities, and of the left. These forces had often been thought to be the only ones that would defend Jews against anti-Semitism. Nevertheless, within that union of interests there were a great many divisions which became increasingly apparent in the wake of the Irish and Catholic anti-Semitism of the 1940s. More recently, the most pronounced outbreak of anti-Semitism occurred among blacks; if there have been pogroms in America, then they were conducted by blacks, mainly in Harlem. In the 1930s, the 1940s, and later in the 1960s the Harlem riots were in every respect equivalent to pogroms. This is true in spite of the fact that black rioters, like the seventeenth-century Cossack hetman Bogdan Chmielnicki before them, were not motivated solely by anti-Jewish animus; they were anti-white, just as he was anti-Polish.

Owing to their special position in American history, the blacks' anti-Jewish rage often was seen as black rage, not as anti-Semitism. In this way inhibitions against anti-Semitism that prevailed in American public opinion after the Holocaust were breached. Some Jews foresaw a future where once more they would stand alone exposed to hostility. More often, however, they pinned their hopes on restoring the old alliances. The Jewish community, too, could not react to their recent allies as to pogromchiks—at least not in effective unity.

NOTES

1. Hannah Arendt, *On Violence* (New York, 1970), pp. 41 ff.

2. Ibid., pp. 51 ff.

3. For an elucidation of the term "ideology" and related terms as I use them, see my essay "The Dynamic Elements of Culture," *Ethics,* LXV, no. 4 (July 1955), 235–49.

4. Premonotheistic, pagan societies, based on mythological cultures (see the essay cited in note 3), need not set up such exclusions. Cf. Eric Voegelin, *Israel and Revelation* (Baton Rouge, La., 1956), pp. 1–11.

5. See my exposition, "Anti-Semitism in the Perspective of Jewish History," in C.H. Stember, *Jews in the Mind of America* (New York, 1966), pp. 273–83.

6. James Parkes, *The Conflict of the Church and the Synagogue* (Cleveland, 1961); for a brief, popular exposition, see Parkes, *Anti-Semitism*, (Chicago, 1963), pp. 57–73.

7. Léon Poliakov, *Histoire de l'antisémitisme: de Voltaire à Wagner* (Paris, 1968); cf. Guido Kisch, *The Jews in Medieval Germany* (Chicago, 1949), chap. 5.

8. Cf. Abram Vossen Goodman, *American Overture: Jewish Rights in Colonial Times* (Philadelphia, 1947).

9. Cecil Roth, *A Life of Manasseh ben Israel* (Philadelphia, 1945), pp. 282 ff.

10. See Bertram Wallace Korn, *American Jewry and the Civil War* (Philadelphia, 1957), chaps. 4–7.

11. Frankin Hamlin Littell, *From State Church to Pluralism: A Protestant Interpretation of Religion in American History* (New York, 1962), introduction.

12. See Ray Allen Billington, *The Protestant Crusade, 1800–1860* (New York, 1938); John Higham, *Strangers in the Land* (New York, 1967).

13. See Charles Samuels and Louise Samuels, *Night Fell on Georgia* (New York, 1956); Leonard Dinnerstein, ed., *Anti-Semitism in the United States* (New York, 1961), pp. 87 ff.

14. Higham, *Strangers in the Land*, pp. 185 ff., 286 ff.

15. Ibid., pp. 277–86; Morton Rosenstock, *Louis Marshall: Defender of Jewish Rights.* (Detroit, 1965), chaps. 5–7.

16. Arthur Goren, *New York Jews and the Quest for Community* (New York, 1970), pp. 134 ff.

17. See Jacob Robinson, *And the Crooked Shall Be Made Straight* (Philadelphia, 1965), pp. 213 ff.

18. Ben Halpern, *The American Jew: A Zionist Analysis* (New York, 1956), pp. 15 ff.

19. Idem, *Jews and Blacks: The Classic American Minorities* (New York, 1971), chap. 4.

20. See Ismar Schorsch, *Jewish Reactions to German Anti-Semitism, 1870–1914* (New York, 1972).

21. See Jacob Toury, "Plans for a Jewish Political Organization in Germany (1893–1918)," *Zion,* XXVII, 3–4 (1963), 165–205 (in Hebrew with an English summary).

22. Harry L. Lurie, *A Heritage Affirmed* (Philadelphia, 1961), chaps. 1, 2.

23. Korn, *American Jewry and the Civil War,* pp. 68 ff., 72 ff. Moshe Davis, *The Emergence of Conservative Judaism* (Philadelphia, 1963), pp. 101 ff.

24. Korn, *American Jewry and the Civil War,* pp. 124 ff.

25. Goren, *New York Jews,* pp. 159 ff; Samuels, *Night Fell on Georgia,* pp. 174 ff., 188 ff.; Eugene Levy, " 'Is the Jew a White Man': Press

Reaction to the Leo Frank Case, 1913–1915," *Phylon,* 35, 2 (1974), 212–22.

26. Samuels, *Night Fell on Georgia,* pp. 178 ff.

27. Rosenstock, *Louis Marshall,* pp. 182 ff.

28. C.H. Stember, *Jews in the Mind of America.*

29. An unpublished Brandeis University study by Zvi Ganin covers the developments in Boston and New York thoroughly.

GRAENUM BERGER

14 The Role of Communal Workers in Jewish Self-Defense

I am neither a professional historian, nor a social scientist, nor a full-time academic, but an action-oriented administrator of contemporary Jewish institutions and communities. I have spent my life studying the works of historians, social scientists, and, most of all, the throbbing Jewish people, their organizations and their communal structures, in an effort to assist them in acquiring more knowledge of the Jewish historical experience, to intensify their active participation in Jewish familial and communal life, to exhort them to retain or develop anew a distinctive Jewish lifestyle. I prayed that this combination of factors would miraculously commit them to the continuity of the Jewish people against all the betting odds of discrimination, persecution, and destruction from the outside as well as from ignorance, indifference, assimilation, intermarriage, self-destructiveness (low birth rates and abortion) of their own doing. I have attacked these problems as a Jewish communal professional. In the contemporary scene those who work in this capacity may have come to occupy the most strategic position in defending and sustaining the Jewish community, particularly in the United States.[1]

My special assignment for this seminar was to examine the

attitudes of Jewish communal workers on the subject of violence and defense in order to evaluate whether their role is different from that of other types of leaders in the past and present. Leaders were once divinely designated, inherited, appointed, elected, arrogated —to name just a few means by which they rose—or they sprang up spontaneously when the situation warranted. The subject is worthy of a more comprehensive investigation, for the documentation, if and when it does exist, is both scant and scattered.

The Emergence of Organized Defense

Leadership for both offense and defense in previous periods of Jewish history was exercised by kings, judges, military commanders, scholars, businessmen, and guerrillas. Occasionally even ordinary working people attained stature of heroic proportions. The profession of Jewish communal worker, apart from that of rabbis, religious functionaries, and teachers, is of comparatively recent origin, arising only in the last century and most dramatically in the last fifty years. The ongoing functions of the Jewish community— tax collection, religious rites, slaughtering, marriage, divorce, operating hospices for travelers and the sick, dispensing charity, ransoming captives, endowing poor brides—were usually assumed (more definitively after the destruction of the Second Commonwealth in 70 C.E.) by well-to-do laymen, by designated but usually unpaid volunteers, or by learned individuals and ordained rabbis who did not possess pecuniary resources.[2] In Eastern Europe the machinery of the kahal (the administrative body of the community) was conducted in part by paid personnel, but except for the distinguished laymen—shtadlanim or court Jews who knew their way among non-Jews—we know little of the roles of the rank-and-file communal workers in dealing defensively with militance from the outside.

During the Maccabean period Jews had learned through bitter

experience that if they wished to survive they might even have to set aside their most sacred rites. Thus they finally and reluctantly agreed to violate the holy Sabbath by fighting their enemies on that awesome day. Without the leadership of Mattathias this fundamental policy in the defense of Jewish life would not have been adopted, for the high priest was not prepared to alter the law.[3] Would that the Israelis had been equally vigilant on October 6, 1973 (Yom Kippur), when war erupted.

Throughout Jewish history, particularly in ancient Israel, there have been occurrences of violence and militance (or defiance) as a result of disputes over person, property, or territory—even to the extent of war, as in most societies. After 70 C.E.—except for the ill-fated Masada episode, the Bar Kokhba revolt some sixty years later, and an abortive uprising in the seventh century—Jewish experiences were largely limited to self-defense on a local level, not always even involving the entire community, rarely in concert with other Jewish constituencies. If Jews survived the assault, they seldom gained power from the experience and did not acquire the means to counteract attack more successfully the next time. Thus the same misfortunes were repeated throughout the period of Jewish exile. It was not until the Russian pogroms after the 1880s, the development of the shomrim during the earliest settlement of Palestine, the forming of Jewish brigades in World Wars I and II, and the creation of the State of Israel that paramilitary and military preparedness began to be manifested effectively.[4]

Prior to that, over the long span of history, Jews per force enjoyed what modicum of peace they could find in the intervals of surcease from discrimination, persecution, death, and exile. Special pleading, bribery, concealment, and escape were the common instruments of their diplomacy and tactics. Occasionally, to avoid unremitting depredations, they converted to the dominant faith or assimilated into the majority culture. Some practiced Judaism in secret and, as in the Inquisition, were frequently burned at the stake. They even resorted to Masada-like martyrdom through group suicide in York (England), in Germany during the Crusades, and following the Chmielnicki savagery in Poland during the mid-seventeenth century—much as suicide went against the traditional grain of the Jewish people, as evidenced by the fact that even today Jews have lower rates of suicide than almost any other group.[5] The remarkable liturgical acrostic prayers written to prepare Jews to accept death voluntarily *al-kiddush ha-Shem* rather than be raped, forcibly converted, or slaughtered are evidence that for medieval Jews suicide was often a means of defense—the only alternative to dishonor and spiritual defeat. During World War II suicides occurred in the Nazi death camps after inmates were subjected to every kind of barbarity that evil minds could devise. Officials of the Jewish community councils often took their own lives rather than participate in the selection of individuals who they knew would eventually reach the death chambers.[6]

Hannah Senesh, at the age of twenty-three, was literally suicidal in her effort to rescue Jewish people. With fellow paratroopers she dropped behind the lines over Yugoslavia, made her way underground to Hungary, was captured, brutally tortured, and finally executed in 1944. Would her life have been spared had Rezso Kastner, a Jewish official, exerted himself in bargaining for her release? In the subsequent trial in Israel on charges brought by Malchiel Greenwald, Kastner was accused of neglecting many other Hungarian Jews in favor of helping his family and friends while cooperating with Nazi officials. The court found him guilty, but the Supreme Court reversed this verdict. While Kastner made good his defense in court, in 1957 he was violently assassinated in front of his own home.[7]

In contrast to the violence involved in individual, group, or mass suicide, one can describe in greater detail the most common form of defense that Jews have used throughout history, namely bribery in one form or another, as the immediate response to threats from the outside in order to save their own lives, to save their property, and to defend an entire Jewish community. I call such acts bribery whether they were surreptitious, or presented in the form of official tribute, or disguised as special taxes; whether they were exacted from an individual, a special group (usually those with property), or from an entire community. Bribery became almost an institution in Jewish life—or, in the case of some of the taxes mentioned, it *was* an institution. The victims accepted it as a normal feature of their experience. In the summer of 1966 I made a study of personal and social pathologies among Jews in different parts of the world, trying to contrast their behavior with that of the native populations. The paper was being prepared for an international conference of Jewish communal workers. There was little material on South America, so I spent part of that summer visiting Jewish communities in Venezuela, Brazil, Uruguay, Argentina, Chile, Peru, Colombia, Panama, and Mexico. As I went over a list of "deviant behaviors," which included divorce, separation, premarital and extramarital sex, prostitution, alcoholism, homosexuality, juvenile delinquency, and adult crime—all problems with which Jewish communal workers are partially occupied—the response was generally the same everywhere: we have none; we have very little; we have not had an incident for many years. So I took another approach and started to break down adult crime into homicide, manslaughter, assault, robbery, arson—and when I mentioned bribery the reply was instant and questioning: since when is bribery a crime?

How did Jews in the early days of their settlement in America respond to threats and attacks on Jews in other parts of the world? In the 1840s the Damascus affair startled the Jewish world. Leading Jews in Damascus were tortured, and one died when the blood libel charge was leveled against them following the disappearance of a superior of the Franciscan convent and his servant. Investigations of the "ritual murder" led to the Jewish quarter, where confessions were forced upon the alleged culprits. Jewish leadership in France and Britain took up the cause and protested vigorously. The American consular representative in Syria, one Jasper Chassaud, in his report to the Secretary of State, then John Forsyth, almost gleefully accepted the ritual murder libel against the Syrian Jews. Sir Moses Montefiore and the Jewish Board of Deputies of England importuned Lord Palmerston, the British Foreign Minister, to use the moral and diplomatic force of Great Britain and its empire to stop the persecution. The British government in turn persuaded the United States to act in the same condemnatory way as an expression of its humanitarian concern for the threatened Jews. How did the American Jewish community, then numbering only 15,000, act? According to one authoritative account, "Only after all these events had taken place and when, without Jewish knowledge, the American State Department had already placed itself officially on record in favor of humanitarian intervention, did the first mass meeting of American Jews . . . take place . . . in New York City on August 19, 1840."[8]

How different was this belated action of a tiny, insecure minority from a meeting that I attended in Madison Square Garden in 1971, when 18,000 people crowded into that indoor arena to protest continued refusal of the Soviet Government to allow Soviet Jews to emigrate. There was an overflow audience of thousands in the streets vociferously greeting the speeches of Senator Henry M. Jackson, of recently freed Russian Jews, and of others. This meeting had been preceded by unabashed advertisements in major newspapers, letter-writing campaigns to congressmen, the State Department, and the president himself, and announcements on radio and television. How bold American Jews were in 1971 with nearly 6,000,000 Jews in the United States and how fearful in 1840. True, Jews had pressed their own and other governments to take action in the intervening years on many occasions, but never quite with the air of confident militancy that has emerged in recent years.

In Russia the iniquitous May Laws (May 3, 1882) prohibited Jews from dwelling in or acquiring property except in the Pale of Settlement. There were expulsions from various communities, intolerable overcrowding, denial of economic opportunities, and organized physical persecution. In response, distinctive self-defense units began to emerge. There was wholesale emigration of Jews from Russia during the period that the laws were in force (they were revoked in March 1917 after the Revolution). The resident

Russian Jewish leadership was concerned with other issues besides Jewish well-being. Their preoccupations were reflected in the militant revolutionary socialism and its counterpart among the Jewish Bundists and in the nascent nationalist, sectarian Labor Zionist movement, to which they lent their support. These movements were new phenomena among the Jewish people, disillusioned with the not fully realized freedoms initiated and promised almost a century earlier during the heyday of the French Revolution and the Napoleonic period. Those emancipatory developments had raised many hopes, but their most pervasive outcome seemed to be the arousal of chauvinistic nationalisms and the awakening of the long-dormant forces of nativistic anti-Semitism.

The ideological movements which had sought to overthrow the royal, military, clerical, and bourgeois hegemonies throughout Europe inevitably produced reactions from the Right that somehow managed to coalesce enough forces to quell their turbulent currents. In every such reaction anti-Semitism seemed to gain in force, and Wilhelm Marr coined that very term in 1879. The wide circulation of the *Protocols of the Elders of Zion* and the anti-Semitic reaction associated with the Dreyfus Affair convinced Jewish intellectuals and their youthful followers that anti-Semitism was a permanent part of the problem to which they must direct their attention. They began to formulate answers for the normalization and continuity of Jewish life by urging the creation of a permanent homeland in Palestine, although for some Jews any haven, even in Africa, South America, or elsewhere, might have been an equally desirable alternative in order to flee to freedom, attain economic security, and enjoy some measure of autonomy.

Outright pogroms before, during, and after World War I were to some extent countered by self-defense units including some even bearing arms. But these efforts were not always universally approved by Jews. Jewish self-defense was encouraged and often inspired, however, by Jewish writers such as Hayyim Nahman Bialik, Ahad Ha-am, and later Vladimir Jabotinsky. Defense organizations were often led and abetted by teachers and their students; they in turn enlisted Jewish workers such as butchers, woodsmen, and coachmen, who were physically strong and courageous and who could also wield a knife, an axe, or a whip expertly to defend themselves, their families, and the honor of the long-abused Jewish people. Jews who had been forced to serve in the armies as conscripts brought back with them a knowledge of military organizational methods and the skills to use all weapons with effectiveness. The long-held belief that Jews were a cringing people who avoided any face-to-face encounter and conflict, who were devoted to peace at any price, was now seemingly coming to an end. No longer would they simply bare their throats for easy slaughter by organized or drunken hoodlums or by "unofficially" organized persecutors; nor would they abjectly obey official discriminatory decrees, although these were to be enforced by state military personnel. There are reports that they used blasts of a shofar as a communication system.[9] But Hitler's ovens, gas chambers, and mass shootings later proved that the Jews had not learned the lesson of total defense sufficiently to combat a massive, evil machine powered by the full force of a modern nation state and offering no opportunity for resistance or escape.

Despite constant provocations, Jews probably never learned to hate sufficiently and universally so that the full impact of this emotion could be put in the service of defense. Writing some years ago about the role of his fellow Jews in battling for the establishment of the State of Israel, Menahem Begin asked: "Was there hate in our actions? In our revolt against the British rule of our country? To such a question, the sincere answer is Yes. But was it hatred of the British people as such? The sincere answer is No."[10] Thus, even in an underground leader of the Irgun, writing in a book in which he chose to have Rabbi Meir Kahane, the leader of the Jewish Defense League, write the foreword, one can find no admission of unbridled hate.

The emerging militancy of Jews was viewed by the rank and file more in terms of a class struggle than as a defense of distinctively Jewish rights. Yet, even when this attitude associated itself with the "coming world revolution," by and large Jews often established their own "national" groups, such as the Bund, a Jewish unit within the overall political organization. This caused Lenin to refer to the Bundists as Zionists who were afraid of seasickness.

When Jewish rights were violated abroad, Jews resorted, by dint of their occasional influence on the governments of France, England, Germany, and the United States, to protesting such acts on the part of foreign states (Syria in the Damascus Affair, Italy in the Mortara incident, Russia in the pogroms, etc.) with the hope of stopping the outrage. If this failed, Jews called for cutting off diplomatic and commercial relations.

Shtadlanim were prepared to exercise their often powerful international financial muscle. The leadership perforce had to be constituted by outstanding and well-to-do Jewish laymen, such as Montefiore, Cremieux, Rothschild, Schiff, Strauss, and Marshall. It could not have been made up simply of well-meaning Jewish communal workers. Laymen created and led such organizations as the Board of Deputies of British Jews, the Anglo-Jewish Association, the Alliance Israélite Universelle, and later the American Jewish Committee and other communal relations bodies. Rabbis, too, were often in the forefront of protests in behalf of Jewish rights —generally in association with key lay leadership, although there is evidence in the literature of American Jewry that the rabbis often spoke for themselves, or at best their congregations, and only rarely as representatives of the Jewish community at large, until they became the presidents of national bodies.

In America during the period of violence which grew out of the slavery issue, Jews and their leaders, including rabbis, could be found on both sides of the controversy. In the South some Jews were slaveholders and they defended the Confederacy. One, Judah Benjamin, even became its vice-president, and when the Civil War came to an end at Appomattox he was forced to flee the country.

With the creation of the American Jewish Committee in 1906, the B'nai B'rith Anti-Defamation League in 1913, and the second American Jewish Congress in 1928, for the first time professional

Jewish leadership emerged and became involved in the development of policy and the execution of a program. But up until World War I, and even for a decade or two thereafter, Jacob H. Schiff, Felix M. Warburg, and Louis Marshall were the names usually associated with statements in defense of the Jewish community. Cyrus Adler, a native-born Jewish scholar, was the exception, but it is not clear whether he acted as a layman or as a professional in his association with the leaders mentioned above. Rabbi Judah L. Magnes emerged as a distinctive professional servant figure when he became head of the New York Kehillah. Later Morris Waldman, John Slawson, and Bert Gold, executives of the American Jewish Committee, and others like Benjamin Epstein, Arnold Forster, and Isaiah Minkoff became the formidable spokesmen, backed by staffs all employing a retinue of experts and professionals. Today the budgets of the principal Jewish communal groups run into millions of dollars annually and each is housed in its own imposing edifice.

The first major demonstrations in which Jews acted militantly and in distinctively Jewish groups, even when allied with other ethnic organizations, occurred in their involvement within the labor movement. A number of the leaders had been trained in underground movements in Europe, which involved constant risk, heroism, and spartan discipline, and they tended to build up a climate of unprecedented militancy in their behavior.[11] Many immigrant Jews had brought in their baggage a recently found liberalistic, socialistic, or revolutionary fervor, and they soon organized to use it to protest against the indecent sweatshop conditions, the unhealthy working and living environment, the working conditions in the factories with their multiple hazards of fire and accident, the low pay, and the lack of job security.[12] The unions, which were well-disciplined and under Jewish leadership, began to make demands on their exploiting Jewish employers and resorted to the one weapon that they could use with authority, albeit not with impunity, the strike. The articulate Yiddish press aided and abetted their efforts, educating reluctant Jews and exhorting them to act.

The employer, with the support of the existing laws and the police, did not hesitate to retaliate by locking out and dismissing his workers, seeking eager replacements from the floodstream of impoverished immigrants who had fled from Russia to the *"goldene medina."* It was not until the Triangle Fire in 1911, when 140 young shirtwaist Jewish women workers were burned or leaped to their deaths, that Jewish militancy, pressed to the extreme, began to show signs of making headway.

But once again Jews with a passion for moderation and compromise called in leaders such as Louis Marshall and Louis D. Brandeis, who had already developed a reputation for resolving major human and legal disputes, and initiated the celebrated form of arbitration agreements, "protocols of peace," which stood as classic instruments for the resolution of difficulties within the Jewish industrial and commercial communities. Employers were forced to bargain with the union thereafter. In some respects this arbitration paralleled the procedure of the boards of Jewish conciliation, which had dealt with individual, domestic, and family problems within the Jewish world. Here public-spirited Jews responded with vision to the protests against unfair employers. The government, although it usually sided with the employer, was not yet a major object of Jewish wrath.

Other problems of Jews in New York called for a different kind of response and discipline. Prostitution, both juvenile and adult crime, and a kind of Jewish "mafia" were beginning to arise with the unmanageable immigration and the resulting social dislocation and moral decline. Men had left their wives and families behind. None had been prepared for the breakdown in Jewish family and community values which by and large had controlled their lives in the shtetl and even in larger European Jewish communities. Jewish criminals were charged with poisoning the horses of drivers in order to intimidate or eliminate business competition. These unholy practices, so uncharacteristic of Jews, drew unfavorable criticism from the public, the press, and the police commissioner of New York. Jews were accused of being wild, bestial, dirty, and immoral, of bringing their evil foreign ways to what was innocently described as a once staid community. Obviously this gentile criticism ignored their sobriety, their phenomenal educational motivation, their introduction of advanced cultural forms in the theatre, press, and literature, their unusual commercial and industrial energy, and their philanthropic generosity—which a few writers did happily record for posterity.[13] The natives had too soon forgotten their own American history, the violence which had attended the development of New York from its onset, the hooliganism that marked the period of the Civil War, the Irish rebellions, the riots of the blacks, and the problems that accompanied every new influx of immigrants from every part of the world. Each recurring wave of migrants had to experience the same slanderous attacks.

As a response to these problems, the Jewish community formally established for the first time a kehillah, an organized way of dealing with the problems that arose internally and with threats from the outside. It was formed with great labor. The well-established and better-endowed German Jewish constituency was unnerved by the raw, noisy, new, and poorer Eastern European Jews. Capitalists confronted radicals. Employers were embarrassed to sit down with workers. Struggles for power were everywhere evident. Somehow the kehillah movement, most notably the New York Kehillah, was kept alive from its onset in 1908 until its gradual demise in 1922. It ushered in changes which ultimately led to a Jewish community better organized to serve the philanthropic interests of Jews. Under the leadership of Samson Benderly, Jewish education underwent a great transformation, utilizing the newly developed theories of progressive education as expounded by John Dewey and William H. Kilpatrick at Teacher's College of Columbia University. The youthful rabbi Mordecai Kaplan introduced the concept of the broadened synagogue-center, which ultimately influenced the character of almost all Jewish religious institutions as well as their rabbinic leadership. The New York Kehillah promulgated a research bureau to provide sound information, to make possible the assessment and answering of charges leveled against the Jews and to provide the background necessary for intelligent handling of the social and communal problems that emerged from immigration, congestion, and social dislocation.[14]

The emergence of the professional worker as community leader was manifested most dramatically by Judah L. Magnes, a fervent exponent of Jewish community organizational discipline and of a forthright approach to dealing with problems. Yet he was partly responsible for the ultimate dissolution of the kehillah, certainly for its weakening, because of his attitude of passionate pacifism and his opposition to America's entry into World War I. In succeeding years Magnes's stand repeatedly raised the question and problem of whether a professional has the right to take independent, personal positions at variance with the views of the dominant community leaders or the self-perceived interests of the overall Jewish community.

World War I and Immigration

When the war broke out in 1914 Jews were indifferent to the fate of czarist Russia and were therefore often accused of being pro-German. The established leadership of the Jewish community was largely of German origin. Recent immigrants who had suffered under the czarist regime were adamantly and unashamedly anti-Russian. However, the subsequent ruthless behavior of the German Kaiser and his army as they trampled over their European neighbors; the sinking of ships by submarines frequently without warning; the growing fear that the fragile balance of power in Europe would be upset by a total German victory; the role of Turkey, which then controlled Palestine, in siding with Germany; the disruption and destruction of whole Jewish communities by the uncontroled ravages of war in Central and Eastern Europe; the prospect of a socialist revolution in Russia that would replace the crumbling czarist monarchy; and the possibility that England would declare for a Jewish homeland in Palestine—all this ultimately contributed to a complete change of sentiment in the Jewish community, so that overwhelmingly it threw in its lot with the Allies. Tens of thousands of young Jewish men went off to war, and the National Jewish Welfare Board was established to work with Jewish recruits in the camps and at the front. Amid the rising tides of nationalistic sentiments aroused by the total collapse of the Romanoff and Hapsburg empires and often seeking expression in anti-Semitism, fundraising campaigns were undertaken to provide relief for the impoverished Jews caught in the European battlegrounds.

By 1917 opposition to the war would have been unpopular. Yet Magnes, then a prominent Jewish leader, still took a pacifistic position on principle. At that time such a stand was deemed inimical to Jewish interests abroad. Substantial support was withdrawn from the kehillah, and this ushered in its premature demise. Magnes suffered greatly in loss of prestige and position, but he was not defeated as a person and ultimately went on to head and develop the Hebrew University on Mount Scopus in Palestine. He never gave up his views on peaceful resolution of any conflict, and in Palestine he sought an accommodation with the Arabs even to the point of advocating a binational Jewish and Arab commonwealth.

After World War I Jews with pacifist and socialist platforms were elected to public office in New York State, but the reactionary forces that soon came to dominate American political thinking drove them from their posts, and one suspects that they were opposed as much for being Jews as for their liberal outlook.

Jewish communal workers came to the fore during World War I with the creation of the massive relief organizations in the United States which were essential to assist the Jews of Europe, then suffering from unparalleled economic, educational, religious, and familial dislocations. Russians, Poles, and Rumanians vented their anti-Semitism in full-fledged pogroms. American Jewry sent experts (Boris D. Bogen, Joseph Hyman, Israel Friedlander, and others) to study and help repair the damage. But a reading of the literature gives little information as to the attitudes of these investigators regarding violence, war, or Jewish militant self-defense organizations. Communal workers participated avidly in major fundraising campaigns,[15] which openly stressed an allied victory and the hope for ultimate restoration and rehabilitation of families and communities. Some, including a number of Jewish scholars, participated in the postwar conferences for the securing of minority rights, urging that such rights be accorded to European Jewish communities and hopefully guaranteed by the newly created League of Nations—even though this stand in some cases went counter to their adopted American views in favor of individual citizenship rather than group identification as a minority, at least for Jews in the United States.[16]

Some Jewish communal workers became advocates of a Jewish homeland in Palestine. This stand developed prior to the Balfour Declaration and was reenforced by it, but most saw the Jewish homeland largely as an option rather than as the major thrust of Jewish interests and felt that any such state would have to be established and guaranteed by the international community rather than by the force of Jewish soldiery—despite the fact that Jewish settlers in Palestine had already demonstrated their ability to defend themselves quite creditably. These leaders did not yet see Palestine as a land that might have to be taken by force should the Arabs and the surrounding nations resist Jewish immigration. But in response to the realities of their situation, Jewish settlers in Palestine had organized their own self-defense for decades, from the beginnings of the nineteenth-century Bar Giora movement with its distinctive military garb,[17] to the Shomrim, the Hashomer, and finally the Haganah. The movement for self-defense was broad based. A reading of various biographies of Israelis points to the involvement of intellectuals and communal workers as well as workers in the defense units. Their later service in the British Army also proved useful in the tactics as well as larger strategies that were used to counter repeated Arab attacks during the riots of the 1920s and 1930s.

Open immigration to the United States and elsewhere has always been the policy keynote of American Jewish communal organizations. In the first quarter of the twentieth century they exerted strenuous efforts to counter the invidious campaigns for more restrictive immigration. These efforts ultimately met defeat, but not before several million had found their way to the American shore. The rising nativistic anti-Semitism of the 1920s, allied with disgruntled labor organizations, resulted by 1924 in laws designed to keep out Jews, Asiatics, Eastern Europeans, and Mediterranean groups. Quotas were established based on the census of 1890, when there were relatively few Jews in the United States.

With the end of World War I, Jews had to set up more permanent self-defense units in Poland, Rumania, and elsewhere in order to survive. As a group they did not prosper from either side in the civil war that raged in Russia. Everywhere boycotts threatened their economic life. The numerus clausus kept them out of the universities and the professions. Pogroms were unremitting between the two world wars.

No doubt some American relief money ultimately passed into the hands of the self-defense units wherever it was possible for it to be forwarded surreptitiously, but at best this form of support was feeble help. Reading the reports of various Jewish communal workers during this period of ten to twenty years, one is struck by the picture of abject misery that emerges, the desperate pleas for relief. The possibility of direct action and advocacy or of calling for support through more militant local action seems not to have been real or feasible in the minds of the suppliants. Formally, the Jewish world protested any attack through the United States government or, when they had an opportunity, in the halls of the League of Nations far away in Geneva. But it was the Jewish organizations, with their recent foreign roots, that adopted strong, independent positions urging both international action as well as freedom for Jews to migrate abroad, including to Palestine.

While Jews were fighting for open migration to rescue their brethren from Eastern Europe, they also tried to get them out of the New York area—to farms in the East, the Midwest, or Texas, as in the case of the Galveston movement. Similarly, Jewish organizations tried to encourage Jews to change their occupational patterns, urging them to become artisans and even setting up special technical schools for them. Jewish agricultural schools and the Jewish Agricultural Society were founded with funds donated in substantial sums by the philanthropic banker, the Baron Maurice de Hirsch. Many of these programs and benefactions affected the lives of tens of thousands of Jews for decades thereafter, even though the basic concept of these projects ran counter to what the Jews in their newfound land generally wanted to do with their lives. American Jewish leaders felt these policies were necessary in order to counter the bigotry engendered by Jewish concentrations in the cities and in relatively few trades and services. The experience during this period led to similar efforts at relocation and retraining during the Nazi period, after World War II, and, more recently, with the emigrants from the Soviet Union.

Leftist Jews and Anti-Semitism

After the liberalism of the Wilson administration and America's failure to get involved in world affairs through the League of Nations, the nation went into a tailspin of reaction. Heightened by unemployment and the depression of the early 1920s, although nothing like the inflation that Germany experienced during the same years when money literally became worthless, the atmosphere was sufficient to "keep foreigners out of the country" who were allegedly taking away jobs. The Russian Revolution also had its repercussions in America, where there was a witch hunt to contain and imprison any menacing "Reds." Jews identifying with Russia as their country of origin or showing sympathy with the emergent communist movement were in double jeopardy. Extreme anarchists like Emma Goldman were actually deported to Russia as early as 1919.

The struggle against radical Jews had its counterpart in the division within many sections of the Jewish community—unions, *landsmanschaften,* anti-Zionists, and various individuals who identified themselves totally with the Soviet regime created troublesome schisms from which the Jewish community suffered for a number of decades. The conflicts not only disrupted the Jewish groups and brought negative publicity, but their disturbing influence had an effect on the character of local Jewish community organization personnel, an effect which has not been completely extirpated even to this day.

The development of native anti-Semitism took a blatant form with the assistance of that great, confused, industrial and mechanical genius, Henry Ford. Ford ushered in a cheap automobile that revolutionized transportation; he was the first to pay five dollars a day to workmen; he financed a "peace ship" which unsuccessfully attempted to end the war in Europe; he considered history "bunk."[18] Apparently he had enough spare time to listen to evil counsel against the Jews, and through the *Dearborn Independent,* the newspaper he supported, he managed to spew forth widely the spurious *Protocols of the Elders of Zion* as well as other vicious anti-Semitic articles for a number of years.

This aroused the Jewish community to counter these widely publicized attacks. First Jewish leaders tried through sober rejoinder to inform the public that the documents were forgeries, that Jews were not involved in a world conspiracy, that Jews represented a wide spectrum of political and social opinion, but that these were individual traits and not part of any concerted racial history or devious economic, social, or religious design.

Jews appealed to Ford directly to desist, occasionally they threatened to boycott his automobile in favor of the costlier and more prestigious Dodge and Buick. Nothing was of any avail until 1924, when Aaron Sapiro, a former rabbinical student who had moved into law and assisted in developing labor unions, more particularly farm cooperatives, was attacked by Ford's newspaper for alleged involvement in a Jewish conspiracy to control American agriculture. The Jewish contribution to American and world agriculture was already most notably marked by the life and work of David Lubin, a Russian born Jew who died in 1919. Sapiro brought a million-dollar suit against Ford, who finally denied that he was an anti-Semite and settled out of court in 1927. He even wrote a public letter of apology.

But despite his disavowals, Ford had already sown memorable anti-Semitic seeds, which blossomed a few years later through the fluent voice of Father Edward Coughlin, who used the recently developed medium of radio communication to spread his venom more widely than any newspaper could have done. The unemployed millions during the 1930s did not need much encouragement to find a scapegoat for their continuing poverty. In 1942 Coughlin was finally ordered to desist by the hierarchy of the Catholic Church, but he had an open forum for nearly a decade.

Thus, when Hitler came to power in the German elections of 1933, the American Nazi Bund had already found a fertile audience for the exploitation of their own form of anti-Jewish propaganda.

The 1920s and early 1930s were attended by considerable violence in the United States that took on a peculiar configuration. Jewish gangsterism began to emerge on an embarrassing scale, including acts associated with the smuggling and illegal manufacture of alcoholic beverages during America's bold experiment with prohibition. Jews were dangerously involved in gambling rackets and often paid for this involvement with their lives. Jewish hooligans invaded the dress and suit industries, so that the garment and trucking business was haunted with bribery, crime, and violent deaths. This activity reached its peak with the prosecution of a group of Jewish criminals known as Murder Incorporated, whose swashbuckling manner and fast living made them heroes among some sections of Jewish youth. New YM-YWHAs were established to attract Jewish youth and in part to counteract such noxious influences.

Another area of violence on a smaller scale was that associated with the establishment of unions in the Jewish communal field during the 1930s. Workers militantly presented their demands against their own Jewish communal agency employers. Stirred partly by radical influences, partly by genuine humanitarian sympathies for the unemployed, and partly by the support given to the emerging union by the National Labor Relations Act, these workers had suffered greatly from the prolonged depression, which exacerbated their already inequitable economic and labor conditions and reduced them to borderline poverty. They were vehement when the government used armed force to repel protesting marchers on Washington. Political change became one of the hallmarks of their future interests. These workers eventually became a dominant force in Jewish communal work as many of them moved up the ladder to head important communal organizations.

This development was paralleled by student movements on college campuses where Jewish students had a large enrollment. The radicalization of the students was often contrary to the positions taken by the lay leadership and the even more conservative professionals who still headed most of the Jewish communal services. But some rabbis became identified with the leftist tendencies in the quest for some more rapid reform of the political system.

There were demonstrations, picketing, and strikes as the unions sought recognition and the establishment of their legitimacy. But the militancy of these groups did not always express itself when it came to supporting specifically Jewish struggles—whether the issue was opposing Arab attacks on Jews already settled in Palestine or combatting the British restriction on immigration of more Jews, particularly refugees from central Europe, to Palestine. Even in combatting Nazism abroad or its proponents on the American scene, Jewish radicals showed a weak record, preferring to use their energies to support the Loyalist cause in Spain. If they attacked the American Nazis it was largely because they saw them as they saw Franco, as obstacles to the export of Soviet-style socialism to America or to Spain. Strangely enough, the militancy of these groups allied them with the forces that were also urging isolation and pacificism within the United States. Senator Nye's investigations of the munitions industry in the mid-1930s gave rise to demonstrations for "scholarships not battleships" and parades for "no more war," activities in which Jews were conspicuous. The establishment of formal American relations with Soviet Russia in 1933 encouraged avid sympathies for that once condemned and internationally isolated country. During the period of the United Front, as the detente of that heady decade was called, exaggeratedly favorable attitudes were constantly being expressed regarding the noble political experiments undertaken in Russia on behalf of all of the peoples of the world. Many Jews believed that the establishment of an "autonomous" Jewish province in Birobidjan, on the outskirts of Siberia, heralded a new Jewish emancipation that could well outshine reestablished Palestine as the Jewish homeland. Although that barren region did attract thousands of loyal Soviet Jews, its pretentions as a substitute Jewish state were never realized, and the extravagant promises of the Soviet leaders and still more extravagant hopes of those who wished to believe them remained unfulfilled.

Although considerable disaffection and disillusionment with the Russian Communists set in with the infamous Kirov trials in the Soviet Union, and later with the revelation of the apparently incomprehensible Stalin-Hitler pact, there was still sufficient residual ideological strength in the leftist Jewish groups in America to frustrate any common Jewish stand against any Soviet action. The conflict among Jewish communal workers was reflected during the period of the pact when some came to work with buttons flagrantly declaring that "the Yanks are not coming." This posture was suddenly reversed when the Germans violated their sacred agreement and mercilessly attacked Russia. When the surprise Japanese attack on Pearl Harbor on December 7, 1941, finally convinced the United States that it must formally join with England, France, and the others in the war against the Axis powers, the old buttons were discarded and new ones immediately replaced them with the slogan calling for the opening of the "second front" that only days before the leftists had campaigned against.

The Response to Hitler

Jewish leadership unfortunately misinterpreted the rise of Hitler to power as simply a reaction to the economic problems born of the inequities of the Versailles treaty. America had tried to assist Germany with the Dawes plan, but the depression made it impossible to continue financial assistance to the already shaken Weimar Republic. Jews both in Germany and the United States felt that once Hitler came to power he would—like most politicians, even demagogues—act responsibly. Leaders of the American Jewish Committee even approached Hjalmar Schacht, the financial expert of the Hitler regime, and offered Germany immense loans in the hope that this assistance (another form of not-so-subtle bribery) would temper and even terminate the daily Nazi attacks upon the Jews. But they did not reckon with the by then well-established fact that Hitler had meant what he had written about the liquidation of the Jews and that he would proceed to strip them of their resources, their rights, their pride, and their strength. The instruments for the "final solution" were already in motion.[19]

The leadership of the American Jewish Committee was opposed to any boycott of Nazi Germany and thereby lost considerable prestige among the rank and file of the Jewish community. German Jews were equally opposed to boycotts and public demonstrations since they felt they would suffer more drastically as a result. The professional head of the American Jewish Committee declared that the proposed boycott had alienated the sympathies of non-Jewish German-Americans and had even produced a counterboycott by German-Americans, although in fact such efforts were insignificant.[20] Naomi W. Cohen's history of the American Jewish Committee is worth reading in its entirety for a vivid picture of the period and how the principal Jewish communal relations organization in the United States struggled to define an effective Jewish defense position.

Other Jewish organizations, such as the Jewish War Veterans and the American Jewish Congress, were more militant. There were newly formed anti-Nazi and anti-Fascist leagues, and there were periodic protest meetings against Hitler. There were boycotts of German goods, and attempts were made to avoid all contacts with Germany in business and tourism, even by staying away from the 1936 Olympic Games. If one attempts to assess how effective the Jews were in stirring up their own ranks, as well as American and world opinion, against Hitler's Germany, it can only be summed up as total failure. The only substantial success was in helping tens of thousands to escape from that country, mostly well-to-do and distinguished individuals—scientists, psychiatrists, doctors, dentists, lawyers, artists, writers, social scientists—who not only made a sterling contribution to the intellectual and professional development of the American and American Jewish communities but, through their aliyah, also laid the foundations for much of the great academic, scientific, and professional strength within Palestine and the future State of Israel.[21] The rescue of these captives was a success story from the outset, but it did not affect the fate of the great mass of Jews in Europe.

Unfortunately, not enough influence could be brought to bear even on Franklin D. Roosevelt, who was almost universally supported by Jewish voters in his four presidential campaigns. Many more Jews might have come either to the United States, to Palestine, or elsewhere had Roosevelt been more concerned. There is considerable evidence that American apathy in the presidency and State Department prevented a much larger migration of refugees to the United States and that neither the president nor the State Department was prepared to press England to open the doors of Palestine for fear of alienating the Arab world, whose leadership during World War II was identified with and supportive of the Nazi cause.[22] Roosevelt did give serious consideration to the settlement of some German Jewish refugees in the hinterland of Ethiopia, endorsing an outrageous plan evolved by Italian Fascists who wanted to colonize that recently conquered and impoverished land and hoped to attract the resources of the Jewish world. Roosevelt hoped that this plan would diminish the force of demands for greater Jewish immigration to the United States and Palestine. But Hitler vetoed the proposal since he had his own plans for the Jewish future.[23]

World War II brought about an alliance of virtually all groups within America. Hundreds of thousands of Jews fought in the Allied armed forces. They backed the war with their financial resources and made substantial contributions of their skills and scientific knowledge to the creation of food, weapons, and, of course, the atom bomb. They supported the creation of special Jewish brigades on the Palestine-African front, which were ultimately to provide the special military intelligence and skill that would prove indispensible in the Haganah's struggle with the British and in the war that followed against the Arab states after the Palestine Partition and the establishment of the State of Israel. Although most American Jews were not openly supportive of the more violent Irgun and Sternist tactics, nonetheless substantial sections of the American Jewish community applauded every act of sabotage[24] and even the assassination of the Right Honorable Walter Edward Guiness, Lord Moyne, in 1944 by two Palestinian Jewish youths.[25] Demonstrations and pageants held in the United States reflected a spirit of unabashed truculence.

Up until 1945 the Jewish community, despite the existence of many Jewish communal relations organizations and a growing professional fraternity that did communicate with one another, was divided on how to cope with all the assaults upon Jews in the United States and abroad. Some Jews liked to pretend that the problems did not even exist. Others feared that by venting these issues in public they would only spread the anti-Semitic idea through contagion. Some advocated attaching repulsive reputations to the bigots so that they would be shunned by respectable society. Others urged that Jews should pressure the press and radio to censor anti-Semitic remarks, but they usually met with no success since censorship ran counter to the constitutional guarantees of free speech, press, and assembly. Some wanted to expose the anti-Semite intellectually and hoped that in a fair presentation an intelligent citizenry would recognize the sheer error of these poisonous positions. A few activist groups, such as the Jewish War Veterans and various youth groups with political motivations, wanted to use militant means by breaking up meetings and attacking speakers at their anti-Semitic rallies. Some organizations invoked the law to prevent such meetings and publications, but they ran into court objections over the denial of democratic expression. Still others preached tolerance toward Jews in the simpleminded appeal that their fellow Americans should give Jews "a break."

Alliances were formed with non-Jewish groups, liberal churchmen, progressive labor unions, minority group organizations, and independent intellectuals who understood that if Jews continued to be the object of discriminatory attitudes this would ultimately spread and encompass others, repeating what had occurred in Nazi Germany. Non-Jewish speakers, publications, meetings, and conferences were financed entirely with Jewish funds to propagate these messages. Widespread efforts were made to publicize the Jewish contribution to American life in the fields of commerce, the arts, the sciences, philanthropy, medicine, psychiatry, and the recent war effort. Some Jews relied on the rhetoric of patriotism, preaching that the United States was the freest, the greatest democratic country in the world and in history.[26]

The revelations of the Holocaust in retrospect had no immediate impact on changing the defense mechanisms of the American Jewish community. At first Jews were stunned and frightened; later many became angry or contrite. But in the immediate postwar period Jews, like everyone else, were wearied of the prolonged fighting and wanted to get back to normal life. The major organizations (e.g., the American Jewish Committee), flushed with new resources, undertook studies on the origins of totalitarianism, hoping to uncover clues as to the psychology of prejudice and how to counter virulent anti-Semitism should it arise to plague another part of the Jewish world. Others (e.g., the American Jewish Congress) fostered closer intergroup relations. Campaigns were undertaken through both legislation and education to protect and extend democratic practices through which, it was assumed, Jews and other minority groups could prosper and achieve a greater measure of security.

The discovery that militant Jewish leadership did exist in the Warsaw Ghetto, in some concentration camps, in underground movements in Yugoslavia, France, and elsewhere, was memorialized through heroic novels, plays, innumerable documents, studies, pageants, and annual religious services. One such testimony to heroism, chronicled in the records of Yad Vashem, warrants recounting. Thus Yosef Gottferstein wrote:

"The Jews of Kelme, Lithuania, were already standing beside the pits which they had been forced to dig for themselves—standing ready to be slain for the Sanctification of the Name. Their spiritual leader, Rabbi Daniel, asked the German officer in command to allow him to say some parting words. He agreed, but ordered the Rabbi to be brief. Speaking serenely, slowly, as though he were delivering one of his regular Sabbath sermons, Rabbi Daniel used his last minutes on earth to encourgage his flock to perform *kiddush ha-Shem* with dignity. The German officer cut in and shouted at the Rabbi to finish, so that he could get on with the shooting. The Rabbi concluded: 'My dear Jews! The moment has come for us to perform the precept of Kiddush Hashem. I beg one thing of you: don't get excited and confused, accept this judgment calmly!' He turned to the officer and said: 'I have finished. You may begin.'

But at Kedainiai the Jews were already inside the pit, waiting to be murdered by the Germans, when suddenly a butcher leaped out of the pit, pounced on the German officer in command, and sank his teeth into the officer's throat, holding on till the latter died.

When Rabbi Shapiro, the last Rabbi of Kovno, was asked which of these two acts he thought was more praiseworthy, he said: "There is no doubt that Rabbi Daniel's final message to his flock concerning the importance of the precept of *kiddush ha-Shem* was most fitting. But that Jew who sank his teeth into the German's throat also performed the precept in letter and in spirit, because the precept includes the aspect of action. I am sure that if the opportunity had presented itself, Rabbi Daniel would also have been capable of doing what the butcher did."[27]

It is interesting to note that the boldest acts of defiance in the ghettos, camps, and underground often came from the rank and file, from socialist and Zionist youth groups who often fought desperately to the bitter end. Only such contentious groups had gained experience at fighting against desperate odds in their own self-defense organizations, which arose from their cruel victimization by the Polish and other regimes since the end of World War I.[28]

The unveiling of the full horror of the German death camps was traumatic for American Jewry, which in some part will never forgive itself for not having forced the American and Allied governments to undertake the rescue of the Jews and destruction of the instruments that led to their wholesale execution. The numerous articles and studies that have dealt with this subject range from religious rejections of the theory of the "death of God" after Auschwitz,[29] to accusations against the Jews themselves for not sacrificially resisting their destroyers,[30] to factual portrayals of the role of the Jewish leadership in both assisting Jews to escape and giving them every possible physical and spiritual comfort, even keeping some of them alive while under absolute Nazi control. Evidence indicates that at times Jews even supinely assisted the Nazis in their unprecedented genocidal program in order to save their own skins and perhaps some of their relatives and friends.[31]

Whether we would be better able to deal with such a situation again hopefully will never have to be tested. Undoubtedly Jews would exert more pressure behind the scenes and openly, as they have done in the 1970s for Soviet Jewry. But should another war cut off contact with Jews in jeopardy, the possibility of influencing an enemy's internal policy is reduced to nil.[32]

The zealous manner in which Jews in the United States and elsewhere fought openly and clandestinely to create and support the State of Israel was in part a reaction to the helplessness they had felt during the Holocaust. The victories of the Israeli army in four wars with the Arabs have instilled a sense of pride everywhere in the Jewish world, a feeling that now "we can take care of ourselves"—at least with aid from what friends we have abroad.

Renaissance and Acculturation

The postwar period brought a new blush of extraordinary wealth to the Jewish community. The long depression and the war period had forced Jews to defer their long pent need for greater freedom of movement, but finally they were able to focus on such issues as breaking down the barriers against admission to the best colleges and most sought after professions, which they had been denied by *numerus clausus.* Restrictive covenants in the ownership of certain properties had still not been totally obliterated. The Jews burst out of their old immigrant and secondary settlement neighborhoods and sought new, larger, and better homes in the best urban apartments, cooperatives, and condominiums, thus creating whole new Jewish sections in the mushrooming suburbs. They established imposing new synagogues employing the most creative architects and adorning these structures with bold, imaginative art works. New Jewish community centers and YM-YWHAs, hospitals, children's institutions, old age homes and residences, camps, and day schools proliferated in every Jewish population center in the country. Fundraising bodies for the relief of Jews abroad, for Israel, for the massive and expensive local structures, and for a broader social welfare program expanded enormously. The Jewish communal professionals and the lay leaders of these vast philanthropic enterprises, (the gross philanthropic product is said to be in excess of a billion dollars annually) came to occupy the most important leadership positions in the American Jewish community. In the process the central federation and welfare funds not only began to develop the policies, but undertook in many instances to provide the resources in all matters of Jewish defense.

There was no monolithic position with respect to either the character or the future of the American Jewish community. The survivalists, who wanted to put more stress on Jewish religion,

Jewish education, and support for Israel, had to contend—often bitterly—with those who felt that the new mood of expansive liberalism in an open society offered different challenges and opportunities for American Jews. The latter argued—and often persuasively—that every effort should be exerted to work more harmoniously and cooperatively with other American groups, even if it meant accepting what was deemed an inevitable trend toward assimilation or, to use the happier term coined by obliging sociologists, acculturation. Government support for domestic Jewish agencies was eagerly sought by Jewish leaders. This inevitably forced many of them to become virtually nonsectarian by name, constitution, and program.

Jews went out of their way to support the black cause of total integration within the American community, particularly after the 1954 Supreme Court decision on desegregation, a decision toward which Jews had played a not insignificant role as amicus curiae. Liberal Jewish youth, often with parental and communal encouragement, went in large numbers into the black ghettos and into the hostile South to teach, labor, agitate, and march with their black fellow citizens toward the finally recognized opportunities for real freedom to move, work, vote, and lead. Jewish communal workers, rabbis, and lay leaders contributed generously to the movement, mounted platforms, spoke eloquently, demonstrated arm and arm with the black leaders. On a few occasions Jews were bloodied, and in at least one instance two young Jews were killed outright in a celebrated case where the perpetrators were finally brought to justice.

Interfaith and intercultural meetings also have abounded. Ecumenicism had a new rebirth when Pope John XXIII convened a Catholic assembly in Rome to reassess his church's attitude toward the Jews. Subsequently, under his successor Paul VI, a schema was adopted which deplored anti-Semitism and stated that the blame for the death of Jesus must be attributed to some of his contemporaries and not to the Jewish people as a whole. Jews eagerly furthered the dialogue that had begun by supporting conferences and even chairs of Christian-Jewish studies at universities and at the Holy See, hoping once again that a greater knowledge of the historical and contemporary Jew might reduce the possibility of future hostility.

With their new wealth, Jews also made signal financial contributions to universities, parks, museums, art and music centers, demonstrating bounteously their total dedication to the best in American culture.

When synagogues and Jewish centers in both the South and the North were smeared with anti-Semitic symbols, bombed, and burned, Jews were concerned, but these acts were usually dismissed as the products of sick minds and marginal groups and not a reflection of a deeply rooted American attitude. According to the studies of the day, anti-Semitism was definitely "vanishing."[33]

Yet, in the period of McCarthyism many individual Jews suffered severely because of their alleged or real radicalism. Some lost lucrative jobs. Some went to prison. A shudder went through the Jewish community when Julius and Ethel Rosenberg were convicted of spying for the Soviets and executed, for the case could not be free of disquieting overtones even though both the prosecuting attorney and the judge who pronounced sentence were also Jews. When the unhappy period of reaction was over, Jews once more rushed about their self-appointed task of being liberal in the open by joining and fostering every avant garde movement that would further extend freedom to every section of the population— women's liberation, gay liberation, campus revolutions, antiwar campaigns and movements that permitted premarital and extramarital sexual relations, abortions, easier divorce, legalized sale of marijuana—all causes which were supported by militant demonstrations and often marked with violence and bloodshed. Jewish names were not absent among both the offenders and the victims. In the process, there was danger that the Jews had once again left themselves almost defenseless against reactionary attacks, often coming from high places. They became vulnerable to charges of attempting to change the American community and, some said outrightly, of corrupting its moral fiber.

A New Wave of Activism

A rude awakening came at the time of the miraculous victory of Israel over the Arabs in the Six-Day War of 1967. In the glow and relief of its aftermath, Jews suddenly developed a new, albeit false, sense of invincibility; but, when appraised soberly, the same aftermath also bitterly disclosed that there were even fewer supporters of Israel among Christians and national states than before, and raucous voices were raised charging that Jews were unbridled conquerors, desecrators of Moslem and Christian shrines, destroyers of Arab morale, and perpetrators of genocide against the Palestinians. During May and June 1967, American Jews, feeling the threat of an impending holocaust, feverishly united as they had never done before with outpourings of funds, widespread demonstrations, and selfless offers of volunteer support for Israel. For once all of the major Jewish organizations banded together to speak with one unequivocal voice on behalf of Jews everywhere. For the time, at least, it was recognized that no longer could Jews afford the luxury of conflicting opinions on the issue of sheer survival. The unity was temporary, however, for the historically pluralistic attitudes, positions and organizations characteristic of Jewry did not disappear. When the war was over and peace did not come to Israel with this overwhelming victory, a sense of impending doom overcame the American Jewish community again as it began to take stock and recognize how perishable were the fruits of victory.

American Jews also learned that their numbers were eroding through the lowest birthrates of any ethnic group, cut further by promiscuous abortions, widespread intermarriage, and outright assimilation through indifference to or even rejection of the Jewish tradition. Jewish youth, despite their high educational achievement, advantaged family backgrounds, and middle-class economic status, were as likely as anyone else to become drug addicts, abandon marriage as a sacred form of heterosexual relationship, and join esoteric or ultrafundamentalist Christian and Eastern religious sects. The Jewish family was showing distinct signs of disintegration, with infidelity, desertion, separation, and divorce on a marked statistical increase. At the same time many of our most serious and concerned young people on the university campuses were voicing complaints that they had not had a proper and mature Jewish education and that not enough was being done to support their search for healthier adult Jewish experiences—this despite the half-century of Hillel foundations and the very substantial development of departments of Jewish studies in several hundred American colleges. It was becoming obvious that we had not done enough to prevent the Jewish cultural extinction taking place in the Soviet Union and that the several million remaining Jews, nominal yet uninformed, would need the help of free Jewry to emigrate and resettle in Israel and other parts of the Jewish world, if for no other reason than to reestablish their Jewish identity. Despite the vaunted wealth of American Jews, there were still hundreds of thousands of neglected Jewish poor among the aged, the large religious families, and the rising harvest of broken families; these groups required specific Jewish ministration since public institutions and public funds could not be relied upon to provide what was needed to fulfill their lives in human decency and as Jews.

This disillusionment, deepened by the recession and inflation in the United States and throughout the world and further intensified after the 1973 war against Israel, with the conveniently maneuvered energy crisis and the inordinately escalated fuel price increase, once more gave Jews cause to wonder whether they were really going to continue to enjoy the fruits of freedom and prosperity in the later part of the twentieth century.

When the established Jewish organizations were not prepared to act quickly enough on the above mentioned problems, grass-roots groups arose to embarrass and force entrenched Jewish leadership and institutions to evaluate what they were doing. Their neighborhood militancy succeeded in winning the assignment of sorely needed public funds for unequivocally Jewish programs serving

Jewish people exclusively. The same activist approach succeeded in obtaining greater support for autonomous Jewish college youth programs. Grass-roots groups have aggressively fought for the right of Jews to continue to live in communities which are undergoing racial integration, so that Jews and their children could continue to enjoy high educational standards and safe schooling, adequate police protection on the streets, and comfortable, clean, and secure housing in communities in which Jews had made significant investments in their own homes, in commerce, and in their own institutions. Some groups have on occasion defied the opinion of all the major Jewish organizations by using vigilante tactics to counter the attacks of hoodlums, drug addicts, and other criminals against the aged and the helpless Jewish merchants still living in marginal neighborhoods. They have affronted the established leadership of the American Jewish community by doing more than offer resolutionary protests against the Soviet Union—by picketing, rioting, and even destroying alien property. These are militant, even violent, expressions of the frustration that some sections of the American community have felt in light of recent events.

An examination of the most recent positions taken by the various American Jewish defense agencies indicates that they may be enlarging their areas of concern and expanding their repertoire of methods, but business as usual is still the prevailing pattern.[34]

One approach is the endeavor to counteract what is called "insensitivity" on the part of non-Jews to abiding Jewish interests, a new term which takes the sting off of the former designation of anti-Semitism. There is more recognition now that we have a real stake in all aspects of international Jewish communities—isolated Israel, shrunken Syrian Jewry, massive but hostage Soviet Jewry, and always threatened Latin American Jewry. The major organizations are continuing to commemorate the Holocaust and advocating the passage and adoption of the genocide convention, but they also include in their almost unlimited range of concerns such issues of universal significance as the combatting of worldwide hunger and starvation.

"Universalism" and Self-Defense

When it comes to domestic affairs, these organizations include in their agenda antipoverty programs, legal aid services, manpower and minimum wage matters, revenue sharing and governmental fiscal policy, education, housing, voting, women's rights, affirmative action on behalf of other minorities, even advocacy of preferential treatment and quotas—all under the rubric of economic and social justice for all people. In the field of civil liberties and individual freedom they have taken positions on the invasion of privacy, capital punishment, criminal justice, censorship, obscenity and pornography, abortion, amnesty, aid to parochial schools, prayer and devotional observances in schools, shehitah, governmental support of child care agencies that want to remain Jewish, and the repeal of Sunday blue laws. While the majority of the organizations seem to favor what they take to be progressive stands, vestiges of a liberal-radical past, nonetheless there are serious differences, often on religious lines, over such vital issues as school busing, abortion, parochial aid, voting rights, equal rights, affirmative action, censorship, amnesty for war resisters, in some of which the traditionalists have not so strangely found fellow abstainers in the Anti-Defamation League and the Jewish War Veterans. The spectrum of concerns is much too broad for any collective of Jewish agencies to encompass and to arrive at a consensus, and in many respects this diffusion of attention keeps them from concentrating on the defense of specifically Jewish interests, which, after all, are their raison d'etre.

All this reflects a new fear that has arisen in the Jewish community that all may not be as healthy as may appear on the surface. The established Jewish leadership is quietly taking a new inventory of what it must be doing to protect the American Jew in the face of a possibly continuing economic decline; in the face of periodic anti-Jewish outbursts from high government officials; in the face of increasing unemployment; in the face of the growing Arab stranglehold on the disposition of their share of the world's fossil fuel and tremendous influence in establishing a ruinous price structure for oil which could dislocate and even bankrupt countries almost totally dependent on imported oil for their industrial and domestic continuity; in the face of what is known in some circles as "Israel's intransigience" about not immediately returning conquered Arab lands without any agreed foundation as to what constitutes the legitimacy of Israel's own survival; and in the face of the desertion of so-called longtime congressional friends of American Jewry and Israel.

There are those who say that the only way Jews can defend themselves in the United States is by supporting programs for the greater extention of democracy through additional laws to safeguard fair employment in every area of American life and assure fair and equal education from the preschool to the graduate and professional levels—despite the fact that such statutes and administrative directives have come to be interpreted by impatient and overly zealous minority leaders, on their rapid rise to a greater sharing of power and wealth, as requiring extraordinary, compensatory affirmative action, which seems to affect Jews more adversely than any other section of the population. Blind adherence to such a position not only exceeds the requirements of equity and fair play but indeed rescinds them since the effect would be to discriminate, and in fact to threaten, the economic, social, and political position long fought for by the Jew in America. Jewish advocates of the "universalist" point of view would use the vast communication media now available to educate all in religious toleration so that no group would suffer any disability under the American constitutional system. Such Jews would organize, both on a national and a local basis, civic groups with broad coalitions to combat any vestige of prejudice and discrimination that might arise in the campaign to grant equal opportunity to all.

But there are others, still a minority among American Jews but a group that is growing in numbers, who are demanding a halt to indiscriminate total involvement in all sorts of issues. They want a slowdown and a careful stocktaking, more selectivity of interests, and closer regard for the quality and quantity of return on energies invested, greater consolidation of the efforts of the various agencies often doing much the same thing; they want a turning inward, perhaps even a withdrawal in some areas, because they honestly fear that currents of reaction are taking hold everywhere in the world and that the Jews, numerically fewer and quite assimilated to the western mentality, are losing their specifically Jewish intellectual, moral, and emotional strengths, their financial base, and their always uncertain political influence. If so, as in the past when the world has grown either indifferent or hostile, it may be necessary for Jews to build new walls around themselves to defend against the threat of violence to their lives and their civilization.

NOTES

1. Jacob Neusner, *American Judaism* (Englewood Cliffs, N.J., 1972), chap. 2.

2. "Council of the Four Lands," in the *Encyclopedia Judaica* (Jerusalem, 1971), V, pp. 995–1003.

3. Moshe Pearlman, *The Maccabees* (New York, 1973), pp. 78–80.

4. Yigal Allon, *Shield of David, The Story of Israel's Armed Forces* (New York, 1970).

5. Jacob P. Marcus, *The Jews in the Medieval World* (Philadelphia, 1960 [1938]), pp. 44, 47, 115, 131, 134, 179, and 451; *Encyclopedia Judaica*, XV, pp. 489–91, and XVI, pp. 848–49; Louis I. Dublin, *Suicide* (New York, 1963), pp. 75–79, 102–9.

6. Isaiah Trunk, *Judenrat* (New York, 1972), p. 443.

7. Anthony Masters, *The Summer that Bled: The Biography of Hannah Senesh,* (New York, 1974 [1972]).

8. Joseph L. Blau and Salo W. Baron, *The Jews of the United States, 1790–1840: A Documentary History* (New York, 1963), III, pp. 924–30.

9. "Self-Defense," in the *Encyclopedia Judaica,* XIV, pp. 1123–29.

10. Menachem Begin, *The Revolt* (Los Angeles, 1948), p. xii.

11. Max D. Danish, *The World of David Dubinsky* (New York, 1957).

12. Leon Stein, *The Triangle Fire* (Philadelphia, 1962).

13. Moses Rischin, *The Promised City: New York Jews 1870–1914* (Cambridge, Mass., 1962); Norman Hapgood, *The Spirit of the Ghetto* (Cambridge, Mass., 1967 [1902]).

14. Arthur A. Goren, *New York Jews and the Quest for Community, The Kehillah Experiment, 1908–1922* (New York, 1970).

15. Jacob Billikopf, "The Ten Million Dollar Campaign," in *Trends and Issues in Jewish Social Welfare in the United States, 1899–1958,* ed. by Robert Morris and Michael Freund (Philadelphia, 1966), pp. 141–42.

16. Oscar I. Janowsky, *The Jews and Minority Rights, 1898–1919* (New York, 1933).

17. *Shield of David,* pp. 11 and 13.

18. From the testimony of Henry Ford during his libel suit against the *Chicago Tribune,* July 1919. *Oxford Dictionary of Quotations* (London, 1966 [1941], p. 209.).

19. Naomi W. Cohen, *Not Free to Desist: A History of the American Jewish Committee, 1906–1966* (Philadelphia, 1972), p. 162.

20. Ibid., pp. 163–64.

21. Laura Fermi, *Illustrious Immigrants: The Intellectual Migration from Europe, 1930–1941* (Chicago, 1968).

22. Arthur D. Morse, *While Six Million Died: A Chronicle of American Apathy* (New York, 1968 [1967]).

23. Richard Pankhurst, "Plans for Jewish Mass Settlement in Ethiopia 1936–1943," in *Ethiopia* (Addis Ababa), XV, no. 4 (1973).

24. Ben Hecht, *Perfidy* (New York, 1961).

25. Gerold Frank, *The Deed* (New York, 1963).

26. Arnold Foster, *Approaches, Strategies and Methods of Combatting Anti-Semitism,* National Jewish Community Relations Advisory Council (New York, 1968), pp. 48–51.

27. "Kiddush Ha-Shem Over the Ages and its Uniqueness in the Holocaust Period," in *Jewish Resistance During the Holocaust.* (Jerusalem, 1971), p. 473; cited by Emil L. Fackenheim in the *Encyclopedia Judaica Year Book* (Jerusalem 1974), pp. 155–56.

28. *Studies of Polish Jewry 1919–1939,* ed. by Joshua A. Fishman, YIVO Institute for Jewish Research, (New York, 1974).

29. Richard L. Rubinstein, *After Auschwitz* (New York, 1966).

30. Hannah Arendt, *Eichmann in Jerusalem: A Report on the Banality of Evil,* (New York, 1964 [1963]).

31. Trunk, *Judenrat;* Arnold Paucker, "Some Notes on Resistance" in

the Year Book XVI, Leo Baeck Institute, East and West Library, (London, 1971). Salo W. Baron relates that he tried to persuade Leo Baeck to leave Germany during the Hitler period; but Baeck stated that "he could not leave his flock" and went with them to Theresienstadt and stayed until they were freed. See Albert H. Friedlander, *Leo Baeck, Teacher of Theresienstadt* (New York, 1968), p. 211.

32. Recently the Soviet Union repudiated a trade agreement with the United States because, under pressure from the American Jewish Community, the United States Congress had inserted into the agreement a proviso that Russia must permit a greater migration of those citizens who voluntarily wished to leave that country. Russia accused the United States of interfering in its internal affairs.

33. Charles H. Stember, *Jews in the Mind of America* (New York, 1966).

34. *Joint Program Plan for Jewish Community Relations, 1974–1975,* National Jewish Community Relations Advisory Council (New York, 1974).

HAIM COHN

15   Law and Reality in Israel Today

As a member of the legal profession, I am quite unable, and quite unwilling, to approach the subject of violence and defense in general terms and from a general viewpoint without first exploring it in legal terms and from the legal point of view. Puristic methodologists might say that it should rather be the other way around—that one should first attempt to find out pragmatically in what ways the people of a nation have solved the practical problems inherent in the dichotomy of defense and violence and then look at their laws and evaluate whether they reflect their achievements or their aspirations. Such a method would not, however, hold for Israel. The simple reason is that we found our laws ready-made for us by the British, in full force and effect at the time we started to embark on the task of molding a national character in the new State of Israel. You will, therefore, have to bear with me—before I go into the idiosyncrasies of this new national character of ours—if I turn first to some of the intricacies of our general law.

The general rule in Israeli law is that a person is not criminally responsible for any act or omission which occurs independently of the exercise of his will. There are of course exceptions to that rule, but they do not concern us here. We are concerned with one particular instance of the application of this rule, and that is the exclusion of, or the constraint on, the free exercise of a person's will by what is technically known as "necessity" and, in popular language, as self-defense. This is a constraint upon the will, says Blackstone in his *Commentaries upon the Laws of England, 1746,* because a man acting in self-defense does "that which his judgment disapproves and which, it is to be presumed, his will, if left to itself, would reject; as punishments are only inflicted for the abuse of that free will, which God has given to man, it is highly just and equitable that a man should be excused for those acts which are done" by constraint (vol. IV, p.27). It does not matter that even when acting in self-defense a man may act upon rational reflection, namely, by choosing the less pernicious of two evils set before him. Still, his will cannot be said to exert itself freely, being rather passive than active; or, if active, he acts rather in rejecting the greater evil than in choosing the lesser.

Violence for Self-Preservation

It must be understood that our law does not render an act of violence lawful, even if committed in self-defense. The violence remains what it is, a *malum in se,* a criminal act. The law only provides the actor who acted in self-defense with an excuse absolving him from criminal responsibility. In the language of our criminal code, "An act or omission which would otherwise be an offense may be excused if the person accused can show that it was done or omitted to be done only in order to avoid consequences which could not otherwise be avoided and which, if they had followed, would have inflicted grievous harm or injury to his person or to his honour, or to his property or to the person or honour of another whom he was bound to protect, or to property placed in his charge; provided that in so acting he did no more than was reasonably necessary for that purpose, and that the harm inflicted by the act or omission was not disproportionate to the harm avoided" (Section 18).

At first glance one might say that doing violence to the person of another in order to avoid injury to one's property should not really be excused; but it is necessary to keep in mind that this is the law of Israel today only because it was the law of England in the nineteenth century, and at that time the English had no more highly valued interest to protect than property.

However that may be, you will recall that the first biblical instance of the law of self-defense is that of smiting the thief found breaking in (Exod. 22:1), and it is only much later that the smiting is justified by talmudic jurists for the reason that the thief must be feared to be not only a thief but also a potential killer (Mekhilta, Mishpatim 13). This assumption of the potential killer in the burglar was not intended so much to change the character and enhance the justification of the act of self-defense as to provide a kind of ex post facto vindication of the burglar's death. It is as if to say that he would have had to die anyway for his murder, so better let him die before committing his murder. We find the same sort of *ratio legis* imputed to the biblical law of capital punishment for the rebellious son (Deut. 21:18). He is condemned to prevent his eventual end as a murderer (Sanhedrin 72a).

Under this law there must be a reasonable, even an exact, proportion between the harm inflicted by the act of self-defense and the harm avoided. You need not put it, as Blackstone did, as a choice between a greater and a lesser evil; the two evils may be equal, and then the law allows you to avert the evil threatening you. You may put it this way: the evil threatening you is from your own legitimate point of view always the greater evil as compared with the same evil threatening another person. Still your reaction must always be proportionate in order that it may be excused, and this proportionality is bidimensional. Objectively, on the one hand, the harm avoided must be proportionate to the harm inflicted; and subjectively on the other hand, you may do no more in self-defense, whatever may be the actual result.

It has been observed that both the objective and the subjective tests are unjust and illogical. If I have done no more than was reasonably necessary to avert the evil threatening me, then I should in all justice be excused for whatever harm I actually did; and if I am excused because of the constraint by "necessity" on the free exercise of my will, then I should be excused if in a state of panic I exceeded the limit of what was reasonably necessary to avert that evil. The requirement of subjective proportionality appears to disregard altogether the well-established psychological data of human reaction, and the requirement of objective proportionality is just another instance of the injustice inherent in attaching criminality to unintended results. Self-defense is thus degraded to a matter of luck. I am lucky if the result achieved is not more harmful than I intended it to be, as I am lucky, indeed, if even in a state of panic I manage to make my proportionate measurements. As a matter of legal theory, these incongruities are easily brushed aside with the assertion that the act committed in self-defense remains what it is, an act of violence, a *malum in se.* Any consideration of benevolence shown to the violent actor on account of his motives of "necessity" may be legislatively restricted in any way thought fit and proper, and the restrictions are thought necessary in order to prevent the excuse of self-defense being taken as a license for violent revenge.

In other words, the proportionality of self-defense is a desideratum of legislative policy. The proportionality is, so to speak, superimposed on the self-defense for purposes of avoiding its misappropriation. It would come to this: that the act of violence, even though committed in self-defense, is a criminal act but that the actor who acted in self-defense is entitled to be excused for his criminal act. This excuse, however, is accorded by the will of the legislator for reasons of policy, only on condition of proportionality. Immanuel Kant has already found that no legislative command can have any effect or any prospect of obedience if it collides with natural instincts of self-preservation. The threat of legal punishment is, because of its uncertainty, set at nought in the face of certain physical danger *(Metaphysik der Sitten, Einleitung in die Rechtslehre, Anhang II)*. When I find myself in danger of death and kill my attacker in order not to be killed by him, I exercise a right born of the instinct of self-preservation *(inculpabile)* that no legislator can effectively restrict. Any restriction on the exercise of this right must be self-imposed. The technical word is *moderamen:* it is, therefore, not a matter of law but of ethics.

The apparent contradiction between the subsisting criminality of the violent act, even though committed in self-defense, and the right to self-defense for self-preservation, is that *aequivocatio* which prompted Kant to classify the laws of necessity with the "equivocal" laws. These "equivocal" laws have different meanings and different purposes according to who looks at them and who implements them. The man who acts in self-defense to preserve his life has not, cannot have, and need not have any law other than or superior to his right of self-preservation; but for the court any individual right of self-preservation may be subordinate to other general laws. As Kant rightly says, the concept of "laws" is not used in the same sense in the two instances.

While it may well be true that any law which would purport to restrict a man's right to save his own life from real and immediate danger would be ineffective, the law may well effectively restrict a man's right to protect himself from lesser evils. Though his acts also may be instinctive when he defends his honor or his property, there is not then, at any rate, the overriding right to self-preservation in collision with legislative intervention. Indeed, when a man kills in order to save his own life the legislative requirements of proportionality are normally fulfilled: the death of the potential killer is a harm not disproportionate to the death of the killer in self-defense. Shooting the potential killer was presumably no more than was actually necessary in order to forestall his shooting first. Thus it is that, however great the incongruities in theory and practice, the implementation of the law does not present much difficulty and does not create injustice.

The defense of necessity is raised rather frequently in cases of violence, but it is normally easy to distinguish between a bona fide act of self-defense and the usual affray in which both the complainant and the accused are actors and victims alike. Nor is it normally difficult to assess whether a bona fide act of self-defense exceeded the proportionate measure. The standing and invariable rule in Israeli courts is that even though the accused who acted in self-defense cannot be excused because he exceeded the proportionate measure, the fact that he acted in self-defense is to be taken into consideration as a highly mitigating circumstance for purposes of sentence. In cases of homicide self-defense will normally reduce the offense from murder to manslaughter or, as you say in America, to murder in the second degree.

Let me give you an example from my own judicial experience of an act of self-defense which could not be recognized in law as sufficient cause for excuse. There were two rival and hostile clans in an Arab village, and one morning one attacked the other, resulting in fierce shooting on both sides. The men who were indicted for murder were members of the attacked clan, not the aggressors, and they claimed very naturally that they shot back in self-defense. The court held that they were in danger of their lives but did not grant that they shot in self-defense only. We said that there was a distinction between self-defense in a spirit of fight and self-defense in a spirit of self-preservation. The fighter conducts a war, and the fact that he is defending himself from aggression serves him only as the cause for his warfare. The true self-preserver, however, hates war, abhors fighting, and spares no effort to get out of it; any violence he commits in self-defense he commits unwillingly and only under the force of circumstances. The law protects the man who defends himself under constraint, not the man who uses his self-defense as the cause of fighting. In the language of a great English judge, it is not the law that a man who is threatened must take to his heels and run; what is necessary is that he should demonstrate that he is prepared "to temporize and disengage." In the case before us it was clearly proved that those sincerely convinced that it was their duty to defend themselves against their aggressors not only waged war against them but rejoiced in the opportunity to join battle. The language used by them both in their police statements and in the evidence in court was the language of fighters who took up arms to settle their bloody account with their enemies, not of peaceful people who were helplessly coerced into acts of self-defense.

This same case also affords an illustration of the difference between national and international law on the subject. The respective rights and responsibilities of the fighting village clans are, of course, determined under national law. They differ considerably from those of belligerence under international law. I dare say that had the rights and responsibilities of those accused fallen to be determined under concepts of international law, they would in all probability have been entitled to acquittal.

Aggression and Self-Defense Among Nations

Needless to say, violent attacks also are unlawful under international law, and, though consensus has not as yet been reached as to how aggression ought to be defined, for our purposes we may take it for granted that the international crime of aggression consists of unlawful violence by one state against the other. In the United Nations Charter all sorts of paper remedies against acts of aggression are provided, but it also is laid down in Article 51 that "nothing in the present Charter shall impair the inherent right of individual or collective self-defense" if an armed attack occurs against a member of the United Nations and until the Security Council has taken measures necessary to maintain international peace and security. This inherent right of individual or collective self-defense is but a reiteration on the international plane of that natural and overriding right to self-preservation that we have encountered before. It cannot be denied to anybody, nor can it be abrogated, even by the Security Council. All the Council is supposed to do is to make the exercise of the right of self-defense superfluous and redundant by taking more effective action itself to restore peace and security.

Still we find on the international plane, too, parallels to the proportionality requirements of national law. It is not only that the Security Council may take action and thereby actually paralyze a self-defending state, but, much more importantly, it is currently the general consensus that "the right of the parties to a conflict to adopt means of injuring the enemy is not unlimited." The language here is from a resolution of the International Red Cross Conference, and the limitations there referred to apply to aggressors and defenders alike. It is true that there is no restriction on the defending state in international law insofar as the scope and purpose of warfare are concerned. Once engaged in a war of self-defense, a state may well embark on what has become known as total war. Such restrictions as are imposed by modern international law are known as "humanitarian," and are for the greater part laid down in the so-called Geneva Conventions. That these conventions are honored mostly in their breach does not necessarily detract from their character as international law. Humanitarian restrictions on the amount and nature of violence admissible in the exercise of one's right of self-defense, coupled with and interdependent with the very same humanitarian restrictions imposed on the aggressive violence itself, provide the international counterpart to the national proportionality requirement.

It may be of interest to note that in the special committee set up by the United Nations to define aggression, an exception to the definition was proposed in the following terms: "The temporary use of force in the exercise of individual or collective self-defense, until the Security Council can act to restore peace and security, shall not constitute aggression, if such force is reasonably proportionate to the wrong and necessary to repel an aggressive act." Many members of the committee considered the requirements of reasonableness and proportionality as "consistent with established concepts of law as well as with humanitarian aspirations," and the smaller nations welcomed them as assuring that no nation could use every breach of the peace as a pretext to use excessive force in retaliation; but the Soviet representatives objected to the concept of proportionality "as placing an unreasonable burden on the victim for the benefit of the aggressor." Neither the definition nor the exception has yet been approved and accepted, and the requirements of proportionality and reasonableness have so far not been superimposed on the right of individual and collective self-defense in international law. If, as I have tried to show, the superimposition of these requirements on the right of self-defense in national law has given rise to all sorts of legal and logical objections, particularly to the apprehension of legislative ineffectiveness on the international level, these objections and apprehensions would be all the stronger.

A state attacked by its enemy would have done nothing if it only repelled that attack. In order to defend itself effectively, it must deprive the enemy of the means and thwart the enemy's desire to attack again. In order to do that it cannot be restricted by proportionality requirements unless proportionality is redefined for purposes of international law to cover any action required to subjugate the aggressor. However, any such redefinition would, I fear, be self-defeating.

For more than a generation since the establishment of the State of Israel, the population has virtually and actually lived in a state of permanent self-defense. Even before the establishment of the state, the Jewish population of Palestine had to be in a state of permanent preparedness to repel attacks of violence. It does not matter much that the violent actions of self-defense may actually have been carried out first by underground and eventually by standing armies. It does not matter, firstly, because there is not a single household in Israel which did not produce at least one soldier; but secondly, and more importantly, what we are concerned with here are mass reactions, and these flow from the conscientiousness of the people as a whole.

However much one would like to avoid generalizations, it may readily be asserted that the people of Israel, sharing with all human beings a natural instinct for self-preservation, have at all times been deeply and acutely conscious of their inalienable right of individual and collective self-defense. Under the necessity of circumstances forced upon them, they have, from their very beginning until the present day, concentrated the best of their talent and resources on their defense or, as it is sometimes synonomously called, their security.

Israel has repeatedly had to defend itself against enemy attacks directed to the total destruction of the state. The people have responded by repelling the attacks of those who declared that Israel be thrown into the sea. One cannot know for certain what might have happened had the Security Council or one of the superpowers not intervened and procured a ceasefire whenever Israel was on the verge of defeating an Arab power. I am content to leave it at this: that Israel is no better and no worse than any other nation at war, and that its urges of self-defense do not stop at the repulse of actual attacks but seek to deprive the enemy once and for all of the means or the desire to repeat attacks in the future.

It is a common experience that if you are constantly exposed to violence and have to defend yourself against it day in and day out, you soon become insensitive to the limits to which you may go. Whether it is that you would not trust your attacker to observe any limits on his part or that in the course of violence your own moral standards are suspended—albeit temporarily—it seems that constant violence, even in self-defense, is not easily compatible with moral sensitivity. Aware of the grave dangers involved in this psychological factor, Ben-Gurion insisted from the very beginning on the innoculation of the Israel Defense Forces with the dogma of *"tohar haneshek"*—the purity of the arms—thus preaching and teaching in his rather naive but imperturbable optimism that no shot may be fired except for a necessary and justifiable purpose. As Ben-Gurion's officer in charge of legislation, one of my first assignments from him was to have a soldier's use of a firearm without actual necessity made a criminal offense. I can testify to the fact that during the War of Independence in 1948 and 1949 this law was observed and enforced very faithfully, if only for the reason that we did not have enough armaments and munitions to allow unnecessary shooting. But since we have, alas, become learned in war, all sorts of psychological factors of warfare may have superceded dogmas of purity.

After the War of Independence we could pride ourselves on the fact that, however bitterly we were attacked and however desperately we fought, there was no hatred in our hearts against our enemies. We could claim that however much violence we used in self-defense, we used none in malice. The book *Siah Lohamim* ("Tales of Fighters"), which records reflections of soldiers on the war, is a testimonial of unique grandeur to the humanism and love of peace which were well nigh universal at that time. If Israelis have changed since then, and not all have, it is not only because war and violence have become perpetual but also because the composition of the army has changed. Serving now in our armed forces are tens of thousands of soldiers who have come from Arab countries and who nurture a deeply inbred hatred of their former overlords and oppressors. Prejudices and resentments are infectious, and self-defense against ferocious and uninhibited attackers does not need much persuasion to be infected with hate and ill will. If many people today are tired of wars, that does not necessarily mean that they have come to love their enemies.

The Problem of Retaliation

It is difficult, if not impossible, for a soldier engaged in active warfare to know and observe the limits of self-defense. Moreover, it is one of the exigencies of war to retaliate, and as far as retaliations are concerned, the biblical "an eye for an eye" may well have been the last limitation ever imposed on man. While self-defense remains the conscious exercise of a right which, in the nature of things and if only by definition, must have certain limits; retaliation is but an instinctive exercise of power and it requires, to a much larger degree than self-defense, that self-imposed moderation which pertains to the realm of ethics. Within the framework of planned, organized, official army operations, such retaliations will normally be undertaken with certain well-defined strategic objects, and the very planning beforehand of such operations provides the necessary curb on vengeful excesses. Nonetheless, in every war there are sufficient opportunities for soldiers to attempt partisan acts of retaliation, however unlawful they may be. It has been said to be only natural for soldiers whose comrades were tortured or maltreated by the enemy to take their own revenge on enemy soldiers falling into their hands. Natural or not, it is a fact that in the Israeli army only very few exceptional cases occurred in which individual soldiers repaid atrocities in kind, and in each case they were brought to justice.

The soldier, and virtually every Israeli has been a soldier, returns to civilian life with a heavy burden of violent experiences and memories, disillusions and resentments, and more often than not with a conscious or subconscious feeling that having luckily escaped death, now is the time to get out of life all he can. One might have thought that the long years of experiencing legalized and organized violence and the resulting egocentric urges of self-indulgence would precondition the Israeli to violent conduct after his discharge from the army. Happily, nothing could be further from the truth. In fact, our criminal statistics show that the incidence of violence in Israel is lower than in most other countries. I shall give you some figures for 1973. From among 135,678 registered offenses, there were 183 woundings, 217 attacks on public or police officers, and 7,320 simple assaults, totaling 7,720 offenses of violence or about 5 percent of the whole criminal activity. If you add to that 27 murders, 13 manslaughters, and 75 attempts at homicide, you have another 113 offenses of violence which make for one per thousand more. Another interesting feature of the crimes of violence is that while only 36 percent of all criminal offenders were caught and brought to justice, the number of offenders caught and brought to justice for crimes of violence, including homicide, amounts to 90 percent. These figures show only the number of offenders convicted; we have no statistics on cases of violence in which the accused successfully pleaded self-defense.

While the incidence of violence as a whole is thus of no disquieting dimensions in Israel, there are some particular forms of violence which are rather more widespread in Israeli society than anywhere else. Curiously enough, we have had for several years the world record, proportionately of course, of matricides and uxoricides, the killing of wives by their husbands and of husbands by their wives. This is the more remarkable since under the religious laws prevailing in this country both Jews and Muslims can dissolve their marriages by mutual consent. It appears, however, that for many getting freed of the marriage ties is not enough if they do not get physically rid of their spouses. One man shot his wife in the presence of the assembled rabbinical court during the very divorce proceedings. Needless to say, unless there was some immediate provocation, these are mostly acts of revenge for years of suffering or for adulterous treachery; perhaps here and there such acts can be traced to the primordial right of the husband to kill his adulterous wife.

More serious is the Israeli situation with regard to violence on the highways. The courts abound with cases of drivers who vent their anger on other drivers by overtaking them, not granting them the right of way, or otherwise annoying them—sometimes even by alighting from their cars and treating the other to a sound thrashing. Recently an old man in his seventies was killed when he was struck in the head by another driver who had known him before. It seems that all the nervous tensions of the Israeli and all his repressed criminality turn loose when he is driving a car. There has also developed a particular pattern of criminal behavior in youngsters who steal cars and then, driving them wildly, endanger the lives of all users of highways.

Criminologists now tend to ascribe all violence to what they call situational stimuli, meaning that all acts of violence are the result of conscious or subconscious choices between alternative reactions to provocative external factors. (Much work has been done on this subject by the Institute of Criminology of Tel Aviv University, which has published two volumes of the *Annals of Criminology* that contain some papers on the sociological aspects of violence in Israel.)

According to the theory of situational stimuli, violence is the outburst of a defense mechanism, just as aggression is the expression of fear from and self-protection against an imaginary or even real evil. Psychoanalysts have made a very valuable contribution to the discovery of the psychological processes and the origins of aggressions. Applied to the subject matter of our present investigation, it would appear that violent self-defense is to be distinguished from unlawful violence and that while the former is a defense action undertaken consciously, the latter is a defense action undertaken unwittingly. The purpose of the former is to avert a real and immediate danger, whereas the latter is a reaction to imaginary or potential danger. Legally speaking, however, the difference between them is, of course, that it is only the reality and immediacy of the danger that gives rise to a possible justification of, or excuse for, the act of violence, while in the absence of such reality and immediacy man is expected and required to conquer his fears. Still, there may be some small, albeit wholly academic, consolation in the fact that all violence is really defense, and the vistas of research opened up by this thought may well be worth exploring.

Afterword

SHLOMO SIMONSOHN

With the passage of time and generations, a once independent Jewish nation in Palestine passed into a different state of mind in its attitudes to violence and defense in the Middle Ages. This process of change is relevant not only to medieval Jewry as such but also to that broader stage in the history of the Jewish people which bridges the gap between the independence of ancient times and our modern emancipation—eventually leading to the reconstitution, revival, and national renaissance of the Jewish people in Israel. The change in attitudes over the centuries also may help to explain the attitudes of modern Jewry on the subject of violence and defense.

In ancient times, so far as we know, the Jewish nation was a normal nation, and its attitudes to war and violence were normal, like those of other nations. At a later stage, for a variety of reasons, those attitudes changed. Something that had existed throughout biblical times eventually became the backbone, the motto, the essence, with a different emphasis than it originally had, and developed into a Weltanschauung, into a philosophy, and eventually into a basic attitude permeating all Jewish reaction to what was going on outside its own courtyard and affecting it in that manner throughout the Middle Ages, at least as far as Ashkenazic Jewry is concerned.

Let us consider two passages. One is the final speech of the last commander of Masada, Elazar, who defended the fortress against the Romans toward the end of the Jewish War, as described by Josephus in his work *The Jewish War* (VII, viii., 6). The second passage is a slightly different text on the same event but by someone else. Here is what Josephus has to say after Elazar, the commander, has decided that all was lost:

He had no intention of slipping out himself or of allowing anyone else to do so. He saw his wall going up in flames and could think of no other means of escape or heroic endeavor. He had a clear picture of what the Romans would do to men, women, and children if they won the day, and death seemed to him the right choice for them all. Making up his mind that, in the circumstances, this was the wisest course, he collected the toughest of his comrades and urged it upon them in a speech of which this was the substance:

My loyal followers, long ago we resolved to serve neither the Romans nor anyone else but only God who alone is the true and righteous lord of man. Now the time has come that bids us prove our determination by our deeds. At such a time we must not disgrace ourselves. Hitherto we have never submitted to slavery, even when it brought no danger with it. We must not choose slavery now and with it penalties that will mean the end of everything if we fall alive into the hands of the Romans. For we were the first of all to revolt and shall be the last to break off the struggle. And I think it is God who has given us this privilege, that we can die nobly and as free men, unlike others who were unexpectedly defeated. In our case it is evident that daybreak will end our resistance, but we are free to choose an honorable death with our loved ones. This our enemies cannot prevent, however earnestly they may pray to take us alive, nor can we defeat them in battle. From the very first when we are bent on claiming our freedom that suffered such constant misery at each other's hand and worse at the enemy's, we ought perhaps to have read the mind of God and realized that His once beloved Jewish race had been sentenced to extinction. For if he had remained gracious or only slightly indignant with us, He would not have shut His eyes to the destruction of so many thousands or allowed His most holy city to be burned to the ground by our enemies. We hoped, or so it would seem, that of all the Jewish race, we alone would come through safe, still in possession of our freedom, as if we had committed no sin against God and taken part in no crime, we who had taught the others. Now see how He shows the folly of our hopes, plunging us into miseries more terrible than any we had dreamt of. Not even the impregnability of our fortress has sufficed to save us, but though we have food in abundance, ample supplies of arms, and more than enough for every other requisite, God Himself without a doubt has taken away all hope of survival. The fire that was being carried into the enemy lines did not turn back of its own accord towards the wall we built, these things are God's vengeance for the many wrongs that in our madness we dared to do to our own countrymen. For those wrongs let us pay the penalty not to our bitterest enemies, the Romans, but to God, with our own hands. It will be easier to bear that our wives die unabused, our children without knowledge of slavery, after that let us do to each other an ungrudging kindness, preserving our freedom as a glorious windingsheet. But first let our possessions and the whole fortress go up in flames. It will be a bitter blow to the Romans, that I know, to find our persons beyond their reach and nothing left for them to loot.

One thing only let us spare, our store of food. It will bear witness when we are dead to the fact that we have perished not through want but because, as we resolved at the beginning, we choose death rather than slavery.

Such was Elazar's appeal.

To sum up, the appeal of Elazar to the defenders and the remaining population of Masada was to commit suicide before the Romans took the fortress and thus avoid falling into the hands of the enemy alive. Nearly a millennium later, a paraphraser of Josephus, a man who was really a novelist and apparently was not familiar with Josephus's original writings but only with a fifth- or sixth-century translation, wrote a history of the "Jewish war" in Hebrew (Josephus did not write in Hebrew). This was written in central or southern Italy around the middle of the tenth century. We do not know the man's real name. He is commonly known as Josippon, a nickname which does not mean anything and is apparently derived from the fact that people confused him with Josephus. Here is a translation of what he put into the mouth of Elazar, the last defender of Masada. First, Elazar was supposed to have writ-

ten or proclaimed a lamentation, which is something we do not find
in Josephus, and then he addressed the people as follows:

And now my brethren and friends, have mercy on your wives and
children and on the old among you. Have them not led into merci-
less slavery to groan in the hold of their captors with no one to
redeem them. If you do so, you will forgo your places in the world
of justice and lose the way of true life, since you will have no future
in the life of lives [this is a reference to the world to come], have
mercy on them and kill them with your own hands, let them be
sacrifices, burnt offerings to God. Let not your holiness be stained
with the filth of the nations and have yourselves and your souls sin
to God.[1]

The charge continues in this vein. There is a distinct difference
between the address delivered by Elazar as written, or as reputedly
written or attributed to the defender, by Josephus, and the speech
attributed by Josippon to Elazar. The first is a more or less normal
appeal by a commanding officer to the defending force of a fortress
shortly before collapse in which he advocates suicide in lieu of
surrender. The second is the same. There is, however, no reference
here to independence, to slavery in the political sense of the word,
to subjugation by the Romans, or to national pride. There is only
reference to the true life, the world of justice, the world to come,
God, the redemption, and all that goes with it. And, of course, in
the end there is the suggestion that the defenders kill the women
and children and then commit suicide.

How did this come about and what became of it? First of all,
medieval Jewry did not know and did not read Josephus either in
the original or in translation until the sixteenth century or perhaps
the late fifteenth century. Until then European Jewry was not
aware of a text differing from the paraphrase of the tenth century.
The book that medieval Jewry knew as the description of the
"Jewish war" was attributed to a man called Josef Ha-Cohen, or
Josippon. It was this version and not the original that we know
today. If medieval Jewry had before its eyes an ideal of self-sacrifice
in the face of destruction and of valor in the face of overwhelming

forces, it was the speech of Elazar in the vein described rather than the speech of Elazar as described by Josephus.

In the one thousand years between the events of the first and tenth centuries, the attitude of Jewry—first in Palestine, from Palestine to Italy, from Italy to the Ashkenazic communities of the Rhine region, and from there to all of medieval Ashkenazic Jewry —developed in the following fashion. What I have described, or what Elazar described in the words of Josippon of the tenth century, is really what is called, in medieval terminology, *kiddush ha-Shem,* the "sanctification of the Name."

Kiddush ha-Shem existed. It exists in the Bible and is mentioned there in various forms that differ in context and meaning. It first appears in Leviticus 22:31–32: "You shall faithfully observe My commandments: I am the Lord. And you shall not profane My holy name that I may be sanctified in the midst of the Israelite people—I the Lord who sanctify you." Obviously, there is no reference here to suicide in the face of danger. However, after the destruction of the Second Commonwealth there is the first reference to such an explanation: namely, in Lydda in the second century a group of sages got together and tried to formulate what they termed the laws of martyrdom—the circumstances under which a Jew had to offer his life without committing any form of transgression. Martyrdom was one of the three possible forms of expression of *kiddush ha-Shem;* the other two were exemplary ethical conduct and prayer, neither of which concerns us at this stage.

Martyrdom was first formulated by second-century sages who declared *kiddush ha-Shem* to be obligatory in three events: idolatry, loss of chastity, and murder. A Jew had to suffer death rather than violate these taboos. The last two do not concern us here, but the first bears directly on our subject. In the course of the centuries following this formulation, the sages of the mishnaic and talmudic period delved further and further into a variety of texts and finally came up with something that amounted to what was not only the form but also the expression of what the Bible was supposed to have intended by that statement in Leviticus—that the main expression of *kiddush ha-Shem* is martyrdom. This attitude found its expression in poetry, chiefly composed in Palestine and under Byzantine rule between the second and sixth centuries, which reached Europe by long and circuitous routes, its first stage being southern Italy.

Needless to say, sources for that period are very scarce and for the most part nonexistent. However, there are a few, and these few seem to fit in very well with a theory about the propagation of Palestinian rather than Babylonian culture in southern Europe, excluding Spain—that is to say, in Italy and the surrounding areas which eventually created Ashkenazic culture from the tenth century onwards. Again, by way of illustration rather than methodical and chronological description, I offer a passage translated from an undated letter which we assume to have been written some time in the ninth or perhaps the tenth century.

The holy congregation of Otranto [Otranto is at the southern tip of Italy] has lost three leaders as a result of the execution of the accursed decree [reference is made to a Byzantine order]—their names are Rabbi Isaiah, a prominent and learned man, a humble saint the like of whom we have not seen; Rabbi Menahem, a pious and scrupulously observant scholar; Mar Elijah, their disciple, an upright man who was a merchant. Rabbi Isaiah pierced his own throat with a knife. Rabbi Menahem was thrust into prison and Mar Elijah was strangled. But, the Lord be praised, not a letter of the Torah was burned there, for the fire was first kindled in our town, whereupon we speedily notified by secret messenger. Both here and there calamity prevailed for two days, but on the third we issued forth from the darkness into the light.[2]

The Hebrew terminology employed by the writer is identical with some of the phraseology in the speech attributed by the tenth-century paraphraser of Josephus to Elazar of Masada. It is found, again more or less in the same phrasing, in the poetry and chronicles written by contemporaries and eyewitnesses of the 1096 persecutions in the Rhine region in southern Germany. Thus these expressions, these attitudes, traveled from Palestine to southern Italy, where they were formulated in literature and in what was the basic historical description of the "Jewish war." Some time between the tenth and the eleventh centuries, this formulation was introduced into central Europe by Jewish immigrants from Italy. From the eleventh century and for nearly another millennium, this state of mind and attitude continued very nearly unchanged within Ashkenazic Jewry (Sephardic Jewry had a distinctively different attitude to the same problem).

For the ideal of *kiddush ha-Shem* hundreds of thousands of Ashkenazic Jews sacrificed their lives throughout the centuries and in a manner that became almost stereotyped in the course of time. In many ways this attitude has prevailed among large sections of Jewry to the present day, including of course the Holocaust period.

The change that has come over modern Jewry, at least sections of it, is a change that takes us back in many ways to a situation that existed two thousand years ago. Still, this attitude, this trend of mind, this philosophy, has not disappeared altogether and still prevails in many ways. Though at times it takes on different forms, it remains the underlying conscious or unconscious attitude of many Jews everywhere.

NOTES

1. *Sefer Yosippon,* ed. by D. Guinzburg and A. Kahana (Berdichev, 1896–1913).

2. A Hebrew letter from Bari (?), published by Jacob Mann in his *Texts and Studies in Jewish History and Literature,* I (Cincinnati, 1931), pp. 23 ff., with Mann's comments, pp. 12 ff.

CONTRIBUTORS

Yohanan Aharoni, until his recent death, was professor of archaeology, chairman of the Department of Near East Studies, and head of the Institute of Archaeology at Tel Aviv University.

Salo W. Baron is professor emeritus of Jewish history, literature, and institutions on the Miller Foundation at Columbia University.

Graenum Berger is a Jewish communal worker and former consultant to the Federation of Jewish Philanthropies of New York.

Haim Cohn is a justice of the Supreme Court of the State of Israel.

Michael Confino is professor of Russian history and chairman of the Department of Russian and East European History at Tel Aviv University.

Lenn E. Goodman is associate professor of philosophy at the University of Hawaii.

Ben Halpern is professor of Near Eastern studies at Brandeis University, Waltham, Massachusetts.

Joel L. Kraemer is a senior lecturer in the Department of the History of the Middle East and Africa at Tel Aviv University.

Yuval Ne'eman is former professor of physics and past president of Tel Aviv University.

Harry Orlinsky is professor of Bible at the Hebrew Union College-Jewish Institute of Religion in New York.

Emanuel Rackman has recently been named president of Bar-Ilan University in Israel. Previously he was professor of Judaic studies and consultant to the chancellor at the City University of New York.

David Schers is a lecturer in the David Horowitz Institute for Research of Developing Countries, Tel Aviv University.

Shimon Shamir is professor of modern Middle Eastern history at Tel Aviv University.

Shlomo Simonsohn is rector of Tel Aviv University.

Uriel Tal is professor of modern Jewish history at Tel Aviv University.

Ephraim Urbach is professor of Talmud and Midrash at the Hebrew University, Jerusalem.

George S. Wise is past president and lifetime chancellor of Tel Aviv University.

INDEX